OPUS DEI

OPUS DEI

A Templar's Credo
for the Advent of the City of God
in the City of Man

MANUEL S. MARIN

Library of Congress Control Number:		2007905593
ISBN:	Hardcover	978-1-4257-7922-1
	Softcover	978-1-4257-7913-9

This book was printed in the United States of America.

To order additional copies of this book, contact:
Xlibris Corporation
1-888-795-4274
www.Xlibris.com
Orders@Xlibris.com
32558

CONTENTS

DEDICATORY:

TO: Father Rafael María Fabretto

I dedicate this book to **Father Rafael María Fabretto,** whose initially failed project gave me the opportunity to ride with the *continuum*, where all miracles happen.

PREFACE

I am convinced that some of the things I express in this book are going to be considered offensive by some people. I would like to apologize beforehand if I make somebody feel insulted.

I would also want to clarify that this book is about *agape-love*—self-sacrificing, giving love to all, both friend and enemy—or spiritual love of God, love of ourselves, and love of humanity, which is why I will never get tired of advocating peace and pleading against war—any kind of war, including wars of self-defense—and against hate, including racial, ethnic, political, and religious hatred. I also exhort people to oppose individualism, as practiced in a strictly capitalist society, and nationalism, and this may also be repugnant to some who hold their country and their economic system in the highest esteem. It would be a mistake to think that because I am not an enthusiastic nationalist and overblown patriot, I don't love the USA, my adopted country, or Nicaragua, my country of birth. On the contrary, it means that I love those countries as much as I love humanity. Nothing would give me more satisfaction than to see the United States of America lead the world in a spiritual and economic worldwide crusade, rather than launching imperial wars of aggression and conquest, under the ominous pretext of doing it for the defense of our national security.

Because the USA is one of the few countries in the world with the means to lead a campaign against poverty, misery, disease and oblivion, maladies that afflict most of the globe today, we have the moral obligation to lead it. Also, although I would seem to completely despise the capitalist system of production, what I really hate is greed and avarice, and as a Templar, I believe capitalism is the Holy Grail and the Philosopher's Stone searched for by all esoteric movements related to the Knights Templar. The capitalist system has given us the tools to produce wealth to limits never seen before, and yet, there are people reluctant to share that wealth, in spite of the fact that it comes from the land and natural resources that belong to all, and in spite of the fact that wealth is also human labor invested in the products that workers make, as well as inputs of wits and ingenuity by capitalists and entrepreneurs that galvanize it.

Once again, pardon me for being so blunt about what we have done to ourselves over the history of mankind—the white people conquering and slaving the dark-skinned people, and these, in their turn, helping to preserve and perpetuate this condition of bondage—but we must know the truth, and live with the truth, and the truth sometimes may hurt, and at the end, my message is that blacks, whites, Asians, Indians, and other humans, are just multiple different incarnations of the love of God for humanity.

Manuel S. Marin   Houston, TX, April 20, 2007

1

INTRODUCTION

At the end of March, 2004, I came to Williams Brothers Construction Co. looking for a job as a driver. I could've sought for a different job, but I knew it was useless to try, because although I had a Masters Degree, I was already 58 years old, and had been out of work for too long for an employer to consider me for a job opening other than driving a truck. I needed a job right away to pay for my debts and personal expenses, and I wasn't about to shy away from any work considered demeaning or lowly, or from physical labor, especially since I had just submitted for publication my book *The Axioms of Being and the Renaissance of the Templars*, and figured that the book would sell well. Consequently, all I needed was a temporary job to make a living while I waited for my book to be published. Little I knew that I was no Stephen King, and that I could never make a living as a writer, especially as a writer of philosophy, religion, and spirituality.

I was accepted as a driver—I had some driver experience, but I never did like being a truck driver, so I was taking this job with a bit of displeasure. The day I came to the company's yard at Airtex Dr & I-45 N in Houston, TX, for the orientation, I had a peculiar encounter with Mr. Robert Jones, the person in charge of driver orientation at the time. He connected his computer to the Internet, and played the defensive driving course for truckers offered by The National Safety Council. This was an English presentation. There were also two other Hispanic drivers taking the course.

Once the presentation started, it was obvious that the other drivers didn't understand English at all, and Mr. Jones didn't speak Spanish, so he asked me if I could translate for them, as the presentation proceeded. I acquiesced, and that was the beginning of a somewhat strange spiritual shift in me: something may have taken place in what Mr. Jones later told me he calls the *continuum*. I'll explain shortly what this means, but suffices here to say that things in life happen for specific reasons. Anything you do, and all you do in life, happen for specific reasons, and you get to know those reasons if you know how to ride the *continuum*, if you know how to work in tandem with it, so that you can achieve your objectives. Just don't ever make the mistake of trying to manipulate or outsmart the *continuum* by believing you know the reasons why things will happen the way you want them to happen, because you can never force events and impose your will on it. Believe me; you never know enough to outmaneuver the *continuum*. It is far more "intelligent" than you are, and there is no way you can guess what the *continuum* is up to. Only hindsight can tell you why things happened the way they did—and I am talking about past occurrences only. Perhaps an example may help to understand this notion of the *continuum*.

Have you ever had a plan to achieve a certain goal or objective in your life? You think your plan is perfect, you have taken into consideration all the possible obstacles that may disrupt your plan, and you know how to sort them out. You have everything laid out to the minutest detail, and you are one-hundred percent certain you will achieve your goals, only to find out that there was an absolutely unexpected event or circumstance that you never thought of that thwarted the outcome of your plan. This is what I mean by trying to outsmart the *continuum*. I had a friend who, in a bout of depression, tried to hang himself, but his objective was foiled by a faulty rope that snapped when he jumped off a chair, the suicidal rope tied to his neck. You may think that he would have been successful had he inspected the rope, which is precisely my point—how about the guy who pulled the trigger to kill his own brother, and the bullet misfires, giving his would-be victim time to run away? My suicidal friend is now happy to be alive—and so must be the lucky brothers, one because he possibly escaped death, and the other because he narrowly missed going to prison. Another example follows.

Several years ago, back in Nicaragua, at about 2:30 in the afternoon, I was walking down a street that was completely empty, and it seemed that I was the only person around the neighborhood. I got to the corner at the gymnasium of the school named Maria Mazzarello and the Sequeira ice factory in Altagracia, Managua. At this corner I hesitated, I could either continue walking straight up the street, or make a right turn. I took a few steps straight ahead, stopped, and decided, for no apparent reason, to back up and make a right turn at the corner. When I was about three-quarters of the way down the block, I saw this man coughing like if he was choking, both hands at his throat; his face was already turning purple. I got him up and did the Heimlich maneuver on him, making him spit out whatever was choking him. I patted his back, and asked if he was OK; he said he was, thanked me, and since I was in a hurry, I continued my way home, making a left turn at the next corner. The man was still holding his forehead, looking down at the ground when

I made it around the corner. This was an incident that didn't occupy my thoughts for more than probably five minutes.

A couple of years later I was having lunch in El Chalecito Restaurant, talking to my friend Francisco, the owner of the said restaurant, which had some tables looking out to the street. A shoeshine man walked by and greeted Francisco as he passed. Francisco shouted at him, jokingly: "¡Oye Pepe, no bebás mucho que te puede salir la Virgen María!"—"Hey Pepe, don't drink too much, for you may see the Virgin Mary!" Pepe shouted back that he no longer drank liquor, that he was a changed man. I was intrigued, and asked Francisco what was the meaning of all this dialogue. Francisco told me the story.

"Every time Pepe is shinning shoes for a customer, he tells them about the encounter he had with an angel a long time ago; that he was choking with a bite of tough meat in his throat." Then I remembered Pepe, but I didn't tell my friend anything. He continued, "He says that as he was almost losing conscience, he asked God to help him, and then an angel in the form of a man appeared from nowhere and saved him. That he, Pepe, was looking at the floor for a few seconds, and his angel disappeared!" now Francisco was laughing, "he must have been stunned drunk!" Something distracted our conversation and we left it there.

It is my belief that states of psychic alteration may be induced by situations of extreme danger or fear of death; they may also be self-induced through meditation and prayer; or spontaneously induced through unique interpretation of natural, quasi-natural, or non-natural phenomena. The first one corresponds to Pepe's experience. Examples of the second may be found in individual and communal prayers, meditation and mental trances self-induced in the practice of some religious or magical rituals—ingestion of hallucinogens, like peyote, LSD, etc. may be included in this category. The third one may be found in so-called personal encounters with ghosts, extra-terrestrial beings, supposedly inexistent animals and beasts, and sightings of the Virgin Mary—these may also occur to more than one individual.

Two realities, one that corresponds to the reality produced by states of psychic alteration, the other produced by non-states of psychic alteration, or what we call states of normal consciousness. Which one is more real, or which one is the real one? The fact that 99.99 percent of the time we are under states of normal consciousness does not invalidate the reality produced by states of psychic alterations, nor is the fact that 99.99 percent of people perceive the reality that corresponds to normal states of consciousness invalidates the reality of those who perceive it through altered states of consciousness.

Now that I think about the *continuum*, I cannot but reflect on Pepe's experience. He had a spiritual experience prompted by a situation of near-death. I just had an experience of bumping into an individual being in trouble. As far as I was concerned, what happened to Pepe was just a worldly experience, nothing else, except for my decision to turn around the corner instead of going straight. But for Pepe, it was something mystical, it was an apparition, a spiritual encounter with an angelic being. We both were at the limits of two universes. His universe required somebody to save him from death. My universe required a purposeful decision to make a turn at a street, for no conscious or specific reason at all. The *continuum* brought both universes together, and this prompted the encounter. In Pepe's universe I was an angel sent by God. In my universe, Pepe was an individual in trouble, choking to death, who needed help. Which conception of the world is the right one? If mine, then I have to explain why I made a decision that otherwise I didn't have to make—that in fact was an illogical decision, since my home was at a shorter distance if I had continued straight ahead. If Pepe's, we must accept the fact that the universe of spirituality is next, contiguous, embedded in the material universe, and I was an instrument of God—and God can use anyone as an instrument to achieve His purpose.

The conjunction of two or more universes makes one individual interpret phenomena different from another individual, the difference being on the actual state of consciousness of the individuals in question. The underlying world of possibilities is the *continuum*, a spiritual reality that can be peeked into under certain circumstances. We peek into the *continuum* in our dreams, whenever we use our imagination—either idly or to produce art, inventions, or to advance science. Seers, magicians, visionaries, prophets, and other special human beings can also enter the realm of the spirit and see things that ordinary people cannot see. I theorize that under the stress of imminent death, Pepe managed to utter a prayer, or quasi-prayer, that helped him strip his perception of reality from any of its material cover, leaving the world of the spirit wide open to his consciousness. He saw an angel. I, on my part, didn't glimpse beyond the material world, and all I saw was a man choking to death.

The *continuum* is the "fabric" that joins physical phenomena into a continuous, more comprehensive, system of phenomena whose "perception" may not be physical, but spiritual. It underlies the physical world, and it cannot be anything else than the spiritual realm, the Holy Ghost of some Christian faiths. Pepe's distress originated a disturbance in the *continuum* that propagated to the closest recipient that was I, and made me do what I did. The *continuum* joined his universe with mine and performed the "miracle." Of course, we can always talk of coincidences, or random occurrences of phenomena. If I go to the shopping mall and bump into a friend that I hadn't seen in fifteen years, we talk of a happy coincidence because we don't know the immediate purpose of the encounter. We may say that we both were there, at the right place and the right time, but that there was no purposeful, conscious objective for our encounter. But we don't know that. Our encounter may be an insignificant part of a wider and more extended system of physical interrelationships of phenomena that may indeed have a purpose. In other words, whether we know it or not, we are willing or unwilling agents of the *continuum*, and this *continuum* is the work of God—the *Opus Dei* of this universe, God's will expressed in movement, God's active principle translated into actions that give origin to physical events leading to a purpose that may be interpreted as coincidence or circumstantial occurrence of phenomena, or else, as spiritual manifestations of the work of God, depending on the individual percipient.

Scientifically-minded people will argue that two or more events for which there is no internal or external relationships may happen haphazardly in time and space due to probabilistic determinism—in other words, it is possible for two or more events to occur in time and space with no correlation among them, so that they may be coincidentally manifested by some whim of probability theory. If somebody gets fulminated by a lightning, or killed by a falling object from the sky, we say that the person "was at the wrong place, at the wrong time," instead of seeing in this occurrence some spiritual transcendentalism, some higher hidden purpose that, although not positive for the victim of the lightning, may have a positive ulterior meaning for somebody else. That's the reason why it's easier, at least conceptually, to understand that the flapping wings of a butterfly in the Amazon jungle may be the cause of a storm in the Gulf of Mexico, than to understand how Pepe's struggle for survival and strong faith in God may have influenced me to change the course of my walk home to save his life. We are conditioned to accept linear cause-and-effect relationships (in contiguous space and time), rather than collateral ones, especially if they are separated by space—i.e. noncontiguous in space. Such are the limitations of science.

And yet, if we insist that the phenomena exemplified above with Pepe is a result of mere coincidence, we could try to calculate the probability of the events occurring as they did, and this number would be so staggeringly small, that we would be forced to conclude that chance had nothing to do with it. The chance of I being where I was, at the time Pepe was choking, would have to take into consideration the chance that Pepe was choking (of all the times of his life) at precisely the moment I was walking nearby. And what about the probability that I would make the kind of turn I made, where I made it, at the time I made it? Assembling all these event probabilities at exactly the period of time where everything happened, would be so abysmally small that they would have to occur once in a billion times, if not once in a trillion times, longer perhaps than I and Pepe could have lived, if our lives were separated by one thousand years. If something has zero, or very close to zero probability of occurring by chance, this indicates that the events must have been colluded by some purposeful agent, the *continuum*.

I borrowed this concept of the *continuum* from Mr. Robert Jones. You may have guessed by now that I didn't last very long as a truck driver of Williams Brothers Construction Co. I became a driver instructor instead, working closely with Mr. Jones. This gave us a chance to talk about philosophy and other themes that touched on spirituality and religion. Before I came to work for Mr. Jones I had very much developed my concept of ether as a mantle of both the physical and the spiritual world, but my ether was lifeless. Mr. Jones' concept of the *continuum* gave my ether the spiritual light and the lift that it needed. Hence, my thanks and recognition to Mr. Robert Jones, who with his concept of the *continuum* brought to fruition the idea I had in my book *Non Nobis, Domine: Spirituality, Religion, Mathematics and Physics in the Light of the Postulate of Faith* about the Trinity of Reality, constituted by the physical world, ether, and the *continuum*.

By the way, before we met at Williams Brothers Construction Co., I didn't have the slightest idea of who Mr. Bob Jones was. He seemed to believe that I came to the company at the right time to help him accomplish his objective in reference to the company's training program, and he always used the expression "I've got an angel in my pocket" every time he mentioned my circumstantial or coincidental arrival to Williams Brothers Construction Co. On the other hand, working as a driver trainer was a life saver for me that allowed me to work on my second book *Non Nobis, Domine*, mentioned before, and the present one, *Opus Dei*. Talk about how things and events come together riding the *continuum*.

We said above that Pepe experienced one reality, while I experienced a different one. Let's examine the following statement: "The same underlying reality was visualized by Pepe differently than I did." Hence, it is reasonable to think that "the same underlying reality"—invisible for me and for Pepe—may be the "true" reality, unless Pepe's reality is identifiable with it, or my reality is identical with it, which we will never know. But wait a minute, you will think, how can we talk about something we will never experience, like this underlying reality? Some of you will even argue that the only reality there *is* is the one that 99.99 percent of the time 99.99 percent of the people perceive every day. Except that the very act of denying this "underlying reality," affirms it, because though it *is*—which is why we think of it as a possibility—it doesn't necessarily *exist*, because we never get to perceive it. Such is the power of the works of the Postulate of Faith. This is where all our reasoning apparatus breaks down completely, because we are dealing here with the spiritual world—sometimes also referred to as the world of ideas, which are nothing less than Plato's ideas. What are, then, these ideas? Since they don't reside in the physical world, they would have to be alterations of the ether or the *continuum*, bundles of energy swirling in the ether or in the *continuum*. We will expand on this conception of the world of ideas later in the book. A good understanding of *being* as opposed to *existing* helps to discern the spiritual versus the material.

We must be careful with this typical human tendency to equate reality with existence. If we could never feel the wind, we would probably believe that it doesn't exist, that it isn't real, just like nitrogen, oxygen, neon and other gases exist only in the world of the chemist, and not in the layman's world. For, how can the common, ignorant man, know that there is an invisible gaseous substance known as nitrogen? It doesn't help to say that science knows about it, that it has been known for centuries. Still, for the man of the Amazon jungle, nitrogen would be even more unreal than the spirits he reveres.

Continuing with the theme of the reality behind the reality of the physical world, let's look at one classic example taken from the phenomena called optical illusions. Have you ever looked at the drawing of a cube that sometimes looks like a solid object in the form of a cube floating in space, and sometimes looks like an empty space in the form of a cube carved out of its solid surroundings? The underlying reality of these interpretations is in the lines that make up the cube, but that underlying reality is only visible as straight lines going in different directions. It's only when our brain makes up the cube that those lines become one thing or the other. But optical illusions are still phenomena of the physical or material world. The spiritual realm is outside space and time, and coming back to Pepe's vision, we have to say that what we referred to as "the same underlying reality" *is* (in the sense of *being*, as contrasted with *existing*), which leads to the statement: "The spiritual realm *is*," which is not a statement of existence—as when we say "The moon is at 360,000 to 405, 000 kilometers from the earth"—or, a self-evident truth. Hence, the statement "The spiritual realm *is*" is not an *axiom*, but a *dogma*—although for a lot of people a *dogma* is a self-evident truth. We will later talk extensively about *axioms*, which are statements of the physical sciences, and *dogmas*, which are statements of spirituality.

We will also talk about space and time, especially about objective time (the *ever-present* or *eternity*, without the element of duration) and subjective time (time as we know it). Now, objective time gives origin to the limited *omnipresence* of objects, which makes possible the identification of an object as it moves from a point A to a point B. In other words, in the spiritual realm "objects" are both in "point A" and in "point B" and in their "intermediate locations" all "at the same time," and this makes us perceive (in the physical world) the two objects in two different spatial locations as the same object—there is, then, an invisible link, as it were, that keeps the object from being interpreted by our brain as two different objects when it moves from one place to another. The difficulty about talking of the spiritual world is that our language is geared to deal with the material world, which is why I place some words and expressions that purportedly describe de world of ideas within quotation marks.

But let's elaborate a bit more about our theme of discussion here. When you drop a stone on a pond, there is one possible outcome: ripples are going to form at the surface of the water. Of course, other unexpected things may very well happen, like somebody appearing from nowhere, jumping across the pond and grabbing the stone before it hits water, but the almost sure result is going to be ripples on the surface of the water. When you play bowling and you throw the bowling ball, you may knockout all the pins, knockout just one, two, three, or none of the pins, etc. and your options are always limited. But when you embark on a task to achieve certain results in the future, the possible ways you can achieve your goal are numerous and unlimited, and so are the possible ways of completely missing it. Once you set your first move in action, only the *continuum* can "foretell" the ultimate result(s)—and this *continuum* is the "ultimate reality" behind our reality, it constitutes the background of the physical reality we know and experience on a daily basis. In other words, the *continuum is* in *objective time*—the time element in the unperceived space-time matrix—and comes into *existence*, or manifests itself in space as *subjective time*—time as measured by cyclical or recurrent, repetitive events—flows, and this string of manifestations of the *continuum* is what we perceive as reality. The question is: How do we tap the *continuum* to know what the result is going to be even before we make the first movement? This is a spiritual question that has a spiritual answer: through the power of faith; and since our personal actions are in many cases irrelevant, our first move is always going to be prayer. And this is precisely what happened to Pepe. His intent was to remain alive; his actions to achieve this objective were probably irrelevant, given that he was chocking. Hence, he charged his being with faith in God, thought of an informal prayer asking for Divine intervention, and the *continuum* did the rest. Which raises the question: What precisely is faith? Later in the book we will try to give it an answer.

The world phenomena are linked by *actual* physical cause-effect relationships and by invisible links of *possible* cause-effect relationships. Think of the example of the stone dropped on a pond producing ripples, with just one underlying link. Think of the bowling example, with multiple underlying links. Think of the plans to materialize a given purpose, with its innumerable invisible links that trace whether or not we achieve or miss the stated objective. In relation to this last case, faith is the preparation for achieving the goal, and prayer is the first move that ought to trigger the linkage of phenomena that will produce the miracle of the stated goal or aspiration. The Advent of the City of God in the city of man requires a credo, or system of dogmas—translated into communal faith—and a triggering collective action by one or many individuals (a combination of prayers and doing) to bring about a decent, if ever possible, happy existence for humanity, since it is already a reality in the world of ideas. The Fraternity of the Templars will make it its objective the advent of the Kingdom of Heaven on earth by tapping the spiritual realm of the *continuum* and triggering the so much expected grand miracle of God as a gift to the whole of humanity.

This book is also about love that leads to salvation. But, what is love? Love is doing what is good for others in the same measure of what is good for us. The path to salvation is found in helping others defeat poverty and disease, and this requires an understanding of the rationality of our Christian faith based on love, which means that we must reason out our belief in God, because God is love—and we can only love God by doing what He *is*, i.e. love, but this is a human action that requires an object of our love, which can be no other than our fellow human beings. One way we can rationalize our Christian faith is by laying out the philosophical foundations of *Homo spiritualis* as contrasted with *Homo sapiens*, and thus follow the lead of the Fraternity of the Templars, with the help of God Enterprises and the Orbis Unum Party. This party will pave the way to build the infrastructure necessary for the success of God Enterprises as an economic venture that will spread and expand within the matrix of the capitalist system of production. And once the capitalist Leviathan is capable of feeding and sustaining humanity, then we will have achieved the advent of the City of God in the city of man. Notice that, although the Orbis Unum Party will start being a "party," as our movement gains strength, it will steadily be accepted by all peoples and interest groups, until it will stop being a party to become a movement of the whole of humanity. In addition to this, the Orbis Unum Party will also pursue the preservation of man as a biological entity, and the preservation of nature, including animal and vegetable life, complying as much as possible with the Axioms of Being, specifically with the Principle of Preservation of Life and the Principle of Preservation of the Species.

It is known that the first human beings spread and populated the world in a little over 50,000 years. They lost contact with each other, and even became enemies of each other, giving rise, first to the sense of territoriality, and later, to the concept of nation and nationality. People then were led by an instinct or drive to control territory, and people today are being constantly bombarded with nationalist propaganda. But this shouldn't happen any more in a modern world interconnected by the Internet and advanced communications technology. Now is the time to turn back the tide, and pull together what was separated in the past by the sheer necessity to survive. This calls for a world government, or a system of world governments. A byproduct of this geopolitical integration will be the biological integration of man, thousands of years after the human gene pool was enriched by the emergence of the different human races, soon to be recombined into the new *Homo spiritualis*, a new biological entity recharged with a stronger spiritual energy, and reinforced with a new genetic making upgraded by the contribution of varied races.

The British Commonwealth and the United Nations are examples of embryos of the formation of world governments. Some sectors of the US political spectrum are constantly criticizing the UN out of jealousy, because the UN represents a strong competition to the aspirations of the USA as a world empire of modern times—the Commonwealth can always be readily absorbed into the imperial designs of the US with little or no opposition from Anglo-Saxons and Caucasians. Is it wrong to promote a world government, a world community—where all nations participate almost as equal partners, as against an imperial system of domination, where the leading power is the USA? The national security of the USA can be guaranteed by giving security to other nations, by inviting the USA to participate in this world integration as an important, but equal partner, that can take the lead in many affairs of vital significance to the world community. We can achieve this integration with the help of Party 01—the Orbis Unum party, a party that advocates the globalization of man—which is not a party as such, but a household of the human race, with open doors for all those who would like to return to the *regazo* of humanity. The Fraternity of the Templars could be the forerunner of a government designed for the whole of humanity, with total participation of all peoples of the world.

We know the Templars of the past for the good things they did. If they were the Devil's Bankers, we still want to believe that they had a good purpose in mind, that they did good deeds. Now, if this is not in conformity with history, it doesn't matter, the notion of the Templars in this book has been idealized to transcend the historical records, so that whatever we learn about the Templars of the past will have no negative influence on the Templars of the present and the Templars of the future. In this sense, we can appropriately say that Jesus was a Templar (even though Jesus lived before the Templars), or that every Templar incarnated Jesus in them. What we have to understand here is that once the idea "leaves" the st-matrix (space-time matrix) of our material world, we can place it in the past (make it materialize in the past), as well as in the present or the future. Hence, as far as we are concerned today, it doesn't matter if the Templars never found the treasures they were looking for, the Holy Grail, the Ark of the Covenant, the Philosopher's Stone, or the secret knowledge of the Sufis and Gnostics. What matters is what they did, and the reasons they had for doing it. What matters is that they acted in the name of Jesus, and for the sake of their neighbors, and that they did it with love.

Finally, I intend to contrast in this book the final spiritual defeat of evil as related in John's Revelations versus the material triumph of humanity with the advent of the City of God. I propose here that the capitalist system of production is the perfect tool for the rescue of humanity from poverty and starvation. Our productive capitalist engine is so advanced that we are now capable of feeding humanity for a long time to come. But this requires the appropriate use of the system, with a motivation to help others, and not just moved by personal interests. It requires changing man's attitudes, from those of greed and avarice to those of optimism, philanthropy and frugality. It requires the rebirth of the man of the 21st century with new mental attitudes, to strive with body and soul, to work tirelessly, not only for their own well-being, but for the well-being of humanity. This can only be accomplished with love, love of God, which is the same as love of humanity. It is the objective of the Fraternity of the Templars to materialize the City of God in the city of man, minimizing as much as possible conflicts, fights and power struggles. The Templars are not in opposition to any person or group of persons of any race, credo, religion, national origin, or social status—on the contrary, we are for the rescue of spiritual man, for the making of *Homo spiritualis*. We simply believe that capitalism can be put to better use if we, through God Enterprises, participate and compete freely in the production of goods and services, and do it in such a way that we may benefit the poor with the profits gained.

2

THE NEW SPIRITUALITY

The philosophy of nature and the self that I present in this book is not pantheism, because pantheism or monism is the belief in an underlying divine energy—the one power or cosmic reality—that interconnects everything, and I am not proposing such a conception of the physical world. Rather, the universe, including the earth and man in it, is God's creation, or a manifestation of God's being, which should not be identified with the Deity. And although man was created on the image and likeness of God, man is neither God nor a god, just a plain God-like being. Also, although humans are divine in their true nature and control their personal destinies, they are not an integral part of any divine energy, even as they can experientially realize through proper technique and instruction, like introspection and meditation, that they are part of the physical and spiritual cosmos.

I don't hold in these writings that the mind of each human has "infinite" potential and that the "higher self," unconscious mind, or some such concept provides the connecting link to the infinite, believed to be the repository of vast wisdom and power. Rather, I would affirm that the mind of each human potentially has access to the infinite world of physical and spiritual phenomena, which are both repositories of vast wisdom and power. Furthermore, I do believe that visualization is an important technique that taps the higher self and initiates contact with the ultimate cosmic reality, which is not God, or an essence of God, but an expression or manifestation of God's being; in other words, God's Work (Opus Dei), which I call the *continuum*, is God's active principle operating within and throughout the world of matter. In my book *The Axioms of Being and the Renaissance of the Templars* I hold that God may communicate with man through revelation, and yet man can only indirectly communicate with God through his anima, by means of Jesus Christ, the Saints and the Angels. It is also my belief that introspection and meditation let man know God by knowing himself, but only indirectly, through the so called vast repository of wisdom and power which is the cosmos and/or the *continuum*. Furthermore, I fully agree with the following:

> "The world view of visualization . . . is obviously not Christian. The Bible denies that people are one essence with God or the universe because it declares that only God has eternality [man's anima, soul or spirit is immortal, but not eternal, because God created it]—for He "alone is immortal" (1 Tim. 6:16) [eternal and immortal must be understood here in the sense that God always was, now is, and forever will be]—and only He is an infinite being. Thus the one and only God (John 17:3) who existed from eternity (Ps. 90:2) created the entire material and spiritual universe, including humanity, from nothing. God did not emanate something of Himself in the process of creation so that everything in creation partakes in the nature of God. To the contrary, as the following Scriptures declare, God created the universe merely by speaking it into existence: "In the beginning God created the heavens and the earth" (Gen. 1:1); "The universe was formed at God's command" (Heb. 11:3); "By the word of the Lord were the heavens made . . . For he spoke, and it came to be" (Ps. 33:6, 9)."

> "People are not a part of God. Their minds do not have the "infinite" powers attributed to them by visualization philosophy, nor are they a source of true spiritual wisdom apart from spiritual regeneration or rebirth (Prov. 28:26; Jer. 17:9; Mark 7:20-23; James 3:14-17). Furthermore, visualization has no power to initiate contact with God or gain knowledge of Him [this last part may not be totally true, in my humble opinion]. Biblically, those who wish to personally know the one true God must come to Him by faith through the true Jesus Christ (John 17:2-3; Col. 1:15-20; 2:9; Heb. 11:6; 1 Pet. 2:24)—not by trust in their own inner vision, a spirit guide masquerading as Christ, or by an alleged mystical union with some abstract impersonal concept of the divine."

[Taken from: VISUALIZATION: God-Given Power or New Age Danger? (Part Two), by John Weldon and John Ankerberg.]

Finally, it is my belief that although by the grace and intercession of the Holy Ghost man can directly communicate with God, and gain some knowledge of Him by meditation and introspection, the essence of God (God the Father) can only be known through God Himself reincarnated in Jesus Christ (the Son). The

Holy Ghost provides the means, the *continuum*, to understand and reach to God, but this *continuum*, though it has no physical existence of its own, underlies the phenomenology of the universe. In other words, the *continuum is* a spiritual reality, while the material world *exists*.

The proof of *being* is in recognizing the possibility of existence—that which is possible *is*, but that which is impossible *isn't*. The proof of *existence*, on the other hand, follows verification of phenomena by our sense perceptions—or their extensions thereof. That's why we can say *I am* before we can even say *I exist*, and exactly for the same reason, a mermaid *is* before we can take a look at it, i.e. before we can even verify that it *exists*—a mermaid is because the possibility of its existence in the eternal flow of time is not excluded by the rules of reason. With respect to the question of whether or not *God is*, as far as I know, nobody has ever proved to be absurd *the possibility that God exists*.

Spirituality without ether would be dead—ether faces the physical world on one side, and the spiritual world on the other, so *being* goes from *material being* to *ethereal being* to *spiritual being*, in that order—given that ether is the matrix of both the physical and the spiritual, which means that the physical world *exists* in ether, and the spiritual world *is* in ether. For, how do we hope to explain the spiritual things without making some reference to the ether medium that would facilitate spiritual phenomena without material interference? We dare say that the spirit is really an organized motion of the ether, motion that is much more sophisticated than electromagnetic phenomena. Ether is both the matrix of the material world and the matrix of the phenomenology of the spirit. The so-called "dark matter"—that supposedly is so abundant in the universe, shows all the characteristics of ether, and makes possible the explanation of the Big Bang and the expansion of the universe—would also be the appropriate medium of the spirit, that is to say, the medium were the spirit *is* as opposed to the medium where matter *exists*. The theory of strings that purportedly explains everything, requires at least 10 dimensions to be expressed in mathematical terms: the three regular dimensions of the material world, the dimension of time, and six other dimensions of the spirit—the dimension of time and the six other dimensions of the spirit correspond to the seven heavens mentioned in the Bible and in other esoteric writings. Humans, as living beings, are bounded to the three physical dimensions of space, plus the dimension of time, which is one of the dimensions of spirituality that is directly linked to man. The other six dimensions that explain dark matter or ether, are dimensions of the spirit, since they are barred to human perception—they can only be inferred indirectly, and probably will never be known to us directly by our senses, not even through instruments that would act as extension of our senses.

Physical science has clearly established that speeds beyond the speed of light are unreachable. Material objects cannot move or generate speeds in the ether medium beyond the speed of light. Non-material entities, on the other hand, are not restricted to the speed of light, which means that ether is a medium much more complex than we can imagine the material world to be. We can interact with the spiritual world by means of meditation, imagery, dreams, and imagination, plus concentration. Through varied rituals we can make the spiritual world respond to what we want the material world to be. Ritual is important because it creates the conditions in the ethereal world that will produce changes in our material world in a similar fashion that prayer does. Now, the spiritual world can mimic movement and phenomena of the material world, which is why spirits seem sometimes to materialize, and we can hear sounds of voices that do not come from material beings. With rituals we can also alter and excite the ether medium, so that it produces signals of communication (channels) with the spiritual world. Images are important because they give substance to our perceptions. If we see a house, and we turn around, the house is still there, because we keep the image of the house in our memory. But if the house is destroyed while we are not looking, it is still in the spiritual realm, in a different non-material dimension—the material house may have been destroyed, but its idea is imperishable, which is why we remember it. The destroyed house, on the other hand, will be perceived by a different individual, and will be fixated in a different dimension of the world of possibilities brought into reality. The person who witnessed the destruction of the house will juxtapose the previous image of the complete house to the next image of the destroyed house, and two world possibilities will have become realities to the same individual in the eternal flow of time, and the past is as real as the present. The spirit can visit and explore this world of contiguous realities, which allows the individual to explore the past and the future.

Neuroscientists have not been able to explain how savants can perform incredible mathematical calculations and other spiritual tasks, like producing and reproducing classic music, remembering things to incredible details, etc. because they search for explanations in the mechanical works of the brain. The savants, for whatever reasons that may go from a traumatic birth to accidental brain injury, seem to disconnect from the reality we know, in such a way that they use all their brain power to connect with the world we seldom explore, the reality of ideas, and mathematics belongs to the realm of the spirit. What savants do is no different from what seers and mediums do, except that savants play with ideas rather than spirits, although both ideas and spirits dwell in the spiritual realm.

The Ego

We will say here that the ego is the generator of needs and wants—the ego is at the center of gravity of our bundle of needs. If and when the ego runs out of indispensable human needs, it'll always be ready to create new and bizarre ones, and when it runs out of ideas to turn trivial things into necessities, it will turn into itself and will make of appeasing itself a super need, to be satisfied indefinitely, which is why rich people will make of hoarding money a goal into itself—even if they know that they will never be able to spend all the money they have in less than one lifetime.

Making contact with the spiritual world is something that pertains to the anima. If and whenever the ego imposes itself on a weak anima and tries to make contact with the spiritual world, the ego will only communicate with demons and evil spirits that will cheat both the anima and the ego, making them believe that they are in the presence of good spiritual entities. This is because the ego is always looking for things of the material world, riches, vengeance, sex, etc. The ego is totally incompetent to make contact with the world of good spiritual entities, which is why the prayers of the ego will only be answered by evil spiritual forces. We said before that the ego is incapable of making contact with the spiritual world, and this in no way contradicts the fact that evil spirits can find their way to the self through an anima already weakened by an imposing and ambitious ego. The fact is that God will never listen to the prayers of the ego.

The ego, the anima, and the self are another example of the holy triad. The self is the manifestation and result of the resolution of the conflict between the anima and the ego. The self is what makes an individual unique and totally different from another individual, and yet the self will be driven mainly by either the anima or the ego. We know the difference between persons that manifest a great love for humanity, and thus, are spiritually loaded individuals, and those people who only think about their own interests, reflecting a personality loaded with ego influences. We see here how the duality blends into the triad, which is a manifestation of the unity. In other words, the duality ego-anima resolves into the self (the triad) or individual human entity (the unity). These sacred numbers, one (the unity), two (the duality) and three (the triad) are at the root of the Templars' mysticism, itself derived from Hebrew and Christian theologies.

Ether Disturbance

A moving particle, like an electron moving close to the speed of light, creates a disturbance or excitement in ether similar to an electromagnetic wave. An electromagnetic wave, on the other hand, carries no moving particle with it. It's just a moving disturbance of ether that carries with it a bundle of energy—by the very fact that is a disturbance—that for all practical purposes resembles a particle. Scientists call these ether 'particles' photons, and claim that they have no mass, as it should be. These particles of ether, though they travel at the speed of light, carry different amounts of energy, depending on their frequency. This means that ether, though continuous in its composition—whatever that may be—is deformable in a discrete form that gives origin to the so called quanta of energy, which means that at the speed of light, ether reaches its maximum capacity of longitudinal deformation (refer to wave length, frequency, and energy). Particles can travel at speeds close to the speed o light, but they can never reach the speed of light, because to accelerate those particles to the speed of light would require an infinite amount of energy. Photons, or ghost particles, on the other hand, travel at the speed of light because they are pure bundles of ether energy. The speed of light, thus, depends on the elasticity and composition of ether. An ether excitement or disturbance moves longitudinally and elliptically, like a twister (or whirl or tornado or vortex) so it has spin, but it doesn't have mass. Now the speed of light limits the speed at what material objects can move, or the speed at which the ether can generate movement when excited by a material source (or force), but spiritual entities are free to "move" at speeds greater than the speed of light, because spiritual entities are "pure movement" of the ether medium counter-facing the material world.

The human brain has the capacity to communicate via the senses with the material world, but it also has the capacity to communicate via resonance (like in a resonance box) with the ethereal world—the world of spiritual entities. We receive messages from the ethereal world, and we have the capacity to send messages to that world. Our brain is, in other words, a receptor-transmitter of electromagnetic waves of all kinds, far more complex than the electromagnetic waves that come through our eyes. Our brain is our interface with the material world and with the spiritual world. With the material world we interact via our nervous system and our senses. The brain processes the external sensuous information with its inner-wired brain circuitry (logic), taps other information gathered from the ethereal world, and reacts to the stimuli from the material world (creating images that fix, change, invent, explain, etc. the material phenomena). Our input from the spiritual world is much different than the one we get from the material world, and we cannot process this input with the brain apparatus we use to explain things of the material world—hence the conflict of science and religion, being and existence, matter and spirit, etc. Although we also use reason to process things of the spirit, our main tools to process what comes from the world of electromagnetic phenomena (that resides in ether) are intuition, introspection, mystic awareness, and contemplation, because ether is the means of transmission of both moving particles and electromagnetic disturbances. These electromagnetic disturbances come from all over the universe, but mainly from the ether that fills in the interstices of matter, which is booming with all kinds of electromagnetic energies.

When we die, what comes out of the body is a tremendous convulsion of electromagnetic disturbances (our soul) that shocks the ether. This disturbance—we some day will be able to design machines that will detect these disturbances—impact the ether and get transmitted all over the universe. If we were evil people, our soul will be a cacophony of wild electromagnetic bundles that will wander in the ethereal world and will be reinforced by other cacophonies of electromagnetic bundles, creating friction and heat—lots of heat—and this is hell, eternal damnation (whether or not this heat burns like material heat is something I don't want to know). This is one reason why for the Templars it is important to tend for the terminally ill, so that we can smooth out the electromagnetic bundle of spiritual energy which is about to create a disturbance in ether. If these packets of energy are of the harmonious type—all in perfect harmony—the soul of the deceased will go to heaven where there is a filter that doesn't let in bundles of cacophonous energy. Hell and Heaven, thus, are realities of the ether. But this is only one of many interpretations that tries to relate, as much as possible, to the physical world.

As far as the notion of hell and heaven is concerned, some of the apocryphal Gospels have an interesting interpretation that departs from orthodox Christian doctrine. According to some apocryphal writings, there cannot be hell, because God is much too good to send people to a place of eternal suffering. It is my contention that if there is love, then there must be justice—read about the Principle of Love in my book *The Axioms of Being and the Renaissance of the Templars*—and people have to pay for their sins. Christ came as a way out of this requirement of justice, so that we don't have to be punished for our sins; He gave his blood to wash out all the sins of the world, but still requiring repentance and His acceptance as our savior, as necessary conditions to be cleansed of sin. Christian orthodoxy claims that without Christ we are bound to a hell of fire and eternal damnation. But there is one problem with this concept of hell: If we are talking about spiritual entities in the spiritual realm, any reference to time is invalid, since time and space are not qualities of the spiritual realm, and eternal means "never ending in time." Furthermore, justice requires that the punishment be proportionate to the sin, and we have an additional problem with the application of justice: Mainly that it consists of doing something bad (punishment) for the sake of a good purpose (curbing sinful behavior) in compliance with the *lex talionis*, and only God can do this perfectly, only God is qualified enough to apply the *lex talionis*—that is, without an excessive punishment, which is bad, and without a lenient punishment, which is also bad. This means that if the secular authorities don't punish us for a crime committed, we still will face God's punishment, and since the secular authorities are imperfect in imparting justice, even if we are punished in life, we may still face punishment after death. And that's what hell is, paying for those sins not vindicated by Christ, and since the spiritual world is timeless, paying for our sins in the afterlife may not be an eternal punishment, but a timeless one, whatever that means—and we will only understand the meaning of timelessness after we die. So, don't count out hell as yet, because justice indeed requires punishment, and we don't know if a timeless punishment is also an eternal one, given that we don't have a clear understanding of "eternal" in the life beyond.

Now, tapping into nature through our sense terminals is not like tapping into the ether through our resonance terminals, because the spiritual is far more real than the material. The spiritual is eternal, and though is in constant change and motion, it doesn't change fundamentally in essence. The material world, on the other hand, is always changing.

How the ether interacts with the brain is something we still need to investigate. But if light impacts material objects, something similar must happen when we will something to be changed (miracles). Our pure force of electromagnetic energy, which is our faith, will impact the material world and make it change. But this can only be done by those who ride the ether in the same frequency with the will of God.

How do I know all this? I don't really know, because the things of the spirit cannot be proven, they can only be discerned (intuited, as it were), and then believed. Knowledge pertains to science, and belief pertains to spirituality. The limits of scientific knowledge expand with new discoveries, but the difference between knowledge and belief cannot be dissolved into a continuous and far reaching extension of knowledge. Belief and faith will always be side by side with knowledge, no matter how much we get to discover, and no matter how much we get to know about the universe.

Thought vs. Action

Jesus said that he who desires somebody else's wife has already committed adultery in his heart. This is because the lust for somebody else's spouse is the genesis of adultery—just as conception is the genesis of a human life, which can be interrupted voluntarily or involuntarily (naturally), the thought of sexually possessing a married woman/man is the 'conception' of adultery, which can be carried out always so voluntarily.

The power of the thought is such that we can create realities, *beings*, with just thinking about them—be mindful that I am talking here about *beings*, not to be confused with *material beings*, at least not yet. Likewise, the desire (the lust) for the possession of a married woman, already creates the reality of adultery—and similarly to the case of the child born after conception, the thought of adultery can lead to the 'birth' of an adulterous relationship, though the sin is already committed at the moment of 'conception' of the adulterous thought. We are constantly creating realities that *are*, which could become realities that *exist*. The thought of adultery is the *being* of adultery (adultery in the spirit) and the actual consummation of adultery brings it into *existence*.

Why is it disrespectful to God that we should have sinful thoughts? Because God *is* in a spiritual world, and our thoughts *are* or belong to the realm of the spiritual world—and thus are a source of contamination of this realm—so that God can 'see' the reality of our sinful thoughts, just like we can physically see the repugnant reality of the materialization of anything that is bad, prohibited, or evil.

Our thoughts can indeed create realities. Otherwise, how can we explain the genius of Leonardo da Vinci in his artistic and engineering capacity, the genius of great inventors, or the genius of prodigious scientists like Newton or Einstein, who created things in their minds before they put them on paper or devised experiments to test them? But our creativity can be of two radically different sorts: the creativity of the saints and the creativity of the knowledgeable. The creativity of the saints has to do with faith, while the creativity of the scientists has to do with knowledge of the physical world.

We can define faith as the power of the will to turn into reality the entities of the world of possibilities (faith is the power of the will to bring things from the realm of *being* to the realm of *existence*)—and these 'creations' that result of powerful acts of faith we call miracles. There are two ways miracles can happen: One is by altering the natural processes of nature without physically interfering with them, and the other is by actually doing (making a reality) of what we want to create, which is why we have to be careful with what we desire. For faith has a positive and a negative aspect to it, although faith itself is neutral. In order to have faith, we must imagine the object of our faith, and the objects of faith may be good (positive), or bad (negative), which is the reason why we must always have positive thoughts, and shun negative thoughts and attitudes—this happens in spite of the fact that religious faith is very often associated with positive things only, which is not always the case for secular faith. Furthermore, we can't have what we can't imagine, which is why we must visualize with faith what we want. One thing that is absolutely pernicious is to think of something you want to be or do, and immediately reject the thought because you believe it is impossible to make it a reality—the very act of rejecting your "unreal" thought energizes negatively the force of your faith, killing what your mind had created in the spirit.

Of course, I can't visualize myself as being the King of England, because this is a thought which is out of my sphere of possibilities. When we say that we must create and keep positive thoughts, we mean that we must steer our imagination towards what is in our visual horizon of possibilities, and keep it within the sphere defined by this visual horizon. Anything outside our sphere of possibilities belongs to the realm of wishful thinking, which is a world populated by chimeras. Another mistake we must avoid is confusing hope with faith. Hope is to the ego what faith is to the anima. When we hope for the attainment of something, if it becomes a reality, it is due to the works of probability, and thus entirely out of the power of our will, or due to the works of our own physical efforts—in which case it is something always attainable, if we just produce the effort to make it a reality. When we have faith in the realization of something, probability has absolutely nothing to do with it, and our physical efforts to attain what we expect (with the exercise of our faith) will never come about entirely as a result of those physical efforts, which is why the fruits of faith are always considered miracles. Notice that with respect to hope we talk of probabilities, while with respect to faith we talk of possibilities, for that which is impossible to man, is possible to God if we just will it to be with the power of our faith. Thus, the desire to be the King of England, since it is out of my world of possibilities, could never be attained by hope, but only by faith, except that I cannot cover (disguise) hope with faith, in an attempt to cheat God, which is a good reason for me never to expect to be the King of England.

The Dichotomy of the Self

The dichotomy of *being* and *existence* is both a result and a cause of two different approaches to world phenomena. Questions of *existence* relate to the world of physical phenomena, and questions of *being* relate to the world of spiritual phenomena. If my question is: Where do I come from? My intellectual ego will try to answer the question by using the methods of scientific discourse, and as the inquiry about the origin of man extends farther and farther back in time, the genesis of man as a spiritual being gets lost, and is obscured by the findings about man as an animal species. Science responds to questions of existence, like: What am I made of? What is the chemical and biological composition of the human body? What is the function of the brain, the heart, the lungs, etc? Questions of *being*, on the other hand, cannot be answered by science. When we make an abstraction of space and time, all there is left is our consciousness of *being*, and if we ask what *am* I?, our question cannot be answered by our sensuous perceptual apparatus, and trying to set up experiments will not work either, because our inner being has nothing to do with our outer existence. This is a spiritual question that can only be answered by contemplative introspection, making use of intuition and faith. Physical science is useless when dealing with matters of the spirit.

The ego always opposes the anima. The ego is the obstacle between our spirit and the Spirit of God. The ego wants everything that satisfies the flesh; it cries out for pleasure. The ego is the big impediment we have to conduct our work with God Enterprises. The work of God requires the taming of the ego, so that the anima can carry out its work on behalf of society. The objective and function of the Fraternity of the Templars is to bring about what the anima yearns for and to deflate the ego, so that we can do the work that will lead to the advent of the City of God in the city of man.

Perhaps we will never know whether the Templars found the Holy Grail, the Ark of the Covenant, the Philosopher's Stone, or any of the so-called secret or occult knowledge. But if they discovered or invented financial banking, they probably understood the rudiments of the capitalist system of production. They even had *encomiendas*, a kind of cooperative farming. They also probably understood that there is no need to separate the church from the state in the manner in which it was being separated in their time. In our time, this separation is unnecessary, because for the Templars and for the Orbis Unum party, the needs of all humans must be attended, and those needs are both spiritual and material.

There are universal religious principles that apply to the whole of humanity, including to the so-called atheists, which means that religion and secularism need not go separate ways when, on the contrary, they seem to complement each other. Furthermore, sometimes it's difficult, and even impossible, to separate the material necessities of men from their spiritual and emotional needs, which is why the solution of man's problems requires a unified comprehensive approach by something that integrates state and church, rather than making an arbitrary separation of what comes together in each individual's self.

As we said somewhere else, both science and religion use unproven principles for their system of truths. In other words, they both rely on faith. Spiritual statements of faith, taken to be true, are called dogmas, and dogmas are, thus, truths about the spiritual world.

Can we take as a dogma anything we care to make into a 'spiritual truth' just because we capriciously wish to build our own religious credo, based on our own particular 'dogmas'? The answer is absolutely and emphatically no. A dogma must be intuited by a great majority of humans; the intuition of one individual, or of a tiny minority of humans, will not count as a dogma, but will rather be the foundation of a cult or sect. A dogma must be a spiritual statement that makes sense to the vast majority of people, across all cultures, and through all historical periods; it's a truth of spiritual man in his capacity as *Homo sapiens* evolving towards *Homo spiritualis*.

An axiom, on the other hand, is a truth of the material world. An axiom may be, in fact or in principle, verified empirically, without reference to other empirical statements.

"The same thing cannot *be* and *not be* at the same time." This is the rule of the excluded middle; either something is or is not, but not both at the same time—notice that being is taken here as synonymous with existing. The rule of the excluded middle is used in science and mathematics, and is called an axiom because it stands by itself as a truth—it doesn't need further evidence to validate it.

"One thing is identical to itself" is another axiom. Expressed in mathematical form we say that y=y is an identity, an elementary truth or axiom that cannot be verified or proven by anything else.

"The whole is greater than the part" and "The whole is equal to the sum of its parts" are other examples of what we consider to be axioms, elementary truths that cannot be rejected by our judgment on the basis of additional verification.

We will use *be* for spiritual entities and *exist* for material things. No definitions are given of those terms.

I am vs. I exist

We come back to the Principle of Existence: *I am. I exist*. We said that this principle is Descartes' *cogito ergo sum*. *I am* gives rise—not as in a causal relationship, but rather as a pre-suppositional substratum—to all our spiritual knowledge; and all our spiritual knowledge is based on the statement *I am*. This is a statement of faith, because it doesn't have anything to do with logic. The rest of the individuals that make up humanity *are* because we will them to be. Thus, *'people (humanity) are'* represents another statement of faith. Although we shouldn't try to reason spiritual things out, we can metaphorically say that since *'I am, and people are, then God is'*. And *'God is'* is yet another statement of faith. When Moses asked God about His name, for all reply God told Moses "I am who I am," which really means that God has no name, because God is a spiritual being. We properly attach names to things that *exist*, and not to spiritual entities that *are*. But we dwell in a physical body, and communicate with words, and this human condition (or impediment) forces us to use labels for things like "soul," "spirit," or "anima," which in reality have no name.

In contraposition to *I am*, *I exist* is not a statement of faith, but an axiom that can be immediately confirmed by experience. If I am conscious and perfectly awake, then I can confirm that I exist. I exist is subordinated to I am, because I have to be perfectly conscious to discern my physical existence. That's why I can say that I exist if I am, but I cannot appropriately affirm that I am if I exist, which is why I get the intuitive knowledge that my spirit is immaterial, that it doesn't need a body to *be*, and hence, is immortal. Yet, don't let yourself be misguided by the apparent trend of reasoning applied to this discussion, because asserting the immortality of the soul is also an assertion based on faith (and most definitely not on reason). I am and I exist are so closely superimposed on each other that it is very difficult to separate one from the other, giving the appearance that they are identical statements. The worst part of it is that logic does not work here, and to try to use reason to disentangle one statement from the other has led to all kinds of dead-ends and logical contradictions. Let's face it, I am and I exist reflect two different entities juxtaposed to one another, although to *be* is a necessary (though not sufficient) condition to *exist*, and not the other way around.

Now, all physical (material) knowledge originates from the statement *I exist*, and is based on the same statement. Nothing in science can be sustained without the intervention of somebody who can utter the axiom *I exist*.

I know that the temperature in my neighborhood is 75 degrees Fahrenheit, because somebody read the thermometer, obtaining a reading of 75 degrees Fahrenheit—and that somebody, to get a reading from the thermometer, must exist. I accept his statement that the temperature is 75 degrees Fahrenheit by faith, though if I were to doubt it, then I would get my own thermometer and get the information myself; this, my own personal reading would be trustworthy, because I exist. But again, I must trust whoever made the thermometer that also happens to exist or have existed, because otherwise I would have to make my own thermometer, and to make my own thermometer I would have to trust the laws of physics, these laws were discovered by men who existed, etc. In the final analysis, somebody must exist to make a statement of fact. Therefore, all science relies, depends, and is based on the axiom of existence, mainly *I exist*.

This discussion brings about Descartes' sought for *first principles*, except that they are juxtaposed to one another: *I am*; *I exist*. This is the duality of being that philosophy has been arguing about ever since man learned to think rationally.

Descartes was looking for the initial principle(s) from which everything else could be deduced. He almost managed to find it in his *'cogito ergo sum'* dictum, which should be translated as:

I am, therefore I exist.

The 'I am' is the basic dogma of spirituality. The 'I exist' is the basic axiom of materiality. The problem of Descartes was trying to establish a logical relationship between the *cogito* and the *sum*, when there isn't and there can't be any. The *cogito*, or I think element—which is really consciousness of the anima—happens to be paired to the *sum*, or I exist element—which is the bundle of sense perceptions that make a human body. There is no *ergo* that connects the two; the presence of the two elements over time is what makes a human being. Nevertheless, there is a sense in which we can talk of the *cogito* as being a necessary (but not sufficient) condition for the *sum*, while it is not clear that the sum is a necessary and sufficient condition for the cogito.

In human discourse we should never confuse the subject with the object of a statement. 'I am, therefore I exist' could be expressed as 'I, my anima, perceive my physical body,' which leads me to say that 'I exist.' In the first statement I is the subject, and physical body is the object. If we interpret 'I' and 'anima' as being one and the same, it is inappropriate to say 'I perceive my anima,' because the object cannot function as subject in the same sentence. This kind of problem is discussed by Bertrand Russell at length. [Think of the town's barber who shaves those people in the town who do not shave themselves. If the town's barber shaves himself, then he doesn't shave himself; if the town's barber doesn't shave himself, then he shaves himself]. Kant's antinomies of reason can be said to be a product of the violation of the subject-object rule. The concept of infinity, both in philosophy and mathematics (and even in physics) is plagued with paradoxes, contradictions and antinomies. Just read the famous and interesting arguments of Zeno of Elea to prove that movement doesn't exist. Cantor's proposed solutions only make the paradoxes even more complicated.

The trap of solipsism is the result of extreme or radical empiricism. A person who refuses to accept the being of others will rely only on his/her own perceptions to accept the existence of those other individuals, and since the solipsist only recognizes his/her own being (in a very confused and bizarre manner, if that much) everything else in the field of his/her perceptions has a subjective reality. In other words, the world of a solipsist exists as long as he/she perceives it, as long as the solipsist exists (lives). If empiricism were to be consistent with its own views, it should hold fast to solipsism, and yet, not even the most radical empiricist will accept a solipsist view of the world, such is the power of faith. Because only by accepting the being of others—by nothing else than faith—can we release the material world from our own subjectivity, making it objective the very same moment we realize that other individuals, other beings, can also perceive the world as we do, because they not only exist (to our eyes), but because they are, i.e. they have an anima. Furthermore, the existence of God follows from the fact that the world will continue to exist even when the last of the humans dies—and this is a statement of faith—lest we fall into another empiricist trap, nihilism, the view that once the world ceases to be perceived, it ceases to exist. Because who or what is going to sustain the *objectivity* of the world in the absence of perceiving sentient individuals? Not God, because for a radical empiricist God does not exist.

But the question remains: why would empiricists reject solipsism, when solipsism is the most consequent conclusion of their view that anything to be real needs empirical verification? And although they deny their being by identifying it with their existence, they are forced to get out of their own skin in order to accept the objective reality of others, and once they are cornered with their self-defeating arguments, they have no other recourse than agnosticism, and extreme agnosticism falls into the trap of atheism when dealing with the question of whether or not God is or exists.

Atheism is more prevalent than solipsism, although they rest in exactly the same premises, because it is easier to deny God's being and existence than it is to deny other people's being (though an empiricist accepts other people's existence, as a subjective reality, and only if those people are under the empiricist's field of perception)—think of it, a true solipsist is a god; he can claim that he has the power to create things (including people) by just perceiving them, except that objective reality in the form of a raging bull or a train, in the path of the solipsist, has the power to tramp, maim, or kill even a solipsist god.

When we say 'I am,' we are expressing that we are conscious of anima—the spirit, the soul. When we say 'I exist,' we are recognizing our corporeal existence, our capacity to sense objects, including our own body, directly with our senses or with instruments which are an extension of our senses (or an aid of our senses).

The 'I am' is the origin of spirituality and religion. The 'I exist' is the origin and base of all our scientific knowledge and empirical verification.

Our reason and logic are useful to get to know the world only. Our intuition and meditation are useful to get to know the spiritual realm only. If we use the tools of spirituality and try to apply them to the knowledge of the material world, we can only produce nonsense, rather than knowledge. If we use reason and the scientific method to try to make sense of spiritual things, we produce contradictions, paradoxes, antinomies and a whole range of conflicts between the spiritual and the material worlds—where there shouldn't be any, since they are separated of each other by an insurmountable methodological abyss. But though contradictions, paradoxes and antinomies are not acceptable in the material world, they are perfectly plausible when dealing with the spiritual world.

Science uses axioms as a starting point for their deductions. Religion uses dogmas. Both axioms and dogmas to be believed rely on faith. Axioms rely on the belief that what happened in the past will also happen in the future. If the world were such that every time we toss a fair coin the result is heads, science would say that the next toss is going to result in heads.

The difference between an axiom and a dogma is that axioms are truths given by experience. Dogmas are truths given by revelation or by mystic intuition—which have nothing to do with experience, and dogmas cannot be verified by more than one individual at a time. Science claims that perception and experiment are at its foundation. Religion claims that revelation and intuition (dogmatized knowledge) are at its foundation.

Examples: Science claims that the speed of light is 300,000 Km per second. This is consistent with experiment. It's an axiom, because there is no known explanation of why light travels at that speed. In other words, there is no known chain of events that, linked to each other, cause light to travel at the speed of 300,000 Km per second. This axiom is based on faith—it doesn't matter how many times we happen to measure the speed of light, the axiomatic result given above will always be the same—because as long as we don't explain the phenomena, there is no reason why we should not expect one experiment that may very well give a different measure. It may not be very probable, but it's possible, if and always we don't provide an explanation that rules out that possibility.

We know that other people exist because we can verify their existence through our senses. We hear them talk, we talk back to them, we see them, we can touch them, and we can even smell them. But no matter how real their existence is, we know that they *are* by a sheer act of faith. In other words, we know that they are spiritual entities like us, because we will them to be—this is an act of 'creation,' but then we are like God, we were made by God in His image and likeness, so we have the capacity to create. In reality is God who created people (both in the being and existing sense), but every time we perceive them we 'recreate' them (especially in the being sense), as it were, with the help of God. Don't try to reason this out, because this is all based on faith, and we said before that faith deals with spiritual entities only. If you were to sense some kind of logic in this discussion is probably because we are dealing with things at the boundaries of knowledge and faith. Think of a perfectly created drone or android that looks exactly like a human being—if we know it's a machine (no matter how perfectly it replicates a human), we can never will it to be (in the spiritual sense), because humans by themselves cannot will spiritual entities to be, we cannot create or destroy spirits.

The antagonism (friction) between scientific knowledge and religious belief is produced by a misunderstanding of their methods of determining their respective truths. Science is applicable to nature and the material world, and it relies on logic, reasoning, or other tools that rely on logic and reasoning, like mathematics. Religion uses exclusively the tools of mystic intuition, revelation, and faith for the attainment of its truths. That's why mystic intuition cannot be reasoned out, because any attempt to apply logic to religion gives as a result unsolvable contradictions.

Hence, spiritual knowledge cannot be submitted to the contamination of thought, arguments, the spoken and the written word, without losing all its meaning. If we grasp a spiritual knowledge by mystic intuition or revelation, it must be kept non-polluted by thought and reason, in order to remain a pristine spiritual knowledge. The mistake of those who criticize spiritual knowledge as being unscientific is that they don't realize that spiritual knowledge is indeed basically and essentially unscientific. The material world is the subject matter of science, not of religion. The spiritual world is the subject matter of religion, and ecstatic meditation is the method of mystic spiritualism.

When science tries to apply reason and logic to the universe as a whole, it's going out of its realm, because the subject matter of science is the material finite world, not the material infinite world. When religion tries to explain the material finite world, it falls in great contradictions, because the material world is not the realm of religion.

We call thinking the capacity of the human mind to reason, intuit, and create. Reason is mainly applied in scientific investigations, intuition (as in faith) in spiritual endeavors, and creation (as in invention, imagination, dreaming, divination, artistic expression) in the arts—and to some degree, in science.

Darwinism argues that the world's known species are a product of evolution. They look at bones over time and deduce that from a bipedal hominid called Australopithecus *Homo sapiens* evolved through thousands of years of evolution (in time). Darwinians refuse to include God in this process. They only see nature at work, and for them nature lacks intention. Creationists argue that God created the species as we know them—and all other species that have disappeared—as if they were a final product. Creationists refuse to see other than intelligent design in the origin of the species. The truth is that if God created all the species that are, and the ones that have been, his creation was an act that happened outside of the space-time matrix, which means that all those creatures were created simultaneously. But once God created the world, and with it the flow of time, the stream of several generations of individuals to produce another different individual, a different species, was a necessity of time in order to produce birth and decay. In the end, there is no contradiction between the religious interpretation and the scientific conjecture about the origin of the species. To say that it is not scientific to add one more element, i.e. God, to the theory of evolution is also a violation of the Occam's Razor principle—we are throwing in the element of *veiled emptiness* to 'explain' what screams for an explanation without the God element—because it is an assumption based on the same stuff that those who believe in God use, mainly faith (even if faith in veiled emptiness).

It is important to understand that the duality of man—on the one hand, the man-anima, and on the other hand, the man-ego—is inevitably going to lead to the City of God and to the city of man, respectively. The City of God is the advent of the kingdom of heaven on earth, while the city of man is what we have right now, the secular kingdom of men. This secular kingdom of men is ruled by the ego, and the ego's need for money, sex, power, and the things of this world, which will never satisfy the never ending lust of the ego for the material things and the pleasures of the flesh. The actual condition of the world is an uneven mixture of spirituality and materiality, materiality being disproportionately more prevalent than spirituality. This condition would eventually worsen and would lead to the demise of humanity as predicted in St. John's Apocalypse if we don't stir humanity away from materiality and towards the things of the spirit. If we change our ways, we will not only reach the kingdom of heaven on earth (not without going through spiritual Armageddon first, the final spiritual battle against the forces of the ego), but later will be raised in body and spirit to heaven—a transition we may not even feel, and which is reserved to purely spiritual beings like Jesus Christ, because spiritual power is strong enough to purify the flesh, and this mystery-miracle can be performed only by God.

The duality of ego and anima is important to the understanding of self, because the ego represents our actual existence in time and space, while our anima represents our timeless and incorporeal being (outside, as it were, from space and time). The ego, thus, is going to remember whatever happened in the past, and knows nothing about the future, while experiencing the present. The ego may make projections about the future, it may guess how things are going to turn out in the short run (and sometimes even in the long run), and it may make plans about the future. The ego is very much inclined for science, experiment, and the sense perceptions. Imagination, scheduling, invention, and planning are important for the ego's materialization of ideas in the immediate future. But the ego cannot "see" the future as clearly as it remembers past occurrences. The anima, on the other hand, has "memories" of the past and the future, and "knows" about the present not directly under the ego's field of perceptions. We call this faculty of the anima divination. The anima can tell you about the past, it can tell you what's going to happen in the future, and it can tell you about things not immediately perceptible in the present, because the anima can tap the "pool of memories" of the spiritual realm. But the ego is very imposing, it interferes greatly with the capacity of the anima to visualize things, which is why we don't always have complete access to the "pool of memories" of the spiritual world, and when we do, the "memories" of the things we see are not always clear and crisp, as they would be if they were memories produced by the ego. Some people would do better than others at "seeing" the past and the future, but all of us sometimes dream about future occurrences, or have premonitions about things that will happen in the future. We may sometimes experience déjà vu, which is the same memory as "seen" by the anima, but duplicated by the ego, and placed in the present and the past.

Déjà vu is a "memory" of something that happened in the past, and that it seems that it just happened in the present. Our "memories" of the past and our "memories" of the future are basically the same "stuff," which is why a psychic can speak about the past, as well as the future. There is no space or time in the spiritual realm. Our "memories" are only placed in the flow of time through our perception of physical phenomena. Once we are in the stream of the material world, our "memories" residing in the spirit are placed either in the past or in the future. In fact, our "memories" to our left, and our "memories" to our right of the flow of time get mixed up in the present in the mind of the seer, or in our dreams. How does our spirit "remember" things of the past or the future? This is a mystery that will be revealed. But once the spirit incarnates, we remember only a few things, and forget most other things.

Déjà vu confuses us, because what we experience in the present (and we call déjà vu) seems similar to what we interpret as having experienced in the past, but that our ego rejects (in fact) as never having experienced at all (we sink our teeth into our memories, and conclude 'no, I could never have been in this place before')—déjà vu may also be something that will happen in the future, a 'memory' we have of the future, thanks to our capacity to peak in the timeless world of ideas. It may even be something that we 'remember,' but it's really somebody else's memory. These are all phenomena of the spirit.

A propos of mysteries, we will say here that there are mysteries that will be known by man, there are mysteries that will be revealed to man, and there are those mysteries that man can't simply know. The mysteries that will be known by man are those that man himself will be able to uncover through scientific investigation and mathematical discoveries. We know about mysteries revealed through prophesizing. The mysteries that will never be known to man are those that can't be known for either of two reasons: either man is not physically, emotionally, mentally, or spiritually prepared to know them, or else man lacks the necessary tools of reasoning to understand them. The concept of infinity is one of those mysteries that man can only visualize, but that we cannot comprehend in its entirety. The presence of God may be one of those mysteries that we are neither physically nor mentally equipped to grasp, which may be one of the reasons why not even Moses could stand the presence of God, because it would kill him instantly.

We may also consider the occult as that knowledge that for special reasons cannot be known by the general population. Occult knowledge must remain a mystery to some people, because those people may not be mentally and spiritually prepared to assimilate that knowledge. Just like a 5-year old child is not intellectually prepared to assimilate Integral and Infinitesimal Calculus, there are things of the spirit that many an adult cannot assimilate. Occult knowledge, thus, is not occult with evil intentions—though it is perfectly feasible that evil people can and will keep some knowledge occult, so that others don't enjoy the "advantage" of knowing it. Modern weapons systems are occult knowledge of this latter kind.

The way mystery is related to miracles is typical of the things of the spirit that man is unable to comprehend. Just as there are no mysteries to God, there are also no miracles to God. What is impossible to man is perfectly possible to God. There is no way we can reconcile the opposites, as in the statement "something is or isn't," or "something can't be and not be at the same time." And yet, there must be a logic for the Deity such that opposites can coexist—and here I'm just speculating, since there is no way we can know the thoughts of God, so Einstein's dream to be like God could never be realized. Miracles have a way of being revealed that make them lose the sense of awe when we understand them; if a cancerous tumor gradually shrinks for no reason at all, until it disappears, and we don't know how to explain the phenomena, we immediately consider this mystery of healing a miracle. But if this process of healing is later explained in a rational manner, the notion of confronting a miraculous cure vanishes, as if every process in nature, explained or not, was not a miracle.

The mechanism of faith is very peculiar, because faith taps into that which is mysterious and can only be known to God. The reason faith is so powerful is because it allows—by a supernatural influence from man to God—to move the world of the unexplained and the unexplainable. When we put our trust in God, we are generating a force that operates in the realm of the impossible by the actions of God.

Free Will and Determinism

Philosophers have been arguing about these opposing concepts for centuries, some in favor of absolute freedom and some in favor of total determinism. And yet, freedom and determinism are one in the world of spiritual entities. Absolute freedom of the will, if perfectly contained within God's will, becomes deterministic, which means that our freedom of the will may be both absolutely free and absolutely deterministic at the same time, if and only if it coincides with God's will. An example from science fiction may help to understand this.

In the series Star Trek, there is a group of chapters that make reference to some beings called the Borg. These beings completely strip other beings of their free will for the good of what they call the collective. In other words, the supra-being made up of the individual beings that make the collective dictates how each individual acts—this is complete determinism. If within this context of complete determinism we were to think of the individual members of the collective to have absolute free will, in such a way that whatever they decide to do (or not to do) individually, with absolutely no restrictions, were to be in agreement with the will of the collective, this free will would become determinism, and there wouldn't be any contradiction between free will and determinism. Therefore, if and whenever, our absolute free will is in complete agreement with God's will, with no restrictions whatsoever, then our absolute free will is completely determined by God's will, and this, far from being a contradiction in terms, is the union of the contraries found in the Marxist philosophy. This union of the contraries that resolves into an upper synthesis of elements that hide their contradictions is at the core of a much spiritual philosophy—in spite of the materialistic twist that Marx and others gave to the so-called Dialectic and Historical Materialism. Perhaps, then, we should rethink the elements of materialism that fit well in a spiritualistic philosophy.

As a special aspect of determinism, we can mention spiritual predestination. This belief in predestination negates the necessity of free will, since what do we need free will for if we are predestined to salvation, condemnation, or spiritual annihilation? But, we know that there is free will, and hence, we don't really need an argument to support it. In a dualistic philosophy of man, predestination would imply that all men are born with an ego, but only the predestined ones for salvation would be born with both an ego and an anima—that a man should be born with just an ego would make him like an animal, and a man born with just an anima is contradictory, because the flesh requires an ego, and because *ego-less-ness* would make him a spiritual being, like an angel, which also contradicts the definition of man—so that no matter what the latter do, their anima would always remain immaculate, free of all sin, and thus always ready for eternal bliss. Those born without anima would forever be annihilated—would forever be predestined for annihilation—though perhaps not bound to an afterlife of hell and eternal suffering. Predestination, in other words, leads to salvation for free, without having to do anything for humanity, and to the contrary, even if we sin and commit crimes against God, nature or man, we would still be saved if we are predestined to be saved. Some Protestant religions, with the help of predestination, would be forced to conclude that for those predestined for salvation there is no sin, since by the grace of predestination they have already been pardoned of all sins past, present and future, through Jesus' sacrifice in the cross, and thus cannot lose their ticket to heaven, even if they commit all kinds of heinous crimes. Predestination, interpreted this way, thus, leads to all kinds of bizarre conclusions and theological aberrations.

A spiritual philosophy of non-predestination and free will—and this interpretation is held by Catholics—on the other hand, forces man to earn his salvation, and permits all humans the free participation in God's bid for eternal bliss, without exceptions, special prerogatives or privileges. And since there must be justice, those who committed sin must pay for their transgressions. As to whether or not hell is a place of temporary or eternal suffering, that's a different topic of heated theological debate. Now, as we said before, in the world of the spirit, predestination and free will don't necessarily contradict each other, since the absolute free will of a man that is always in tune with God's will, makes him predestined to salvation, and this renders all theological arguing for or against free will, or for or against predestination, fruitless, since man's anima may partake of both. But there is yet another interpretation of free will and determinism, and that comes next.

The ego is in charge of the needs of the flesh. The anima is in charge of the needs of the self—we defined the self to be a tag or label for both the ego and the anima, without being a different entity. The ego already knows what to do to satisfy the flesh, and it doesn't have to make any decisions—in fact, the ego is never presented with moral choices, and it will take what is convenient to itself—and the ego is, therefore, subject to determinism. The ego's determinations are dictated by hedonism, and thus, it will seek for that which is pleasurable, and it will avoid anything that causes pain. The anima, on the other hand, takes care of the self, which is a duality of ego and anima, and thus, has to make a decision as which way to go. Either it satisfies the ego, the flesh, or else, it will give way to the needs of the spirit. This capacity of the anima to make decisions is what constitutes *free will*.

Free will is the opportunity of evil to be, and the presence of goodness potentiates, or raises the potential for evil, without causing it. Evil is opportunistic, and it may crop up in the presence of goodness. The anima is good by its own nature and pristine in purity, but its sole presence makes the possibility of evil to be, and this is free will. Consequently, the problem of free will and determinism corresponds to the duality of ego and anima in the self. At the spiritual level, the anima is predestined to be pure and immaculate, but it may get soiled by giving in to the excessive needs of the ego. The ego, in other words, is the original sin. If we were to be born ego*less*, we would be like Adam and Eve before the fall, incapable of doing what is evil, or wrong, if not for God's prohibition. For what sense there is in goodness without the capacity to be discerned, to be seen, to be detected? The potential for evil gives to goodness the capacity to be discerned, and God's prohibition was the spark that ignited in Adam and Eve the exercise of their free will. Once they violated the prohibition, the ego came into being, and it would stay with us for every generation to come.

Now, back to predestination. If the anima is in complete control of the self, man is predestined to be saved, and this condition of being completely controlled by the anima is equivalent to being in a state of grace. The *dictatorship of the anima*—being under a state of grace—predestines man for salvation, because the ego is chained and subdued by the spirit, and in this sense, an anima in complete and total control of the self is incapable of doing evil deeds, knows no sin, and basically ignores the existence of hell. In other words, somebody who is in a state of grace is immunized against sin, hell and the devil, which means that for such an individual, sin, hell and the devil were destroyed and do not exist. And so is free will, because an anima in total control of the individual loses its capacity to make moral decisions, for its decisions are always going to be good—there cannot be moral decisions if you are forced to do only what is good, and those incapable of committing crimes are not and cannot be subjected to *lex talionis*, otherwise known as the Law in the Old Testament. Now, this is for an individual whose anima is in complete control of the self, and thus, of the ego. But what about those who are not in control of their ego? They are like a diamond buried in the mud, waiting to be discovered, whose beauty can only be revealed if cleaned of the dirt that covers it. What about those who were enslaved by their ego before they found a way to force their anima to take control? What about their past sins and transgressions? That's where Jesus comes into action. The death of the Lamb of God in the cross redeemed our past debts with Divine Justice. In this sense, if we were already forgiven for our past wrongdoings, and we remain in complete control of the self—if our anima is at the command and control post of the vessel, which is our spirit, our body and our flesh—we necessarily bypass God's Judgment, and for those people living in the grace, there is simply no Final Judgment. These conceptions are at the core of a Pauline theology, but only seldom explicitly making the claims expressed above.

How about those who never found Christ, and never let their anima control their selves? In other words, how about those who never fell in a state of grace, and never will? Will they go to a hell of fire? This is a mystery yet to be revealed, although my ego, filled with a sense of vengeance, tells me that they will be punished in a hell of fire, and yet my anima soothes my self by telling me that perhaps God, in his infinite kindness, will clean the diamond which is their anima, wiping off the dirt and filth, and restoring it to its pristine spiritual purity. But who are we to judge? Are we forgetting that what is impossible to man is possible to God? One thing is for sure, those who are not predestined to fall in the grace of Jesus Christ will never participate in the joy of being citizens of the City of God that will forever establish its rule in this world.

Wait a minute. What are we saying here? We are just affirming that in a community of people whose animas are in control of their selves we will be living in heaven before we "go to heaven," which seems to be a contradiction. It is not a contradiction, because in the world of the spirit there are no contradictions, and terms that apparently are contradictory blend into each other. Therefore the City of God can be brought down to the city of man, and if we do this worldwide and for all humanity, the *continuum* will eventually blend our earthly existence into a spiritual *being* of all, just like the Ascension of Christ into heaven diluted the differences between His bodily manifestation and His spiritual being, as His Divine presence rose to the sky above.

Axioms vs. Dogmas

"What is possible is real," this is an axiom. It may be inferred by the Postulate of Faith, postulate that is at the boundaries of logic and reason. This axiom is similar to the so-called Murphy's Law: "If anything can go wrong, it will." We could also say that it is a dogma, rather than an axiom, except that the dictum has nothing to do with matters of the spirit, but rather is deeply rooted in experience.

The soul or spirit is the avenue or the outlet window of the 'experiences' collected in the 'pool of memories' of the spiritual realm. That's how we 'remember' the past and the future. The soul or spirit is outside of the st-matrix (space-time matrix). The st-matrix is not the same as the 'space-time continuum' of Einstein, because this concept closes the door to the *being* of entities like the spirit or anima. The st-matrix, also known as ether, on the other hand, is discrete and continuous at the same time: discrete in its relation to physical phenomena, continuous in its relation to spiritual phenomena. One of ether's facets faces the material world, the other faces the spiritual world, and this other facet of ether (or the st-matrix) is called the *continuum*.

Reincarnation tries to explain the fact that we can 'remember' memories that don't belong to us, 'memories' that our ego considers foreign to the self. One problem with reincarnation is that our anima never moves from one body to another body—the ego can be overtaken or replaced by another ego, or by evil spirits (possession), but not the anima. When a person dies, the anima of that person is incapable of moving to another body, human or animal, since this would be like resurrecting in a foreign body, and we only know of resurrection in the same body. Furthermore, the spirit of a human in an animal body would be able to 'remember' with clarity some of the memories when the spirit was in a human body, something unknown of in humans, much less in animals. Just like déjà vu, reincarnation is the confusion of the ego confronted with the experiences 'visualized' by the anima. Since the anima has access to the "pool of memories" of the spiritual world, it can pick up 'memories' that belong to another person, which the ego does not recognize as its memories, thus leading to the presumption that we lived another life or lives of the past. Again, it is easier for some people than for others to 'remember' other lives, especially under hypnosis, originating the belief that we lived past lives, and thus reincarnated in the body we now have.

Freud's psychoanalysis is very close to our view here. He was dwelling with a subject that is at the borderline between science and spirituality when he talked about the conscious, the sub-conscious and the unconscious mind.

Here is a simple dogma: "The soul or spirit is." This statement is true and is a dogma—knowledge obtained by meditation or mystical intuition. It cannot be communicated from one person to another, it cannot be argued by thoughts, words, or written discourse. Dogmas are imposed on the human understanding by the sheer power of the will to believe (faith).

Here is an example of an axiom: "Material things exist in the discrete st-matrix." This st-matrix is the space-time continuum of Einstein, except that it is discrete, rather than continuous. The st-matrix both is and exists. Its existence is derived by the Postulate of Faith and by the fact that matter is perceived in space and time.

The space-time continuum of Einstein is not discrete and, hence, does not allow spirits to be, which is perfectly OK, because Einstein deals with the world of material objects only.

The st-matrix, which may also be thought of as a substance, is like a net that sustains matter and allows spiritual entities to be, though outside this st-matrix, which itself is time and space (where everything else exists).

The following is an important dogma: "Spiritual beings are in an ever-present all-encompassing simultaneity." Hence, every spirit shares the 'memories' of the spiritual realm. That's why psychics and spiritual people can tap into the spiritual realm, where these 'memories' have no past or future, and filter them through their own existence into the material world, as 'memories' of the past or the future. This way a seer, a séance, a magician, or a medium can predict the future, talk about the past, and say things about the present that they have no experience of. They can even read people's minds. This is because what's in our minds is also in the minds of everyone else, except that our corporeal existence distorts and shocks our spirits in such a way that we don't know what other people are thinking, and for the same reasons, we don't know the future, and cannot see into the past—I'm talking here about ordinary human beings. Only privileged individuals can tap into the 'memories,' or ideas of the spiritual world, though they do it with great limitations and distortions provoked by the myriad of stimuli of our material existence.

Just as we can tap the myriad bits of information from the spiritual realm, we can impress and even channel spiritual energy on objects and situations in such a way that objects can be charged with good or bad influences. Objects, places, and situations contaminated with bad energies carry on curses and provoke bad things to happen to people. Amulets and sacred objects can emanate good energies that could make a person with the appropriate mindset—that is, the appropriate mind frequency (sometimes also called faith), as it were—absorb those energies that make miracles possible.

This means that our mind can charge objects and situations with good or bad energies. If you suppose that a person's brain under meditation—or on the negative side, under the influence of strong emotions, like hatred, envy, or jealousy—can show areas of the brain on a CAT scan where activity is manifested as change in colors from blue to red, those brain activities are producing changes in the brain physiology, and therefore, they may very well stir the contiguous ether next to the brain surface in such a way that the brain ethereal emanations impinge in the objects or surroundings, producing certain spiritual influences that affect the world and the objects of the world. This is the origin of magic, good and bad, and witchcraft. No wonder alchemists of the past and present conjugate the science of chemical combinations of elements with the spiritual charming of those physical events to produce powerful chemical reactions that do change the world. Ask a shaman whether or not a certain combination of herbs without the necessary rituals of enchantment will produce the same effect on the sick or bewitched person. Concocting a certain drink from several plants, placing it in a glass of water overnight ('agua serenada,' in Spanish) will never have the same effect as if drinking it right after the shaman prepared the cocktail of herbs, and this is very well-known by both the shaman and the patients. Anyone who knows the effects of the *macuá* on both love and money, knows that a *brujo* has to treat it before it becomes effective, since *macuá* is just a bird's nest.

Imagination, creativity, dreams, inventions, etc. are all a product of our tapping the spiritual realm. That's why, with some of the knowledge we acquire in this world, we can create or design things that didn't exist before, except that they were, like Plato's ideas, already in the spiritual realm. In other words, those ideas, inventions or designs are in the spiritual realm (as opposed to exist) before they were created (before they existed) in this our material world.

Logic and reason do not work or function in the spiritual realm, because logic and reason are products of experience—experience of objects immersed in the st-matrix. When we say that a spiritual entity *is* we mean that it cannot be created nor destroyed, except as God may decide to do one or the other. Objects in the material world can be created or destroyed, in the sense of being assembled and disassembled, and they are linked with one another through space and time, thanks to causation and succession.

Let's see some of the axioms of the material world. Take for example the "whole is greater than the part." We have established this axiom through experience. The same thing can be said with respect to the identity axiom: "A is equal to itself" or the axiom that says that "two things equal to a third thing, are all equal among themselves."

When we look at two objects, A and B, no matter how identical they may appear, A is equal to A, and B is equal to B. But if we establish as criterion of equality the concept of humanity, when we say that A is human and B is human, we may conclude that A is equal to B. Furthermore, if B is equal to C, then A is also equal to C, and we don't have to establish this last relation of equality through experience. But all these processes happen in experience, are applied to experience, to the material world, they happen in space and time, or in the st-matrix. We cannot extrapolate our logical tools of reasoning to the spiritual world, which is outside space and time. This is why the equivalent of an axiom in the spiritual realm is a dogma. We force into our understanding the truth of the dogma through faith. The Postulate of Faith is at the very limits of the material and the spiritual world.

Hence faith, mystic intuition, and meditation are the tools of spiritual knowledge. Spiritual knowledge cannot be communicated, cannot be reasoned (without leading to Kant's antinomies of reason, or Russell's paradoxes of thought—remember the barber that shaves everyone who do not shave themselves?), cannot be publicly verified, cannot be verified through experiment. Spiritual knowledge is individualistic in its conception, though its source is public.

We cannot prove the existence of the st-matrix or the space-time continuum of Einstein because it is out of the realm of material scientific knowledge, which is why the st-matrix can only be proved with the Postulate of Faith. There will be, of course, a great number of indicators that this st-matrix exists, but they are only indirect indicators. The st-matrix cannot be probed or tantalized with material objects or measuring instruments, because it is the support of those material objects, and it cannot be abstracted from them.

If the world was such that every time we toss a coin it comes up heads, and heads only (no tails—remember, this is a bizarre world—no matter how fair or ideal our coin is), we would conclude that according to experience (we would make reference to countless past experiences, and say it has always been this way) it is impossible to get a tails outcome as a result of a fair coin toss. Similarly, if in our non-bizarre world we were to think about the possibility that a billion coin tosses were to produce a billion tails in a row (and nothing but tails) we would almost be ready to think of this as an impossibility, were it not for the knowledge we have of probability theory. In a similar fashion (and we don't know whether or not we live in a bizarre world with respect to this example) combining two atoms of hydrogen with one atom of oxygen inevitably produces water—we have never had an experience that contradicts these results. If there was a scientist who was to come up with a statement of probability with respect to this chemical reaction, the rest of the scientific community would treat him like a mad man. Thus scientists most probably also rely on statements of faith to prove some of their statements, just like religion does.

If you don't believe scientists make statements of faith, just ask any scientist how he knows he is going to die, if he has never experienced death. How can anybody, for that matter, say that he or she is going to die, if they have never had any experience that resembles the experience of dying? I am not trying to belittle science. I'm just trying to prove a point, trying to disengage science and religion from this hostile embrace that they exert on each other.

Examples of Dogmas and Axioms

Let's discuss a little about the following dogmas and axioms:

Dogma: "Our mind participates and has access to the pool of memories of everybody else's minds (Orbis), which constitutes one mind (Unum), because spiritual things are not limited by time and space." The spiritual world is filled with ideas that the material world mimics and materializes in the flow of time and the infinity of space. Since we are spiritual beings by virtue of possessing an anima, we, as well as everybody else, have access to this spiritual world of ideas, which explains why we can sometimes 'live' somebody else's life. We can also potentially 'think' somebody else's thoughts.

In the world of ideas *my* ideas would be *your* ideas, and we should be able to read everybody else's minds. In fact, we wouldn't have to, since we would already know other people's ideas, given that our mind would be part of humanity's mind that participates in the Spirit of God, the *continuum*— which is not the same as God. Here we have an example of spiritual knowledge that we cannot elaborate more about. Things get confusing once we discuss them, and words and arguments obscure the issue.

Dogma: "Our memories go in a circle that closes in to our present." They go to the right, which is the future, and to the left, which is the past. The opposite of our present is déjà vu, not the past or the future, but the alternate present that feels to belong in the past, a possibility that never made it into reality.

Axiom: "What is possible is real." We mentioned before that this is an axiom, not a dogma, because it deals with existence of the physical world. We live the best of all possible worlds. We live the most probable of all possible worlds—the present is the actual realization of the most probable world. Alternate possibilities, which are different configurations of our universe, are eventually realized in the flow of time.

Dogma: "Our inventions existed before (and always) as memories not yet realized." Man cannot create anything spiritual, because all things spiritual already existed, and yet he can 'create' ideas (by tapping the "pool of ideas") that later become objects. Ideas cannot be created, nor destroyed; they can only be transformed (new ideas). The reason this is a dogma, not an axiom, is because it deals with the spiritual realm of ideas.

Inventions were in the realm of ideas—they were as real as the objects we invented. Our dreams, imaginations, creations, fantasies are realities in the world of ideas that we copied from the realm of ideas. They are realities if they are not the product of mechanical alterations of the brain, like those produced by drugs, disease or madness.

Axiomatic statement: "We, the Templars, do not condone sex." We will take the position of Saint Paul with regards to sex. Sex is out of our discussion, and each individual has to deal with it on a personal level. We are going to let sex be decided by each individual—the reason being the consequences that sex elicits, including unwanted pregnancy. Sex is both to be enjoyed and to procreate children. We must not confuse both functions of sex. We are not going to condemn sex either.

Every person has to find his or her own limitations with respect to sex. These limitations must be within the wider limitations and prohibitions of secular law: pedophilia, incest, rape, and other aberrations. Here is a good place to talk about one of the consequences of hedonism, which is prostitution. Why is it wrong? Because it doesn't play either of the main functions of sex, pleasure or reproduction—prostituted sex is usually enjoyed by just one partner, and monetary retribution was never an aspect of either function of sex.

As mentioned above, sex has two functions, pleasure and reproduction. Sex as pleasure cannot be regulated by anyone, except as it breaches the formal prohibitions set by secular authorities—things that go against natural law, which are punishable by secular law. Sex in its reproductive function can only be heterosexual.

Sex in its reproductive function is in accordance to natural law. Sex in its function as an avenue of pleasure is also in accordance with natural law. Sex with animals, children and other aberrations is *contra natura*.

And since we mentioned *contra natura*, one of our topics in this book, the misappropriation of goods in a capitalist society, is *contra natura*. The survival of the fittest as a doctrine of domination in our society is *contra natura*, though it may be in accordance with natural law in the animal kingdom.

The so-called "derecho de la fuerza—might is right" is *contra natura*. Conquering other nations, other tribes, other groups of people with the purpose of taking their land, or enslaving them, is not in accordance with natural law, not even if done with the purpose of civilizing them.

Natural Law corresponds to the Principles as expressed in the Axioms of Being.

Contra Natura

The Axioms of Being are Natural Laws. Anything that contradicts natural law is *contra natura*, so anything that contradicts the Axioms of Being is *contra natura*.

Is it *contra natura* to swim? Is it *contra natura* to smoke? Is it *contra natura* to work at night and sleep during the day? Is it *contra natura* to work at all?

Again, intuition and common sense dictate what *contra natura* is: trying to lift more weight than what we are designed for lifting is *contra natura*, says common sense. How about wearing shoes, wearing clothing, driving instead of walking? Is it *contra natura* to live in a house instead of a cave?

God designed man taking into account the whole history of the universe ever since its creation, thus making him optimal as far as man's functionality is concerned, with sexual organs, intestines, hands and feet, lungs, heart, etc that work harmoniously with everything that exists. Was this a good design? The term *contra natura* has to be understood within the context of the Axioms of Being and within the context of God's design. We are not the correctors of 'God's errors,' because we can never outsmart the *continuum*—fixing things in nature may momentarily solve our immediate problems, but we don't know the ramifications of the *continuum*, which means that we may have to pay dearly for our arrogance and boldness in rectifying God's 'faulty designs.' This is why experimenting with genes, as in genetic engineering, may be wrong. Human beings are the result of the workings of the *continuum* ever since the creation of the universe, and the *continuum* could not have designed man with the ability to rectify its work, because man is not God, and thus, cannot act as a substitute of the *continuum*.

Man, in other words, represents the end result of the history of the evolution of the universe ever since God created the world, which is why in a timeless interpretation of creation, Darwin's evolution does not contradict God's work, and science should not be in conflict with religion. Therefore, even the humblest human cell (or neuron) guards the 'memory' of the history of the universe, and this 'memory' is nothing else but the "pool of memories" that every human shares with every other human in the spiritual realm.

Human necessities go from those absolutely necessary to life that are satisfied involuntarily, like breathing, to those that are not necessary to life and can be satisfied voluntarily, like sex.

The beatings of our heart and other involuntary functions of our body are 100% controlled by the autonomic nervous system, while breathing is almost 100% involuntary—though we can hold our breath for a few minutes, at most. Quenching our thirst is also almost 100% voluntary, like eating, since we can decide whether or not we eat or drink, like when we go on a hunger strike. Sex is also 100% voluntary, and we can live indefinitely without sex. There are other "needs" like drinking alcohol, smoking tobacco and consuming drugs that are strictly voluntary—at least at the time we consume them, though in the case of hard drugs, like heroine, their consumption can lead to addiction.

Breathing is a natural function controlled by our biological making, is involuntary, and if we lack air, we feel the sensation of asphyxia and we gasp for air, which is a response of our organism to the need of oxygen. We never really get to have too much air, and there is no such thing as consuming excessive oxygen.

Drinking water to quench our thirst is also a natural function. If our body needs water, we feel thirsty. The response of our organism to too much water is discomfort and a feeling of being sick to vomit. Eating is similar to drinking, and we can get sick of excessive food.

But sex is a different story. Our body response to too much sex is not so much getting sick, but not being able to respond sexually, even if we have the mental necessity to have sex; and this, the mental need for sex is what constitutes sex addiction, with or without a sexual response. This creates a psychological need for sex that can be obsessive. The consequences of unbridled sex are very well-known. People who watch too much pornography eventually get addicted to it.

Drugs like alcohol, tobacco, cocaine, marihuana, and other prohibited substances, may create an urgency to get and consume those drugs. Our organism doesn't know how to make us stop from excessive sex, alcohol and drugs, and the individual becomes enslaved to the desire for those drugs, subordinating his/her life to the satisfaction of these artificially created "needs." This in turn may lead to theft, rape, and even murder. When we are hooked on sex, alcohol and drugs, we become worse than animals, and every other vice follows, including prostitution, extortion, robbery and murder.

Greed and power, which usually go hand in hand, create the same problem. Our spirit gets alienated from the spirit of God, and the spark of conscience dwindles, fades away little by little, until it disappears completely, and we become worse than animals. Once we are willing to kill for money, power, sex and drugs, our spirit is no longer in control of our body, but the other way around. The individual becomes possessed by an evil spirit, his own flesh. That's why we don't condone sex. But we don't condemn sex either, because it serves a positive purpose, the continuation of mankind. Drugs, on the other hand, are not necessities that conserve and preserve life—we condemn the use of drugs because they don't serve a positive purpose beyond the pure and simple satisfaction of the desires of the flesh.

Taking alcohol and drugs is *contra natura* because eventually drug consumption destroys the body, and this works contrary to the instinct of preservation of life—this is a case where extreme hedonism collides with keeping and sustaining life.

The Commandments

Jesus understood that the 10 commandments can be reduced to two commandments: i) love God, and ii) love your neighbors as yourself. These two commandments are juxtaposed to one another, and don't seem to bear any relation to each other, but they nevertheless do. God is a spirit, and you can only love God through your spirit that I will call here the anima. But we are not only anima; we also have a material counterpart that I will call the ego. The ego is individualistic, it only understands the satisfaction of its own carnal drives and needs; it doesn't care about anything, or anybody else, except as a means of satisfying its own desires. The ego wants money, food, pleasure, and rejects pain, sacrifice, exertion, suffering; the ego is absolutely amoral, and when it contradicts our anima, it becomes aberrant, and taints our anima, making it immoral. This ego is a great obstacle in between our anima and God, which means that to love God we must first control and dominate our ego—and ego domination (control) is achieved by doing good things for other people, helping others, loving others. This is why we can never love God if not by loving others—and to comply with the 10 commandments, and hence with Jesus' mandate, we must love our neighbors if we wish to love God. In essence, if you love God, you also love yourself and your neighbors, and if you love yourself and your neighbors, you also love God. Faith without deeds is as dead as a spiritless body.

[Thus, love of God can be attained (expressed) by loving humanity, which is why even an atheist can love God if he/she loves humanity. Will God care if the atheist's ego rejects Him, when the atheist's anima does for other people everything that pleases God? Love of God is thus reflexive, because the love of God bounces back to the individual who loves Him, so that if you love God, God in turn, loves you—and even if you don't love God, God still loves you—because it gives you what you find in nature, and in other people's willingness to do good things on your behalf. The thing to remember is that lack of love is also lack of faith.]

The fact is that atheists who love humanity have already found their way to God, and it matters little if they never believe in God. But those individuals who claim to have been imbued with the love of God, and who fanatically believe in their demons (that they confuse with God), and yet kill and do harm to other individuals, will surely walk into the flames of Hell. God doesn't need the belief and prayers of murderers, or the belief and prayers of those who would gladly murder, or send others to murder innocent people in the name of God, democracy, freedom, and Western Civilization.

Even with the help of the Postulate of Faith—this Postulate only alludes to the necessity of God's existence, based on the possibility of his direct manifestation (as God) to our senses—we cannot prove that God is, but plenty of theologians, including Saint Thomas of Aquinas, have proved that God exists. [In the Old Testament, when God speaks to Moses, God says "I am who I am," which is consistent with what we are explaining here]. The fact is that God's being has to be accepted by faith, and it constitutes a dogma. We mentioned before that we cannot reason out the being of spiritual entities, but we can reason out the existence of things of the material world. Again, we cannot prove the existence of spiritual entities, because spiritual entities don't exist, they *are* (hence the name spiritual beings). The existence of God is manifested to our senses everywhere we look around (though God doesn't manifest Himself to our senses as God). In fact, God exists in and within the material world, and in and within the workings of the universe, including in and within our physical bodies—otherwise, we would not have to wonder who created the world and what the origin of man is. But God may not be in and within us, because our ego may be the cause of an abysmal separation of the Spirit of God that *is*, from our anima. We can only reach to the Spirit of God through love.

To recap, there are entities that both are and exist, like we humans. There is one entity that is and exists, just like we do, but that we can only get to know through faith and love, and this entity is God. There are entities that are, and under certain circumstances may appear to exist or to be in a state of temporal or momentary quasi-existence, and those entities are angels, demons, and ghosts. There are entities that exist only, and those are the inanimate objects of nature. And finally, there are entities who definitely exist, and who would seem to *be*, though in a lower state of being or consciousness, and those entities are the plants and animals at different stages of being.

We must mention here that our imagination can create spurious entities that neither are nor exist, they are just fleeting sparks of our capacity to create—remember that we were made in the image and likeness of God, and thus, we can create things, both material and spiritual, that sometimes cannot be substantiated as either spiritual or material, or both, because of our innate weakness as creators. In other words, because we are little, tiny, weakling gods, we can only 'create' entities that no sooner they are created than they vanish into nothingness. That's how we fill our world of dreams and fantasies with all kinds of 'beings'. But of course, under certain circumstances, we can also become great architects of creation by devising things good and bad, especially through the persistent efforts of science and the investigation of the phenomenal world. Those 'more consistent designs' represent our inventions, which are based on our ingenuity and the discovery of the inner workings of God's creation of the universe.

Natural Law

The Axioms of Being are Natural Law, and anything against Natural Law is said to be *contra natura*:

- The Natural Law of Being and Existence;
- The Natural Law of Mortality of the Body and Immortality of the Soul;
- The Natural Law of Preservation of Life and Preservation of the Species;
- The Natural Law of Nature Conservation, derived from 1 and 3 above;

- The Natural Law of Freedom of the Soul and Bondage of the Flesh;
- The Natural Law of Hedonism: Pleasure vs. Pain;
- The Natural Law of Morality: Complacency vs. Guilt;
- The Natural Law of Knowledge vs. Faith;
- The Natural Law of Love vs. Justice;

Natural Law reflects the duality of man's reality, because of man's inherent dichotomy of spirit vs. physical body.

Because of Natural Law:

- denying the humanity of an individual, or group of individuals, is *contra natura*;
- searching for the 'fountain of youth' is *contra natura*;
- smoking, drinking alcohol, and taking drugs is *contra natura*;
- rape, sexual depravation, child pornography, prostitution, etc. are *contra natura*;
- committing suicide is *contra natura*;
- to lie or to conceal useful knowledge is *contra natura*;
- murder is *contra natura*;
- doing what is harmful to others is *contra natura*;
- destroying and abusing nature and the environment is *contra natura*;
- denying God's being and existence is *contra natura*;
- placing obstacles to spiritual or material knowledge is *contra natura*;
- to abstain from pleasure and seek pain is *contra natura*;
- to interfere with procreation is *contra natura*;
- to torture or inflict pain is *contra natura*;
- to deprive individuals from their freedom is *contra natura*;
- to restrict beauty and artistic creation is *contra natura*;
- to equate beauty with what pleases our senses is *contra natura*;

There are also a whole group of things that are not *contra natura*, and yet are generally accepted to be *contra natura*, like:

- wearing clothing and shoes;
- sexual abstinence or sexual pleasure;
- homosexuality, and other things done for pleasure, without inflicting pain;
- tattooing and adorning your body;
- working at night and sleeping during the day;
- swimming and flying, if we can learn how to swim and how to fly; etc.

One of the lowest and most common acts of inhumanity perpetrated by humans, which are definitively and undoubtedly *contra natura*, are the wars that have devastated the planet and its inhabitants for thousands of years. Another one has been, more recently, the abuse of nature and the environment, which has come as a consequence of the excesses of science. The abuse and pillage of nature have come thanks to the arrogance of the scientific community that erroneously equates knowledge with wisdom.

Televangelists and the Templar's Spirituality

Most religious beliefs preach about love, and there is no doubt that most of them will interpret love as doing something for others. In this sense, the people of the United States of America is one of the most religious and loving peoples in the world. The response to natural disasters, either in the USA itself, or anywhere else in the world, has often been almost automatic and very generous, which attests to the fact that the great majority of Americans have developed a strong sense of solidarity with the suffering of others, and this is certainly a manifestation of love. But this is love triggered by the untimely occurrence of a natural disaster, or by an occasional tragedy, and is not permanent Christian love for humanity, since true Christian love must be constant, lasting, and unrelenting. Love must be the force that moves our lives, which by no means diminishes what Americans do for others in times of tragedy and catastrophe, or whenever the need for help arises.

Then, there are also many religious groups that preach and practice an empty love, for which they seldom give a definition. Fortunately, those are a minority whose fixed intent is with the 'spreading of the word' as a way to salvation. Their interpretation of love centers on faith and the 'spreading of the word'—and they claim that salvation is at hand by faith alone, and not by deeds, which means that their faith, and their love, is empty, and this fact facilitates the turning of their religious beliefs into commercial enterprises. The Catholic hierarchy, on the other hand, is not doing enough for the poor people of the world, but is constantly getting involved on the wrong side of world politics. We heard lately—which is not news, since it has happened throughout all modern Vatican history—that Pope Benedict XVI traveled to Brazil, and gave a speech acridly criticizing Marxism, while giving a lukewarm criticism of the capitalist system, showing the biased view of the Vatican that socialists are more aligned with the devil than capitalists are with God. The Catholic hierarchy and the Papacy have always been strongly pro-capitalist, mildly anti-socialist, and rabidly anti-communist.

Church attendance per se, and by itself, could not be nearly enough to attain salvation. We must be careful of those preachers that claim that just by accepting Jesus as your savior you can win your way to salvation. Remember that faith without actions is empty faith. You can go around the world proclaiming Jesus to be your savior, but if you don't do something for humanity—if you don't love your neighbors—then it's impossible to love God either. You must love God with all your might, and all your soul, and all your heart, but what is it to love a spiritual being with no physical representation? It can't be any of the definitions we have of love, like *Eros*, *agapas*, or *philo*; it can't even be charity, as it was practiced in early Christianity, because God doesn't need of our charity. Hence, there is no direct way of loving God, but through the love, in the Christian sense of the word, of other people, and you can only love God by loving your neighbors.

In this sense, even an atheist, if he loves humanity, has a better chance of attaining salvation than the most faithful of all evangelists that pray everyday but don't do anything for the sick and the hungry. Going to church once a week won't do it either, nor will do it tithing, and giving away what's left in your household—those things you don't use anymore. Giving leftovers is charity in the modern sense of the word, not nearly a resemblance of love. You love somebody, if by giving them what you value, you are making a "painless sacrifice"—for us Templars, love with painful sacrifice is void and meaningless. We give, and feel pleased at giving, and giving with reluctance is unwilling sacrifice, not real love.

Most contemporary televangelists are getting rich with the contributions of the 'faithful'. Notice how these people are constantly requesting more and more money to 'spread the word,' because this is more important than helping the poor—one wonders if you couldn't spread the word while at the same time helping the poor. They insist in carrying the message of love (of empty love, that is) to every corner of the world, and for this reason they need more radio stations, more TV channels, more satellites—like if this was the mission given by Jesus Christ, misinterpreting deliberately Jesus' doctrine. These televangelists rarely spend any money to save the starving people of the world from death by hunger and disease. They preach and ask for money to 'spread the word'—I wonder what they are going to do with the money they collect after the word has already been spread all over the world, if it hasn't yet.

There is a TV station and media religious complex in the US valued at nearly two billion dollars—yes, I wrote billions, not millions—and this religious business is privately owned. The owner of this lucrative enterprise claims to be a Christian, and is incessantly asking for more and more money to buy more TV stations, and build new ones in all the continents of the world, with the objective of 'spreading the word' (who cares about the starving people of Africa?). To be fair, sometimes these people will make token acts of charity to keep the appearance that they are Christians. They will tell you that all you have to do is accept the Lord Jesus as your savior, baptize, and presto! You are ready to go to Heaven—they don't want you to give money to the poor, because that would be unfair competition to them, but they will make sure that you don't forget tithing and giving offerings. It's a business. They want to expand their religious market. These people are the Anti-Christ.

Their churches, that they sometimes call 'crystal cathedrals,' look rather like coffins instead of temples to glorify God. They lost all sense of aesthetic and architectural creativity in the construction of their temples that resemble theaters and palaces more than places of prayer. These preachers sometimes prefer to rent a stadium, or large sports facility, which are suitable for mass gatherings and mass marketing of their religious products—salvation through what they call accepting Jesus as your savior and getting baptized, publicly acknowledging that you are a Christian (of course, they want you to publicly declare that you are a Christian so that other people will follow suit, this is great propaganda gimmickry). I am sure that if God had human-like feelings, God would deeply despise these modern Pharisees that dedicate their efforts to corrupt the Christian faith. But enough talk about these merchants of the faith, and let's have a broader discussion about the Templar's spiritual philosophy, beginning with the following dogma:

Dogma: spiritual beings cannot be created nor can they be destroyed.

We know that other people *are* strictly by sheer faith. And exactly for similar reasons we know that we are going to die a physical death, because we have 'experienced' the physical death of those who died by being witnesses to the corruptibility of their flesh. Dead people lose motion, feelings, their body temperature drops, and after some hours they begin to stink, and if we don't bury them, or preserve them in some appropriate environment, they will begin to rot, grow with worms, and recycle into the natural substances that compose the human body. Now, we never have experienced physical death before, and yet we know we are going to die—by sheer faith, if by nothing else.

But we can never accept spiritual death, because spiritual death cannot be inferred from experience—spiritual entities have nothing to do with experience and perception. In fact, we have already established by faith that other people *are*—meaning that they have a spirit or soul that cannot be created, nor can it be destroyed, because creation and destruction make sense only in the material world of physical objects. Therefore—and this is not a therefore as we use in logic—when we 'experience' the material death of others by faith alone, we affirm their spiritual survival after the said material death, because spiritual entities cannot be created or destroyed in the same way that material things are created and destroyed by the ego.

The duality of anima-ego is even expressed in the Eucharist, whose real meaning is the sharing of the things of this world in one communal spirit with others, in order to be cleansed of our sins and attain salvation. The weekly mass is a gross misinterpretation of this, the real meaning of the Eucharist. Christianity lost its way early in the first centuries, regaining it with the Templars, just to lose it again after their demise. Salvation is both physical and spiritual: The physical part is represented by the bread (the body of Christ), and the spiritual part is represented by the wine (the blood of Christ) of the Eucharist. Even the four accounts of the New Testament seem to have lost their way, since they didn't give much emphasis to the physical salvation, which is an avenue to spiritual salvation. Spiritual salvation is incomplete—and thus empty—without the physical salvation of others, including ourselves, and yet, our individual physical salvation is not as strong a requirement for spiritual bliss as the physical salvation of others.

The genesis of the Moral Principle is found in the Principle of Hedonism. We seek what is pleasurable and reject what is painful, giving rise to the ego's drive for what is pleasurable (Freud called this crude ego the libido): Things that are pleasurable to me are good, and those that are painful to me are bad. The ego doesn't care about how it achieves its pleasure, as long as it gets what it wants (the immediate satisfaction of the desires of the flesh take relevance over everything else, and it becomes an end in and of itself). Since other people have similar feelings to ours (other people are), they also feel pleasure and pain. Thus, causing pain to others is bad, and giving them pleasure is good, and this is the embryo of the Moral Principle (the anima recognizes that other people are and that they have the same drives and needs as we do). Except that sometimes our pleasure may be the cause of the pain of others, and vice versa, originating a conflict of interests between our ego and our anima. Unfortunately, our nature is ego-centered, and more often than not our ego overcomes our anima. Things would be OK if there were enough resources for everyone, and there would be no conflict of interests between the anima and the ego, since everyone could fulfill their heart's desires without causing pain to others, and this would be a case of perfect harmony between anima and ego. But things are not always this way, and sometimes we must make a sacrifice, doing what is good to others at our own expense, and this is love. So, love requires sacrifice, but a sacrifice that is not aberrantly painful—in other words, the feeling of fulfillment brought about by love must overcome the feeling of want brought about by the unsatisfied needs of the flesh—and this is the sacrifice God wants from us. In other words, to make a sacrifice for others we must restrain and overcome our ego with faith (faith in God, that is), and this faith translates into acts of love, which is our way to spiritual growth and salvation. Therefore, salvation of the spirit is attained through salvation of the flesh (ours and other people's flesh). The Eucharist is a symbolic representation of what we said here.

Freud and his psychoanalysis hit the very nerve of these philosophical inquiries, and it is interesting to see how he developed his concept of the ego, the super-ego, the libido, the conscious mind, the sub-conscious mind and the unconscious. Freud's ego is our ego here; his super-ego is the anima; his libido is the wild, untamed ego (the ego unrestrained by the moral principle). The conscious mind represents our personal memories, the sub-conscious mind represents our extended memories in the spiritual realm, and the unconscious mind is the collective memories of humanity imprinted in our flesh (our genes) by millions of years of evolution. The unconscious mind is really a manifestation of God's mind.

Our senses are the filters of reality. Reality is more than we can perceive directly or indirectly (through the extension of our sense terminals like telescopes, microscopes, bubble chambers, etc.), and our perception is the first filter of reality.

Another level of reality filtering is time and space. We can only perceive what's in time and space. Time is associated with our anima (continuity of sense memories), and space is associated with the ego (the owner of our sense terminals). That's why we feel no time has passed if we sleep for eight hours without dreaming, which is similar to what happens to somebody who wakes from a coma after 15 or 20 years of unconsciousness. For the individual who suffered the coma, 15 or 20 years is only an instant, because there is only one string of sense memories before the coma, and another string of sense memories after the coma, with nothing in between—the rest of the people (not in a coma) have a sense of time running 15 or 20 years, because there is no interruption of the string of sense memories that makes up time.

In other words, when there is no awareness of the anima, there is no time, and in the case of the individual who suffered the coma, the anima must have been 'somewhere' in the realm of the spiritual entities. The anima was not destroyed; it came back to the ego (the physical body) that it had left before. When the anima leaves the ego for good, that's death of the physical body, but the anima goes back to the spiritual realm (nobody can say what 'life' after death is, because sense memories can only be produced by the ego, and an anima without an ego has no sense memories—what 'memories' we may have after death, will only be known when we die). But, when there is almost 100% awareness of the anima, without the interference of our senses that are controlled by the ego, like when we fall in a deep trance of meditation, we get a sense of eternity (a "big chunk of time" passes, and we say we had an "instant of eternity," as against an instant of what we consider finite time). A trance of meditation is what comes closer to 'life' after death—does it mean then, that paradise is the same as a positive super-experience of meditation, while hell is a negative super-experience of suspended spiritual existence, similar to a coma? Nobody knows.

The anima in a human "feels" the passage of time, but it is not in space, while the ego exists in both time and space. In fact, the ego exists if and only if the anima is (remember the sentence we uttered before, "I exist if and only if I am"). Things that exist in time and space are physical or material objects. The only entity that seems to be in time is our anima. Other people's anima, just like the rest of spiritual entities, are neither in time nor in space, and yet, they are real entities. Their reality is willed by our anima through an act of faith; their reality is a dogma. And God is because there must be a substratum of our anima and the anima of others—there must be a will to make us be.

The subconscious mind (the realm of the individual anima) is the factory of miracle designs—that's where miracles have their origin, but only as blueprints of what we want. The unconscious mind, made up of the community of the animas (the realm of the continuum and the dwelling place of other superior spiritual beings), is where miracles are actually performed—the community of the animas doesn't constitute God, but it is a manifestation of the presence of God, it is like the pool of the collective 'memories' of humanity sustained by the will of God. The conscious mind (the dwelling of the ego) is the miracle killer—the conscious mind can only do what we can do, within the limitations of our physical and intellectual skills as human beings. Failure is the result of inaction or miscalculation of our ability to do things. Anything that can be humanly done is done by the conscious mind, by the ego—no miracles are worked in the house of the ego, because the ego doesn't even believe in miracles. The desires of the anima are reinforced by faith, but the desires of the ego can only be reinforced by hope. Faith and hope are as different as anima and ego.

Jesus Christ was a miracle worker because He was God, He had direct access to the unconscious mind, and He had total control of his ego—so much so that Satan failed three times at tempting Him. If we can learn to control our ego, to be in permanent contact with our anima, and to have direct access to the community of the spirits, we can also perform miracles. To do this, of course, we need faith—because only faith can transcend our ego. We have to know that the ego is the source of all doubts. The ego is going to advise you that your miracle is impossible, that it cannot be done; that you have to wish only what is within your means to do, that you should stick to reality. Faith cannot work with your ego, because the ego's 'faith' (which is in reality hope) can only result in stubbornness and obstinacy, hardheadedness and doggedness—faith and ego do not mix, and if they do, they lead to waste of resources and ultimately to failure.

Not that there is anything wrong with being constant in our pursuits, to have a strong determination, as long as you realize that you are relying on yourself to do whatever you want to do, as long as you stay focus with what you can do, within your limitations as a human being. Between a strong determination and faith there is an abyss as deep as between your ego and your anima, between your body and your spirit. Determination belongs to the realm of your physical body; faith belongs to the realm of your spirit.

Have you ever noticed how you bring something to your conscious mind, and think of all the possibilities when tackling a problem, just to find out that precisely what you didn't think of, what you didn't take into consideration, is what happens? This is faith in the reverse; this is faith working against you. Have you ever noticed how you come up with some possibility, and soon enough you conclude, "No, it's never going to work that way," and right away you forget about it (you brush it away from your conscious mind) just to find out that what you didn't consider possible is precisely what comes true? This is faith working in your favor, because you transferred your wishes from your conscious mind to your subconscious mind. Yet, even though faith may be working for or against you, the final result may be good or bad—you may win an unexpected prize, or suffer an unexpected event—depending on what your expectations were. The world of probabilities is a world of realities in the making, waiting to come true, and whether or not they come true is the work of your subconscious mind operating in the realm of the unconscious. For faith to be effective it has to be accompanied with a subtle conformity that should not be confused with bitter resignation. This spiritual conformity accepts the realization of the miracle or the non-realization of the miracle with equal ease of mind, because if things didn't come true the way we wanted is because God knows better what's good for us.

Leibniz once said that this world is the best of all possible worlds, which means that there is a host of unrealized possibilities waiting to visit our world of present realities. Our reality is just the tip of the iceberg of the world of possibilities. Everything beyond and behind our present reality belongs to the world of miracles, rejected by our ego as impossibilities—because the ego is blind to the things that are, and things for the ego either exist or don't exist. Our inventions pop out of the world of possibilities and are, even before they are invented (even before we make a prototype of our invention)—that's why we draw a sketch of an electrical circuit in our mind, before we make the electrical gadget that we register as our invention—which Thomas Edison called the phonograph or the light bulb, and Alexander Bell called the telephone. That's why the writer creates a world of science-fiction that is in the mind of its creator. That's why a painter like Dali or Picasso will reflect in the canvas of their paintings a world whose only reality lies behind the "tip of the iceberg of the world of possibilities."

Jesus could make miracles because he knew that what doesn't register in our present world of the senses *is*, except that our senses haven't filtered it yet into our reality—but whose being lies in the world of possibilities, perfectly envisioned by the anima (through an act of faith), but not contemplated by the ego. Miracles are miracles to the ego, but not to the anima, because they pop into our reality all of a sudden, taking our ego by surprise—our anima remains unimpressed with miracles, because it is our ego that suffers the shock of the unexpectedness of the miracle, and whenever we are in the presence of a miracle, it's the ego that suffers the shock of the awe—conversely, when the miracle is not realized, the person of faith would remain unmoved, even when the ego will decry the failure of the miracle to materialize.

Coping with the world entails following a twin path. On the one hand you have to take care of your body, and, on the other hand, you have to tend for your spirit. Body and spirit are juxtaposed in the individual, which means that while we are alive, we must take care of both the body and the spirit. God would never ask for material sacrifices from us, because material sacrifices run *contra natura*. We must continue breathing if we wish to live, we must eat, we must drink, and we must have sex and other bodily and emotional pleasures that make us happy here on earth, while at the same time getting ready for our spiritual well-being after death. Pain and suffering is not something God wants from us. Complete disregard from the things of this world is not in accordance with God's will, because if it was, we would not be able to feel deprived, and pain would not be a measure of our lack of something our body needs. Jesus was never opposed to caring for the physical needs of the individual. His whole ministry was dedicated to curing people from disease, raising people from the dead, and tending to both the body and the spirit of people.

But something happened that changed the whole perception of what Christianity is all about. All through the Old Testament the writers of the Bible worry about the well-being of men. The New Testament also seems to dedicate some time to caring to the physical body of men, and Ecclesiastes is an example of this free poetic writing in the Bible that has to do with the good life and the good living, while we are alive, and against the background of the fleeting and perishable existence of men. Jesus' first miracle was in fact the production of more wine, so that a wedding party would not go awry for lack of something to drink. And then, the whole New Testament is full of miracles that have to do with helping and healing others, tending for the hungry, the sick, those possessed by evil spirits, the desperate and the poor. Up to the end of the period when the New Testament was written, there is this constant worry about the well-being of others, until we turn the second and third centuries of our era, when Christianity concentrates on saving the spirit and completely disregards, even despises, the things of this world, because they have to do with the satisfaction of the flesh. The spirit becomes the primary objective, praying and looking towards God, conversion and following the spiritual guidance of Christ becomes paramount, to such an extreme that Jesus is often quoted as saying that his Kingdom does not belong to this world, which was misinterpreted as if the very same Jesus was turning his back to the attention of the bare necessities of men that have to do with his survival, and more.

It is only with the Knight Templars that we come back to the task of helping the poor—and this only incidentally, because the Templars' mission was to guard the pilgrims against robbers and other dangers in their way to the Holy Land. Of course, through the history of Christianity we see plenty of individual Saints following the very doctrine of Jesus that recommends helping those in need. By the end of the fourth century the Church had become a social institution within the boundaries of the Roman Empire, the clergy no longer cared that much for the tending of the body—even more, it becomes completely reluctant to attend the necessities of the human body, and anything that has to do with the things of this world becomes sinful or related to sin—even sleeping comfortably, wearing good garments and shoes, eating, and, of course, sex, become like a stigma for mankind. In the meantime, a small minority of "Christians" become filthy rich at the expense of the poor with the blessings of the Church.

Suffering becomes a virtue, pain will be rewarded in the afterlife, and although we still hear preaching that we must help the poor, only very few Saints will give up everything to help others, but always with the expressed view that spiritual life was far more important than material well-being. Christianity lost its way, even to our present days. The ritual of the Eucharist was misinterpreted, and the Christian movement became a religious enterprise *per se,* rather than a social movement, whose end was almost exclusively to praise God and to torment the body, so that we would avoid temptation and sin. Faith became an empty bubble that, after death, would burst into nothing. The task of helping others as a means of reaching out to God, which was what Jesus preached, was relegated to a second place, against the primary goal of directly attaining the love of God through prayer and sacrifice— something we know to be impossible. Then came Reformation, and things got even worse, faith became the empty faith preached by the new evangelists, based on baptism, acceptance of Christ as a Savior, and the annunciation of the end of the world that would bring final judgment, and ultimately Paradise or Hell for all men. This apocalyptic view of the world grew stronger right after the birth of the many religious movements that constituted the Reform, and many of the myriad of sects that began to pop up got ready for the final destruction of the world, so many times announced by "prophets" of the doom to be just around the corner.

The Needs and Limitations of Science

Science is the holiest of all the "holy cows," perhaps because it is the result of the highest achievement of the ego. If we think of the desires of the flesh as the illegitimate children of the ego, science is surely its very legitimate child. Ever since the time science took over the privileged position spirituality and religion enjoyed up to and until the 16th and 17th Century, it's almost sinful to say anything against science. And yet we must say it, because thanks to the greatest 'scientific achievements' we had from the 16th through the 21st Century, humanity is now at the brink of extinction. The accelerated development of the knowledge and understanding of nature by the physical sciences came along with an enormous development of technology. We have been able to live longer, and enjoy all the amenities that we now have, thanks to science. Humanity has advanced fast forward at an accelerated pace that, if not stopped, is going to deplete the limited resources that the planet holds. Because of the scientific blunders that have had such a devastating incidence on the environment, new scientific discoveries must be carefully scrutinized as for their future consequences in their practical applications, given that we still have time to save the planet, and with it, humanity. Who can deny the negative impact of radioactive waste, DDT, chemical waste, carbon dioxide, smog, and so many other by-products of modern science and technology? It's as if we had signed a short-term pact with the devil, getting today's comfort in exchange for tomorrow's annihilation, when without the pact, we would have had many more days to live.

Here we try to summarily explain the dangers of science and scientific discovery. Western Civilization would probably be better off if we had stopped scientific and human development at the level of the middle ages. Not that all scientific discovery should have stopped, but that the new discoveries should have been rationalized more carefully so that the natural process would not be disrupted so drastically by human intervention. The problem with technological development is that we are going too fast for what nature can absorb and assimilate; in other words, nature is being adapted to man, instead of man being adapted to nature, and this is a dangerous development. We have had several wake-up calls, and we have missed them. The development of nuclear weapons was a dangerous technological advancement of humanity. We seem to forget that nature has a way of balancing the distortions produced by man, and we will pay dearly for this.

Dinosaurs went extinct thanks to an asteroid that hit the earth some 65 million years ago. This was a disturbance of nature produced by nature itself—a nuclear explosion is a disturbance of nature produced by man. Science and technology keep discovering things that supposedly make man's existence better, and this makes the big egos of science conclude that in the future we will be able to fix things that we un-fixed today—humility is a virtue of the anima, not of the ego, which is why scientists will never conceal a discovery found to be dangerous to the survival of humanity. Science is like a Pandora's Box that may be filled with maladies with no hope in it, and we don't seem to understand that there are some kinds of scientific knowledge that must be kept secret—occult knowledge for the protection of the human race from human folly. Einstein and others who participated in the Manhattan Project carry the guilt of the death of hundreds of thousands of people, and the guilt of humanity's fear of nuclear holocaust. When Einstein said that he wanted to think like God, he was saying that he wanted to be more than a God-like being, he wanted to be God, for if you can think like God thinks, then you cannot help but be God. It was his desire to be God that makes his statement an apostasy, and we make of this apostasy almost a virtue. Humility is in the understanding that this blue marble in space, which is our earth, may be destroyed by the wrong scientific discovery. We must understand that there is a limit to human knowledge, and that we cannot outsmart God by 'fixing' what he created—we are not the correctors of God's mistakes. Adaptation is the key word, and we are not adapting ourselves to the workings of nature, we are trying to change nature, force nature to adapt to our needs, because we came to the belief that we are God, even if we don't explicitly say it. There is a difference between using an existing water fall to produce energy, as against creating it by damming a river, and artificially stopping the flow of water, making a man-made water fall. In the first case we are taking advantage of what nature offers, and in the second case we are forcing changes in nature, changes that may generate unexpected consequences. Think about the unexpected consequences that we may spark by twinkling with human genes and atomic structures. It may indeed be very dangerous to get to know the thoughts of God.

The speed response of nature to environmental changes is determined by nature itself—and this is a reflection and manifestation of God's will and not of man's will.

The laws of nature and natural law are expressions of God's will. Living organisms respond to changes in the environment at the speed that nature determines. If the environmental changes are too fast and/or too drastic, the living organism may not have time to respond and adapt, and a different natural process will dictate that this living organism will cease to exist. But these are all natural mechanisms "invented" by nature. The capacity of nature to synchronize itself to its own changes will also make it synchronize itself to our forced changes in it, but nature may kill us as a result of its own process of adjustment.

Men have grown to believe that once we grasp the mathematical laws that govern the physical world, then we can fix things in nature. But this is an illusion, we can never get to discern the thoughts of God, and if we try, we will eventually mess things up. Our short-term benefits may be paid with a far too high and pricy long-term response of nature. We are on our way to self-destruction, and we don't want to recognize it, because unconsciously, we believe that we can outsmart the nature that God thought. The fact is, we will never be able to outsmart the *continuum*, because whatever we think we can do better, it has already been taken into account by the *continuum*. It is said that the South American Indians used the wheel in toys, but never grasped the tremendous utility the wheel would have had if applied to the hauling of heavy loads. Who knows? Maybe the Incas and the Mayans saw the danger of technological advancement, and chose not to interfere with nature, so they decided to stick to their 'square wheels' instead. If there are no wheels in nature, perhaps it is because the *continuum* didn't "think" we need them. At any rate, the challenge we are facing today is global warming, and we are so "scientific," so arrogant, that we think we can fix what we unfixed—imagine, if we ever manage to fix what we destroyed (with plain knowledge of how we destroyed it), will we be able to fix what we unfixed in nature (with only hindsight knowledge of how we unfixed it)? Science is nothing else than the pursuit of the thoughts of God, and if we persist in trying to unravel what God did, and worse, trying to "fix" it, eventually we will end up like Lucifer, down in the abyss of ignorance brought about by death.

Am I against science and scientific development? Not any more than I am against pleasure and the enjoyment of the good life, because both science and pleasure are children of the ego. And just like the unbridled search for what is pleasurable can lead to pain, and even to death, the uncontrolled development of science can lead to harmful consequences, like the destruction of our natural environment, or even to the extinction of man as a species. The important thing to realize here is that the ego handles science as one of its subject matters, while the anima handles spirituality as its only subject matter; the self, acting as a referee between science and spirituality, has to strike a balance between them with its own subject matter, philosophy.

3

A Short History of the Templars

Right after the first Crusade, nine French knights decided to found an Order, among whose intentions was not to systematically combat the Muslims—as was the Crusaders' main goal. These knights' immediate purpose was not to give assistance to the sick and the poor, as did the Knights of St. John (later called the Knights of Malta) and the Hospitallers, and they were not circumscribed to a given territory, like the Teutonic Knights in the Baltic region. Their main intent was the protection of the pilgrims on their way to Jerusalem and the Holy Places, as well as the protection of the Temple of Solomon and other sacred relics of the Middle East.

The Order of the Knights of the Temple was founded in 1118 by his initial promoter and fist Grand Master Hugues de Payns, along with Geoffroy de Saint-Omer, Geoffroy Bisol, André de Montbard, Payen de Montdidier, Archambaud de Saint-Amand, Gondemar, Rossal y Hugues de Champagne. They were installed by Baldwin II, King of Jerusalem, in his palace near the mosque of Al-Agsa, the only one in the esplanade of what was the old Temple of Solomon. The organization lasted for 196 years and had a total of 22 Grand Masters until the year 1314 when it was dissolved.

This Order was founded thanks to the influence of Bernard de Clairvaux, later to be known as Saint Bernard, with the help of some other people (among them Hugh de Payns and his eight companions). The order was given the official name of the Order of the Poor Knights of Christ—other sources give them the name Poor Knights of the Temple. The members of this order had the special characteristic of being both monks and warriors. Since at first they were not more than nine individuals, they were given the task of escorting the pilgrims on their way from Jerusalem to the banks of the Jordan, at the time frequented as a place of devotion. Under the service of King Baldwin II of Jerusalem, their mission was to escort the pilgrims that would approach the holy city of Jerusalem through the road to Jaffa, infested with thieves and highwaymen. Like most monastic orders of the time, the Templars followed the rule of poverty, obedience, and chastity. Later, after their foundation, they were installed in the Temple of Jerusalem, where they acquired the name of Knight Templars. They remained the same in numbers for about ten years.

It was in 1128 (ten years after their foundation) that Saint Bernard called on the Council of Troyes for the official recognition of the Order of the Templars, who were to be subjected only to the Pope, and free of the burden of paying taxes. With the authorization of Pope Eugene II the Templars began to use their characteristic white robe (the habit of the Cistercians) and the Greek red cross of eight points. They adopted the so-called three perpetual vows (in addition to the Crusader's vow) and the rules concerning the chapel, the refectory, and the dormitory.

Right alter the Council of Troyes the members of the Knight Templars decided to join the Crusader wars to liberate the Holy Land from the hands of the Saracens. It is during these wars that the Templars establish contact with the Arabs and their culture, and it is probably because of the brutality of these wars that they learned to establish a rapport with their enemies, exchanging points of view about the nature of their faith and of their fight. We have to take into consideration that in many instances both the Christians and the Saracens fell prisoners of each other, and probably had a chance to learn from each other. The Templars naturally must have learned that the Muslim doctrine is monotheist and that not all that the Koran teaches, just like not all that the Old Testament teaches, can be literally interpreted and literally applied in real life.

In summary, as a product of the genocidal wars of the Crusades, we have an Order of monk-warriors getting in close contact with both Arabs and Jews, which gave them the opportunity to internalize their opponents' beliefs, or at least expand their own Christian beliefs, in such a way that they became much more tolerant of other faiths and cultures, more than they would if they had never had a contact with those people. This is the beginning of the Templars' process of humanization and globalization, continued in our present days and inherited by the modern Templars of the 20th and 21st century.

Given the theatre of operations of the Templars, two different strains of the organization flourished in the world of antiquity. On the one hand, we had the monk-warriors engaged in the different battles in Palestine and Spain, and, on the other hand, there were the civil-servant Templars of Europe dedicated to the works of the organization. The first ones developed the ecumenical doctrines that characterized the post-crusade Templars, an eclectic combination of the philosophical enlightenment of the Christian faith—enriched by elements of Greek thought—to which elements of the Jewish and Arab traditions had been added. The civil-servant European Templars developed international trade, banking, and finances, plus the system of commanderies. In France they formed no less than eleven bailiwicks, subdivided into more than forty-two commanderies that pursued agricultural production in the estates that had been given to the organization. They also developed guilds of artisans and craftsmen that built the great castles, monasteries and cathedrals of Europe and the Holy Land, including the construction and maintenance of roads of communication among the different cities of the Old Continent. Consequently, the Templar organization grew in numbers and wealth, at the same time that it had a tremendous, and definitely more important, spiritual growth. The Templars became the all-universal reflection of the perfect man, or at least, of the man who searches for perfection in the faith of Jesus Christ and in the application of the Christian doctrine of love of mankind.

Here are some of the achievements of the Templars:

> They accumulated great riches in money and real estate;
> They forged and protected legions of craftsmen and artisans;
> They developed the Gothic art, system that lightened the weight of walls;
> They built or helped to build more than 70 cathedrals in less than 100 years;
> They protected brotherhoods of builders, among others the Sons of Master Jacques and the Sons of Master Solomon, that gave rise to masons and freemasons;
> They rid of thieves the roads and routes between cities, so that commerce would grow;
> They popularized the precursors of the modern checks and modern banks;
> They cultivated great extensions of land to feed men and animals in Europe;
> They practically eliminated hunger in Europe for almost 200 years;
> They elaborated a secret symbolism and a code of communication among their members.

The excellent administration of the order's assets, the fact that they were exempt of taxes, the war booties, the donations and good business transactions, allowed the order to grow rich to the benefit of the common people. The order became, in other words, an ethical multinational organization with ample access to land, property and money. We read in the Catholic Encyclopedia that

> ". . . the most serious charge against it [the Templars] was its insupportable pride and love of power. At the apogee of its prosperity, it was said to possess 9000 estates. With its accumulated revenues it had

amassed great wealth, which was deposited in its temples at Paris and London. Numerous princes and private individuals had banked there their personal property, because of the uprightness and solid credit of such bankers. In Paris the royal treasure was kept in the Temple. Quite independent, except from the distant authority of the pope, and possessing power equal to that of the leading temporal sovereigns, the order soon assumed the right to direct the weak and irresolute government of the Kingdom of Jerusalem, a feudal kingdom transmissible through women and exposed to all the disadvantages of minorities, regencies, and domestic discord. However, the Templars were soon opposed by the Order of Hospitallers, which had in its turn become military, and was at first the imitator and later the rival of the Templars. This ill-timed interference of the orders in the government of Jerusalem only multiplied the intestine dissentions, and this at a time when the formidable power of Saladin threatened the very existence of the Latin Kingdom. While the Templars sacrificed themselves with their customary bravery in this final struggle, they were, nevertheless, partly responsible for the downfall of Jerusalem."

Given the power of the Templars, it was just a matter of time before they would collide frontally with other powerful secular authorities, especially the King of France (Philip the Fair), marking the end of such a magnificent organization that would have revolutionized the world in ways unsuspected to this day. Whatever the reasons Philip the Fair, the Pope Clement V, the Hospitallers, etc. had to destroy the Templars, the downfall of this organization could not have been avoided because the time to bring humanity to a universal fraternity of men and women had not yet come.

It was the night of October 14, 1307 that Philip ordered the arrest of the Templars of his kingdom. They were accused of heresy, sodomy, sacrilege, and other abominable sins—like spitting on the crucifix—then they were taken to cold, obscure and pestilent jails, until they would be condemned and burnt in public spectacles that would make of the Holy Inquisition a "respectable" branch of ecclesiastical justice.

The difference between the Templars and the Catholic hierarchy of the time is the difference between what Christianity was meant to be and what avarice, egoism, and greed made it to be. The Templars were the manifestation of God's love for humanity, and their dual function as monks and warriors, was transformed, once the Crusades were over, in a dual function as spiritual leaders and social workers and entrepreneurs; heirs of the spiritual tradition of Christ, and holders of mundane property, they set as their goal the wholesome advancement of humanity both in its material and spiritual needs.

The great mistake of Medieval Christendom was the separation of church and state. The Templars constituted a very good working model to follow, and yet the blunder of leaving the things of the spirit to the Church, and the "things of this world" to the state proved to be calamitous. There is no reason why the Church could not conduct the secular business of society as well, or even better, than the so-called secular authorities. On the contrary, the religious authorities would be in a better moral position to care for the material necessities of man. Just because the Crusades and the Inquisition—thought to be religious intrusions in secular matters—proved to be wrong, there was no justification for the Church to shy away from caring about the material welfare of humankind, under the pretext that it was a strictly secular enterprise. These matters left to the capitalists and to the insatiable avarice of businessmen and entrepreneurs turned out to be a colossal mistake. The Church, especially the Christian church, should have continued in control of the secular affairs of the state, especially if by way of concession to non-religious leaders, a strictly secular body would be allowed to participate in matters of government, mainly in legislative and judicial affairs, but with little influence in the economic and administrative roles of government.

One strong argument against the separation of church and state is the fact that most people who make up the government happen to be members of a religious group—it doesn't matter what religious denomination they belong to, be it Christian, Muslim, Buddhist, or Scientologist—and they are undoubtedly going to reflect their religious inclinations on the work they do for the nation. Even an atheist could be considered a member of a *religious belief*, since he does *believe* that there is no God, and his belief is going to influence what he does in a government position. The strictly secular human is a myth, an empty concept, because there are no secular individuals. We either believe in some kind of religion, or we don't believe in any religion, or we appear not to care if anybody believes in something, religious or not, but we can never be neutral to human beliefs. Secularism that appears to be neutral to human beliefs (our actual notion of secularism) is dangerous, because it effectively discards morality from the principles of governing, and there is nothing more dangerous than an amoral society—an amoral society is even more dangerous than an immoral one, because the latter at least may be brought back to uphold the basic moral principles from which it strayed, while the first purportedly lacks any sense of morality, good or bad. Furthermore, like we showed in the book *The Axioms of Being and the Renaissance of the Templars*, there is a set of fundamental principles that people of all acceptable religions must advocate, as a matter of being members of the human race, and those fundamental principles cannot help but touch on religious beliefs, and since they are common to all valid religious beliefs, they may be made part of a non-secular policy of governmental operations, where the separation of church and state is a matter of functional convenience for governing, and not a fundamental philosophical conviction that may lead to the justification of anti-human, or even inhuman, governmental actions.

Muslims are far more advanced than we are in the (once secular) management of government by religious authorities, and Iran is the frontrunner of such a system. Now, I am not saying that this would be a foolproof endeavor, especially if led by fanatics and religious bigots, in which case a separation of church and state would be desirable. But we have successfully dealt in more than one occasion with secular dictators and tyrants, and I don't see how we could not manage against a forceful theocracy, if such a theocracy should materialize. The argument that people of other religions would be oppressed by a theocratic government of a particular religious brand would not hold for the Knight Templars, since we espouse a natural or rational system of religious beliefs, a sort of meta-religion, that encompasses all religions that do not contradict the Axioms of Being—Christianity in most of its forms, Islam, Judaism, and other moderate religions—that show profound respect for other people's beliefs, and that would govern without infringing other people's spiritual rights. Even atheists have nothing to fear from the Templars.

But, in any event, we have scores of *de facto* "secular" theocracies all over the world—and the USA under the Bush administration is such an example—it combines the worst aspects of secularism with religious fundamentalism. Furthermore, there is every reason to suppose that people have common religious and moral beliefs that are inalienable—and if a theocracy keeps its governance within the limits of these common moral and spiritual values, we can safely suppose that it would also be able to determine the most common human material needs that the same religious hierarchy would be able to tackle as well, or even better, than any secular government. Ever since before the French Revolution and Enlightenment, these secular governments, product of the liberal doctrine of separation of Church and State, have had their chance to govern and often botched the work miserably. Isn't about time to give the religious authorities an opportunity to give it a try? Furthermore, modern Templars have concluded that one of the big problems plaguing humanity has been the excess of testosterone, which translates into the nefarious rule of men with a proclivity to settle conflicts (among peoples and among nations) by force, leading to bloody, violent and unjustified wars. Under the Templars lead, women would play a more prominent role than they currently play in world affairs.

The liberal concept of separation of church and state—which came as a result of the excesses of pre-revolutionary France, and as a result of the 18th Century Enlightenment, has had negative consequences that we will never be able to fathom completely—one of them being the birth and unbridled growth of the modern capitalist system of production, which drew a wider wedge between rich and poor. The backlash of the early history of the Catholic Church, itself corrupted by unscrupulous clergymen, bishops and popes, associated with absolutist tyrants, and often times insane Kings and Monarchs, is no justification to let the business of government in the hands of worse, or equally corrupt, insincere, and ambitious modern secular politicians, especially the macho types, all too eager to lead entire nations and groups of nations to wars of conquest, or to wars of intervention in the internal affairs of other countries.

As we said before, St. Bernard was the mentor of the Knight Templars. He envisioned an Order completely involved in the mundane aspects of humanity, and although the individual members of the Order were poor, the organization itself would be immensely rich. He thought of the Templars as an organization involved in all activities of human life, so that it could be a reformer, organizer, judge and custodian of human behavior. Therefore, according with what we saw before, the Templars were meant to be a guide for human growth and development within the spiritual rules dictated by Christian ethics and spirituality.

Besides the duality of body and spirit, monk and warrior, St. Bernard established in the primitive rules of the Templars the triad, which was supposedly inspired by the Trinitarians or Celts:

- Accept combat against heretics, even if three against one;
- Respond, among non-heretics, only after being attacked three times;
- As a punishment for a fault be whipped three times;
- Eat meat, attend mass, and give alms three times a week;
- Do the communion three times a year.

Following the rules of the triad, we envision the Templars as having a three-fold mission for humanity: Supporters of the spiritual needs of individual men and women of every credo; supporters of the material needs of individuals of every race; and believers in the one true God, Creator of the Universe. This three-fold mission is reflected in the three branches of the Templars organization: The Fraternity of the Templars, God Enterprises, and the Orbis Unum Party. It is also no coincidence that the founding fathers of the United States of America envisioned a government divided into three branches: The Executive Branch, the Legislative Branch, and the Judicial Branch, as it is no coincidence that some of them were masons or freemasons. It's only unfortunate that—given the welter of cults and Protestant sects that found a home in the American continent, and given the history of religious persecution in the Old Continent—the founding fathers insisted in the separation of church and state.

It is said that the Templars were given the mission to find the Ark of the Covenant in the Temple of Solomon where they would be lodged. Although they dug all over the place, there is no evidence that they ever found anything of importance that had to do with Christ, Moses, or the Jewish tradition. The fact is that after they left the Temple, they seemed to have acquired some architectural knowledge they didn't have before, but this could have been knowledge acquired through the contact with Arabs, Persians, Jews, or through some other Middle Eastern sources.

It is said that the Templars not only constituted a religious and military Order dedicated to safeguard the holy places in the Middle East, but that they were entrusted with a secret mission that led them to the acquisition of esoteric knowledge. Their mission was to rescue the Ark of the Covenant, which contained Moses' ten-commandment tablets. The Ark had been, since the times of King Solomon, the center of the cult in the Temple of Jerusalem as a visible sign of the presence of God on earth. It is said that it had the power to open up the doors to occult knowledge based on the cosmic proportions. It is also claimed that from the Ark emanated such a powerful energy that it could blind those who didn't have a soul pure enough to look at it. For the Catholic Church the Ark had only historical and archeological value, while it is claimed by some modern Templar sympathizers that, for some initiated individuals, like St. Bernard de Clairvaux, the Ark had magic and esoteric value related to the knowledge of the rhythm of the numbers that held the proportions of the Universe. This is what the legend says about the mission of the Knight Templars, but we will look into what really transpired in the process of taking into practice their very original mission.

The destruction of the Order by the King of France seemed to follow a process that was far too easy, given that the Knight Templars were renowned for their capacity to fight in combat. It would be the equivalent of trying to destroy the modern Naval Seals of the US Army, or any other special operations troops. The passivity shown by the Templars when they were arrested seems to point to the fact that they had already learned that the time for the final battle against evil had not yet come. They apparently had learned that fighting evil is something that needs to be carefully weighed, so that the same mistakes of the Crusades would not be repeated. Nonetheless, some of the Templars managed to escape with the ships they had at the port of La Rochelle. In Germany they resisted the order of arrest and became members of the Teutonic Knights. In Portugal they took the name of The Poor Knights of Christ. In Spain they joined other existing orders. That's why many historians believe that a few Templars went underground and continued their mission clandestinely. It is even stranger that Columbus' ships had the Templar Cross painted in their sails, making some believe that perhaps Christopher Columbus was a Templar.

The Templars were targeted for annihilation because they represented an ominous danger to both the State and the Church establishment. A full-blown Templar system of encomiendas would have made obsolete the Church and the State, although this was never the Templars' intention. No wonder the Templars were swiftly exterminated—they represented a potential source of ideological anarchy, this expression interpreted as a viable political system that in time would have dispensed with both the Church and the State.

The legends about the Templars were probably invented as a way of distracting people's attention—the Templars probably never accumulated riches in the form of jewels or precious metals, they probably never had the intention of searching for the Holy Grail and the Ark of the Covenant—why, these things had been taken by the conquerors of Salomon's Temple and we don't know what happened to them. As for esoteric and occult knowledge, I doubt that Christians of the caliber of the Templars would be involved in witchcraft and sorcery. These were all myths designed to obscure the reason for their destruction. This work of slander, skillfully done by the Anti-Christ, was so thorough that even the freemasons and other organizations that claim to be descendants of the Templars don't even resemble what the Templars stood for, perhaps out of fear of being identified with them.

The order to place the Templars under arrest, reads as follows:

> "I, William of Nogaret, in furtherance of the instructions given to me by His Majesty Philip V, hereby order to detain all the Knights belonging to the Order of the Temple and confiscate their assets. Thanks to numerous trustworthy informants, we have learned that the brothers of the Order of the Temple's Militia, hiding the wolf under the appearance of the lamb, and under the habit of the Order, miserably insult the true faith, crucifying once more, in our days, our Lord Jesus Christ. These depraved people have renounced the fountain of divine light and practiced sodomy, the adoration of satanic idols, and the theft of property, they have threaded a mesh of evilness that threatens to destroy our society and our legitimate belief in the Almighty. Signed in Paris in the month of September of 1307."

This was the premonition to the destruction of the Knight Templars. With such an explicit order, the French authorities of the time declared their intention to arrest the Templars. Some time later, following the plans with impeccable precision, the Order had been dismantled, their members had been detained or executed, and their last Grand Master, Jacques de Molay, had been burned at the stake accused of being a dangerous heretic.

Some historians believe nowadays that the treacherous scheme against the Templars was nothing more than vulgar accusations serving as an excuse to annihilate them and to expropriate their vast properties and assets, while at the same time neutralizing their enormous political influence. We propose here that the Pope and the King just wanted to get rid of a competing organization that was making them obsolete, given the Templars spiritual and mundane work to help the socially disadvantaged, the poor and the forsaken. Whatever the reasons for the provoked demise of the Templars, the question remains whether or not the Templars were the depositaries of secret esoteric knowledge, and whether or not the Templars followed a path that deviated from Christian orthodox teachings. Perhaps all those reasons given above remain valid. Perhaps the Templars were a little liberal as to their beliefs, incorporating some elements of Islam and Judaism, as well as some elements of other religions of the Middle East. Perhaps the King of France and the Pope were jealous and apprehensive about the work of the Templars. The crude fact remains that they were annihilated. It happened in Paris, the date was March 18, 1314, on the stake raised before the cathedral of Notre Dame the most important of the accused Templars faced death by fire. They were Jacob de Molay and three other high dignitaries of the Order of the Temple. In a gesture of genuine medieval chivalry and conscious that the glorious organization to which they belonged was going to be unjustly destroyed, the Templars proclaimed their innocence in front of the people of Paris.

It was an act charged with suicidal passion and extreme sincerity that at least let them die reclaiming the dignity that they should never have lost—even as they represented the glorious Knight Templars, those that years before had paid with their lives, fighting for the defense of their faith in the battlegrounds of the Holy Lands. At sunset, in the Island of the Jews in the middle of the Sienna River, their bodies were consumed by the flames.

The spirit of the Templars was not extinguished with the death of their Grand Master, Jacob de Molay in the year 1314 at the hands of the Inquisition. On the contrary, the Knight Templars that remained in Europe manage to secretly reorganize themselves and avenge the memory of their leader in a series of historical happenings whose consequences reached our times.

Nevertheless, several centuries after the disappearance of the Templars we have to ask the inevitable question: Are the Templars still among us? And if they are, what is their mission?

It is a historical fact that many Templars ended up as members of other military and monastic orders. In Germany, a great number of the Templars joined the Teutonic Order. In Spain, many of the Templars were accepted in the different national orders, among others Calatrava, Santiago, Alcantara and the Order of the Hospitallers of Saint John, as well as in the orders of Montesa (Spain) and the Oder of Christ in Portugal. In the XVII century the masons incorporated some of the rites of the Templars—in fact, they even claim to be the heirs of the Templar tradition of the past.

Finally, a lot of legends and myths have been weaved around the Templars, some of which had to do with architecture, astrology, and geometric forms like squares, circles, octagons, etc. Others deal with secrecy, occultism, magic and immense treasures in gold, precious stones and religious relics. It is even said that the Templars sailed to America from La Rochelle and brought back gold, precious stones, and other treasures. Even the finding of a Fort in the Golf of St. Matias, in Argentina, has been related to the Templars. But all of this, so far, has remained legends, myths, or stories waiting to be confirmed or rejected by further historical and archeological discoveries. As for the relationship of the Templars with the modern masons and freemasons, there seems to be a clear connection that could only be natural, given the mission of the Templars as church builders.

One of the main activities of the Templars was the erection of churches and cathedrals in the whole European continent and in the Holy Land, which meant that they had a close relationship with master builders, known as masons. This close relationship was kept, even after the dissolution of the Order. One group of the Templars ended up in Scotland, where, under the protection of Richard I organized the so-called Scotch Ritual, which assimilated some of the Celtic mythology. King Richard created two brotherhoods to preserve the legacy of the Templars—after their persecution and demise by the King of France and the Papacy—the Royal Order of Scotland and the Kilwinning of Heredom. Once the Templars became part of other organizations, by assimilation or absorption, they were able to communicate their knowledge to the master builders of the time organized in fraternities of architects, later known as lodges (of freemasons). It was in the XVIII century that other elements of the Templar tradition were assimilated by the masons, to the point that nowadays the masons claim to be the direct and continuous successors and heirs of the Order of the Templars.

As we mentioned before, the Order of the Templars was created with the express purpose of safeguarding the holy places. This established an association of the Templars with the search and custody of Sacred Relics, giving origin to the Templars' legends about the Holy Grail, the Ark of the Covenant, and the Philosopher's Stone, all of them related to magic, the occult and/or alchemy. The Templars' syncretism of beliefs, which were assimilated from other traditions and rituals, proper of secret societies, made them deviate from Christian orthodoxy and let them open to attacks of heresy. The Templars' mission, as they understood it, was not to exclusively safeguard the Christian faith and the holy places, but to work for the understanding among other religions and beliefs, which made them too liberal-minded for their epoch. That's why they established contacts with the world of Islam, especially with organizations similar to theirs, like the assassins, whose name come from *assaca*, meaning guardian, making them guardians of the Islamic light. The modern concept of the term assassin is a tergiversation of the original concept, which implied valor, especially in combat against the enemies of their faith. The assassins, just like the Templars, were a mystic and religious organization whose objective was the defense of the sacred places of Islam.

Recently, there has been interest in rehabilitating the Sovereign Order of the Temple of Christ. This Order was suspended provisionally by the famous Pope Clement V in the year 1312. This rehabilitation would only be a formality, since there has never been a rift between the Templars and the Catholic Church—contrary to what happened with Martin Luther, the Reform, and the Anglican Church—in spite of the fact that the Templars were plainly justified in renouncing any association with Catholicism, given the persecution led by King Philip and the Pope against its members. Yet the Templars embody all that is to be a Catholic, and more, since we embrace other Christian reformers in a spirit of universal brotherhood, and for the love of God and humanity.

In my book *the Axioms of Being and the Renaissance of the Templars*, I write:

"This calls for wisdom. If anyone has insight, let him calculate the number of the beast, for it is man's number. His number is 666."

"The Order of the Templars has been suppressed for 666 years (a man's number), from 1312 to 1978, when the idea of a revival of the Templars was born. The number 666 is the number of the beast, because an unchallenged system of abuse has been imposed on humanity through 666 years of human suffering; and 666 years is, in this regard, a man's number."

Based on the number 666 of the Book of Revelations of St. John, I express that the meaning of the number is that the reign of the Beast was going to last 666 years, and that, therefore, something must have happened in 1978, mainly the revival of the Templars' movement that marks the end of the period of the uncontested supremacy of the Antichrist over all aspects of human affairs. But this calculation was based on the year 1312, when the Order of the Temple was officially suspended, albeit temporarily, by Pope Clement the V. If we use the year 1307 instead, when Phillip the Fair, King of France, ordered the arrest of the Templars, then the year that should have marked the end of the kingdom of the Beast, and the beginning of a new era for humanity could be 1973. Do we know what happened in 1973? The only thing that comes to mind is the birth of *Creciendo en Gracia*, a movement that their followers refuse to call religious, led by José Luis de Jesús Miranda, from Puerto Rico, who claims to be the Antichrist, except that Mr. Miranda turns around the common interpretation of the meaning of the word Antichrist, and gives it a definitively positive meaning. This raises another interesting question: Are we witnessing the death of the Antichrist era with the birth of the Fraternity of the Templars (1978), or are we witnessing the beginning of a new era with an Antichrist who claims to be leading humanity to spiritual liberation (from sin and hell) and to material deliverance from poverty and misery, right here on planet earth (1973)?

It is said that the Templars of today, just like the Templars of the past, dominate the world of finances through little known discrete enterprises, and that they also have important representation in international Banks and Insurance companies. These "Templars" are behind almost all groups of world re-insurance companies, as well as in the great investment funds. If this is true, those "Templars" seem to be ignorant of the fact that they are soldiers of Christ, and it is only reasonable to think that one day they will wake up to the fact that they are the elected ones, chosen to lead the fight against poverty and misery that prevails in our present day and world. Who these modern "Templars" are, and what they are doing for the masses of impoverished people of the world is not known to me.

Nevertheless—and if it is indeed true that those modern "Templars" exist—like in the past, they would have to live in accordance with the oath of poverty, chastity and obedience in the practice of the Melquisedec priesthood. All the benefits of their enterprises would have to be reinvested in companies managed by the Order, and also money would be given to social programs and charitable institutions. Their companies must be dedicated to licit businesses that are not contrary to the Order's religious and spiritual principles. In other words, they would have to be members of God Enterprises (GEnte), which they are not.

Spiritually (and we must stress here the word spiritually), the Templars are God's militia and ministers of Christ that wait patiently for the second coming of the Lord, expectant of His orders to combat and destroy evil once and for all, in order to inaugurate God's government on earth, all in accordance with a spirit of synarchy for the best interests of mankind. But while we wait for the second coming of Christ, we should start building the foundations of this, the City of God in the city of man.

Bibliography

Addison, Charles G.: *The History of the knights templars.* 1997 Adventures Unlimited Press, U.S.A; First published in London, 1842.

Atienza, Juan G.: *Los enclaves templarios.* Martínez Roca, 1995, Barcelona.

Charpentier, Louis: *Los misterios templarios.* Apóstrofe, 1995, Barcelona.

Fluguerto Martí, Fernando. : *Expediciones al Golfo de San Matías, Patagonia Argentina.* Comunicación personal y en la WEB: www.delphos.com.ar

Melville, Marion: *Nosotros los templarios.* Tikal, 1995, Girona, España.

Walker, Martin: *El misterio de los Templarios.* Edicomunicación, 1993, Barcelona.

Arroyo Durán, Fernando y Fernández Palacio, Jorge L. : *Historia Secreta del Temple, La Mano que Meció Europa.* Artículo publicado en la revista MÁS ALLÁ DE LA CIENCIA No. 138 de Agosto de 2000 (TEMPLESPAÑA).

Knights Templar. From Wikipedia, the free encyclopedia.

Juan de Jerusalén (Lo Inexplicable). De Los Templarios, Martes, 01 de Febrero de 2005.

Della Torre, Horacio A.: *Los Caballeros Templarios—Hechos, Supuestos y Misterios.*

Nicolas Martin y Mateo: *Los Templarios, sus Claves Históricas y Misterios.* Editado por las Revistas Esfinge y Rosacruz.

Abramsen, Elías: *El Poder Actual de los Templarios.* Traducción de un artículo publicado en Malasia sobre los templarios y sus acciones en el Vaticano (Del Malasian Financial News, 25 de Julio 2003).

Gittins, Jonathan A.: *The Rule of the Templars and the Monastic Vows of Poverty, Chastity, and Obedience* (Copyright by Jonathan Gittins, 2003).

4

THE NEW MISSION OF THE TEMPLARS

Before we proceed to describe what the new mission of the Templars is going to be, we must define who the Templars are. We said before that the Fraternity of the Templars, God Enterprises, and the Orbis Unum party, at the time of writing this book, are inexistent entities, because they haven't been organized yet. The author of this book doesn't claim to be a direct descendant of the Templars of the Middle Ages, nor does he claim to be the unique and genuine representative of the modern Templars. I just happen to view the idealized notion of the Templars as a symbol for the fight against selfishness and avarice, and in pro of the rescue of man from misery and degradation. I truly believe that all the contemporary organizations of the Templars should one day get together and decide what they are going to do to honor the name of the holy monk-warriors of antiquity. Templars, masons, freemasons, and all those organizations that symbolize one aspect or another of the glorious Knights Templar, ought to get together to form a sort of Templars' umbrella organization that doesn't necessarily have to be called the Fraternity of the Templars. Whatever we name it, it must be based on similar principles to the ones I propose in this book, and hold objectives similar to the ones exposed in these writings. I, on my part, would be thrilled to be just another member of such an organization, and I hope this book will be an open invitation to all Templars of every nation to get serious about the global fight against greed and avarice, which are the source and foundation of world misery and poverty.

Opus Dei means 'the work of God,' and this work of God necessarily shows the way to the 'advent of the Kingdom of heaven on earth,' for which I wrote a blueprint, credo or manifesto. This credo is constituted by the following parts:

the philosophical foundations of the new spirituality, given in this book and in my book *The Axioms of Being*; God Enterprises, the plan for economic participation in the capitalist system of production; and the Orbis Unum Party that will eventually drop the 'party' qualification to become just the Orbis Unum. God Enterprises is at the very core of the Philosopher's Stone, or the Holy Grail, expressed in the Principle of Love, given that the productivity of the capitalist system is going to lead to almost an inexhaustible source of wealth that will feed humanity, and an inexhaustible source of energy that will move the 'Leviathan,' the system of machines that will output the goods that will clothe, feed, and house the peoples of the world—this inexhaustible source of energy I believe will be found in some sort of cold fusion in the *st-matrix* (space-time matrix), also known as ether or the space-time *continuum*. God Enterprises will be our instrument to conquer Das Kapital through participation in the gambit called the free enterprise system or the capitalist system of production. One more instrument of conquest is going to be the Orbis Unum party or Party 01—the duality, the binary number system that represents all aspects of nature, the perfect circle and the unity, non-being versus being—*orbis* meaning circle, *unum* meaning one, or the unity.

The Leviathan, the Beast, or the Anti-Christ rests on three main pillars: secular authority, religious authority, and the mass media, and they all work within the capitalist system of production. Capitalism is not inherently bad; it's the way the capitalist system operates which may be bad or evil. In the times of the original Templars, there were only the secular power and the religious power—there was no mass media communication, except the one used by Christians to spread the Gospel from person to person, which consisted of preaching and going from one town to the next, making disciples. Mass media has proved to be of enormous importance to capitalism, both to market its products and to keep the general population tightly controlled—news data is selectively weaved to give the general audience a menu of skillfully crafted capitalist-friendly information—under a masquerade of free press.

The Roman Empire was both a secular and semi-religious power. The roman secular authorities soon found out that they couldn't combat the Christians by force and decided to absorb Christianity as the official religion of the Empire. This changed Christianity in a negative way, transforming the movement from one of a populous nature into one inflexible bureaucracy, as it has remained to this day, a departure from Jesus' teachings. Remember that Jesus was never against the secular authorities, but he was always at odds with the religious establishment, mainly the Pharisees and the Sadducees. The problem with religion is that it can't afford to become complacent of the deeds of the secular authorities. The soft-spoken criticisms of the church against the economic inequalities exacerbated by an insatiable capitalist system, alienates the masses that the church is supposed to represent and support.

We are the Knights Templar, the original keepers of the secrets of the Temple of Solomon. Except that there will be no more secrets to be kept, once society understands the need to bring the Kingdom of heaven down to earth, once we achieve the goal of bringing all individuals into the big family of the human race. There will be no wars, no apocalypses, no Armageddon and no end of the world to punish humanity for their evil deeds of centuries past. We are at the verge of conquering the minds and the hearts of men through peaceful and friendly admonitions, and we know that there will be a time when greed will be no more, thanks to the super-abundance of riches that can and will feed us all. This understanding of the need to neutralize the human ego, so that we can all work for the pursuit of individual and collective happiness is not a dream or an utopia, given that at the time of writing this book, billionaires like Bill Gates, Warren Buffett and others, have given up a sizeable chunk of their riches to create foundations to help ease the problems of the peoples of the world, especially the most elementary needs of the peoples of the African continent.

God Enterprises, the flagship of the Fraternity of the Templars, rests on the assumption that billionaires will eventually understand the folly of hoarding money that they know it will be impossible to spend in less than one lifetime. If we assume, for instance, that one of those rich people could live on $2000 a day—amount that could very well pay for the monthly maintenance of four families of four in any third-world country, and we are talking here of sixteen people living soberly for one month—it would take less than 30 million dollars to keep him/her happy for forty years. What would anybody do with more than 30 million dollars, knowing that this amount is enough to keep him/her going for the next 40 years, assuming expenditures of $2000 a day? But even if God Enterprises could not count on those millionaires and billionaires, the organization can be kept going by common individuals with a sense of compassion for others, because once GEnte starts functioning, its very nature will make it impossible to stop growing in extension and wealth.

One country specially, the United States of America, followed by the Western European countries, have, up to now, done the work of the devil, which, in the wider context of God's Work, will lead to the creation of an anti-apocalyptic world order that will embody Saint Augustine's City of God, except that it will be embedded in the city of man. I say the work of the devil, because the capitalist system of production has been Satan's lure to make those capitalist innovators create the productive machinery that has served to exploit and enslave the common man, and yet it will be the instrument to feed and maintain humanity, as soon as we give political power to the leaders of the Orbis Unum Party. The incarnation of the City of God in this planet is not going to be the 1000 years of the reign of the Beast that offers prosperity to all and will cover the necessities of all the inhabitants of the planet earth. This vision of the apocalypse has been grossly misunderstood by some Christians, since Saint John's apocalypse is nothing more than a spiritual representation of what will happen to humanity if our program fails. But it can't fail, because we have already been redeemed, and there is no other way out for humanity than the implementation of the Knight Templars' social order, that has already averted the spiritual apocalyptic destruction of humanity presented in Saint John's Revelations.

We already gave a brief history of the Templars, and have established that historically there was a movement that was stopped only for a little while—some 700 years—but that is here and now to retake the flag of freedom from our ego and from the dictatorship of the flesh and of the 'things of this world.' The Templar's movement has been resurrected and is now ready to take on the task of complying fully with the Principle of Love: Do what is good and fight what is evil. Again, we are not going to concentrate just on the positive half of the Principle of Love, which will be led by the economic and financial work of God Enterprises, but will also prepare ourselves for the counteraction of evil that will try, by all means possible, to stop our crusade for the people. The battles to annihilate evil will be conducted by the Fraternity of the Templars.

We will explain how and why the capitalist system of production is the Holy Grail, the Ark of the Covenant, the Philosopher's Stone of the alchemists of the past. The Templars found them all in the nascent capitalist system of production that they envisioned in their banking operations and the management of *Encomiendas* in the 11th, 12th and 13th Centuries—and in their effort to preserve what was sacred and sacrosanct, and in their effort to do what is good, they ran contrary to the inflated ego of the European bourgeoisie and clergy of their time. Hence, after the Templar's demise, what was meant to be an instrument to relieve the sufferings of humanity became an instrument to enslave humanity, because men did not understand that the ego, the material world, and the flesh, stood between the Spirit of man and the Spirit of God.

In this pursuit of happiness, the Templars will still follow the Rule established at the foundation of the original Order, which is the vow to live a life of poverty, chastity and obedience. But poverty will not be synonymous with misery, chastity will not be synonymous with mortification of the flesh, and obedience will not be the servitude of the zombies. Times have changed, and we the Templars have also changed.

The Knight Templars are considered to be the greatest warriors of the Church (Christ's warriors) always willing to sacrifice their life for the only God of the universe. But, in addition to being warriors, they were, more than anything, monks, spiritual people who made of love the center of their faith in Christ, based on two simple commandments, given by Jesus Himself: "You shall love the Lord your God with all your heart, and with all your soul, and with all your mind," *and* "You shall love your neighbor as yourself" The beauty of these two commandments is that in reality they blend into one. For, how can you love God, a spiritual being, if not through the love of others, as measured by the love of yourself?

The greatest achievement of the Templars was the invention of the concept of banking. The Order of the Templars acquired money and gifts from pilgrims and travelers, giving them in exchange letters of credit that they could cash anywhere the Templars had a preceptory (bank). Travelers that used the Templars "banks" didn't fear being robbed of cash in their way to their destination, knowing that they could retrieve their money once they reached it, and always under the protection of the monk-warriors. Eventually the Templars became money lenders, offering property, cash and money to kings and noblemen interested in their investments. Such practices made them very influential, while the monarchs would go to them whenever they needed cash and monies, which made them the bank of avarice and jealousy. Undoubtedly some of the Templars became corrupt and probably even succumbed to paganism or to something even worse, like heresy or blasphemy. The conditions for the destruction of the Templars had been laid out by the very same services they provided to both the poor and the powerful—they were even accused of usury, and 1307 was the year that saw the demise of the Order of the Templars. In spite of all the good things that the Templars did, it was the implementation of the concept of interest rates for cash loans that injected in their financial system the seeds of insatiable avarice and selfishness that has characterized the capitalist system up to our present times.

One author claims that the remnant members of the Templars went underground and swore to continue their sacred mission. It is said that they reappeared only recently, after adopting the following four directives: The establishment of a new Christendom, the continuation of the Order of the Templars, the defense of the innocent against any natural or supernatural menace, and the eradication of the so-called Order of the Reason. Their battle grounds would be the universities, the editorials and the public arena. Although these modern Templars claim to be capable of providing soldiers to combat natural or unnatural evil, they say that their combat is being held in the courts and the boards of directors. The Templars' modern struggle is said to be directed against what they call godless traitors, the technocratic establishment. The *illuminati* among them claim to have powers given by God. Who those Templars are, and where they operate is a mystery.

In my book the *Axioms of Being and the Renaissance of the Templars* I wrote that the Fraternity of the Templars, God Enterprises, and the Orbis Unum Party are the three branches of the Templars, except that they don't exist at the present time. Notice that the Fraternity corresponds to the first person of the Trinity, the Father. God Enterprises is the visible branch of the Templars, and corresponds to the second person of the Trinity, the Son. And the Orbis Unum Party corresponds to the third person of the Trinity, the Holy Ghost.

Now, the original mission of the Templars may have failed in its search for the Holy Grail, the Philosopher's Stone, and the Ark of the Covenant, because these became idealized objects whose physical existence was not necessary for them to *be*, in the spiritual sense of *being*. Thus the Holy Grail corresponds nowadays to the capitalist system of production with its almost inexhaustible capacity to produce reaches and material things to satisfy the necessities of humanity, and this inexhaustible fountain of wealth will be tapped by God Enterprises. The Philosopher's Stone became the philosophical foundations—the Axioms of Being—of the modern lead Templar organization, the Fraternity of the Templars. And the Ark of the Covenant is the Orbis Unum Party, the soul and primer of the organization that will keep the unity and integrity of the Temple—because that's what humanity is, the Temple of Solomon, and the Knight Templars are here to protect the integrity of this Temple.

As far as the layman is concerned, the Fraternity of the Templars will remain invisible and will organize itself in such a way that only the Knight Templars, within the Fraternity, will know that it is, without necessarily knowing about the rest of its members. The Knight Templars will make themselves visible (will come to view) whenever the order is given to get ready for the final spiritual battle against evil, under the command of Jesus Christ Himself. Because of this, the Templars are fearless and feared warriors that will spare no effort or life to combat the dark forces of hell. God Enterprises will eventually have physical existence in the form of businesses and companies that will generate wealth. The Orbis Unum Party is the soul of the Templars, and will gather the masses of men and women in political support of the organization.

The Templars are going to be a strictly hierarchical organization. The Grand Master will govern the organization for life and with absolute power. Total democracy is vested in the figure of the Grand Master, who will be as infallible as the Pope, but only in spiritual matters—and virtually all matters of the Fraternity are spiritual in character. Since he works for God and the Church, only the Seneschals will be able to depose him. The Seneschals are the coordinators of the organization (the General Assembly of God Enterprises) and are the keepers of the organization's funds and the training programs, and they serve as a liaison in military matters. Next, there are the Commanders in Chief, the Preceptors, the Knight-Brothers and the Sergeants of the Alliance. Finally the Knight-Apprentices are those who are getting trained and prepared to join the organization. The training of the Templars includes one year doing what is good on a daily basis (this implies looking for somebody in need, and giving help)—this very first year of a Templar's training is aimed to the deflation of the human ego; next, the trainee goes through one year discerning what is good and what is bad (or evil) on a daily basis, and communicating their findings to the master on a weekly basis, who will determine whether or not the judgment was right or wrong; and, finally, the trainee will spend one year getting ready to combat evil (this requires intensive military preparation, plus a more intensive, yet spiritual, training through the power of meditation).

A New Mission

We, the Templars, don't worry about building temples and churches—the Templars of the past did plenty of church-building. We are here to put into practice the Principle of Love, which simply stated amounts to do good to other human beings and to ourselves. The definition of Love is stated in the Principle of Love: I must actively do what is good (Love) and categorically confront, i.e. fight, what is evil (Justice). So, to Love is to actively do what is good and categorically confront (fight) what is evil. Hence, how do we Love God, a spiritual being? God sent his Son, Jesus, so that He could be the giver and the recipient of our Love. Jesus said: Love each other like I have loved you. Hence, we love God through Jesus, and since Jesus is no longer with us, we Love Jesus through our neighbors, other human beings, the whole of humanity.

The dichotomy between the ego and the anima brings about two different definitions of love. Love of the ego, which is the love related to reproduction, sex, family life, and the love we feel for our family, friends, pets, etc. Love of the anima, on the other hand is a love that has nothing to do with our relationships, with the family, friends, or any other relationships, but a love that knows no difference between one individual or another, knows no difference between a starving child in Africa and our own children.

The definition of love can be deduced from the following passage of the New Testament:

> "Teacher, which is the greatest commandment in the Law?" Jesus replied:
> "'Love the Lord your God with all your heart and with all your soul and
> with all your mind.' This is the first and greatest commandment. And
> the second is like it: 'Love your neighbor as yourself.' All the Law and
> the Prophets hang on these two commandments."

First, we must love God with all our heart, with all our soul, and with all our mind; love God above all other things material and spiritual. But how do we love a spiritual being? How exactly do we love God?

There are lots of ways we love material things. To begin with, we love ourselves by doing that which is good for us and by avoiding doing that which is bad. We love ourselves by seeking for what is pleasurable to the flesh, which is why we enjoy good food, sex, and the pleasures of the flesh. We also love our wives, our children, our relatives, our friends, and we demonstrate this love by doing that which is good for them, by protecting them from that which is bad or evil. We also love music, and other abstract endeavors, but how do we love God? The answer can only be found in the second commandment 'Love your neighbor as yourself.'

What's incredible about the biblical passage mentioned above is that love goes from the world of the senses to the world of spirituality. We know how to love ourselves. We also want to love ourselves to the maximum extent of the word love, and this should be the measure to love others, and if we love other people—by doing what is good for them, by taking care of them, by protecting them from that which is bad or evil—we transcend the meaning of material love to a higher superior meaning of spiritual love. In other words, we love God by loving others as much (or even more) than we love ourselves, and the first commandment is identical to the second. They become really one commandment, without being two radically different commandments. Amazing how love flows from material beings to spiritual beings!

Marcion never understood that the God of the Old Testament was dealing with people almost totally controlled by the ego, which is why Jahve would seem ruthless and merciless with them. The coming of Jesus is the dawn of spirituality that would make radical changes on men. God gave us the gift of grace, which the people of the Old Testament didn't enjoy, which is why merciless wholesale destruction of men directed by God Himself would be no more after the first coming of Christ. Natural disasters are not the product of direct Divine action, but the result of God's will on nature's work on probability. Marcion's teachings were declared heresy because he was making his understanding of God's actions the irrational actions of an evil God—Marcion was trying to read God's mind in accordance with his own perception of the world, and this is heresy, because you don't question God's actions based on imperfect, and contaminated by the ego, human morality.

The duality of the Principle of Love reflects the duality of the Templars. We are monks and warriors. This duality is also expressed in the book of Revelations, where we are told that Jesus came as a sacrificial lamb, a monk, to manifest His Love for humanity by taking upon Him the sins of this world. Jesus gave us the opportunity to practice the Principle of Love, as expressed in the first part of the dictum given above, yet we disregarded Him. His second coming is going to be as a warrior, because then He is going to expressly lead the combat against all evil, for all times. The confrontation is prophetically shown in the book of Revelations to be inevitable. Finally, the Kingdom of heaven will come to us here on earth, and the Beast, or the Anti-Christ, is nothing other than ourselves. We mismanaged the capitalist system that produces wealth to fight poverty and misery, and appropriated the earnings, the profits, and the money for ourselves. This, the spirit of the Anti-Christ, must be destroyed, in the sense that it's going to be put to good use for the sake of humanity.

We, Templars, pray what Jesus told us to pray, the Father's Prayer. We must pray it every day. We don't ask anything for ourselves, except as it gives us the opportunity to help and Love others. In fact, we must pray once in the morning asking for the opportunity to find somebody we can Love. This person, or persons, that we will be helping on a given day are our passport to Salvation. We, Templars, don't have a definition of Salvation, because by doing something for others we are already partaking of Salvation—whatever else we get from God is a free gift of God, it is Grace. We feel very much honored to be able to help others, because they are being the instrument of our Salvation. Those people should never be grateful for what we do for them—just the other way around, we should wash their feet like our Lord did with His disciples. God doesn't want, nor does he need anything from us. By helping others on a daily basis we are already singing praises to God—and not in any other way. Chanting and playing music to sing the prayers of our Lord is Just Aesthetics for the satisfaction of our spirits. God only wants our Faith and our Love, which is love of humanity.

A Knight Templar never prays asking something for himself, except as an avenue to gain fortitude to help others. God does not need of our daily prayers expressed in vocal sounds; God is satisfied with our daily prayers expressed in actions to help others. The best praise we can give God is love of his children, love of humanity. Preaching is not for the Templars, because we only believe in actions to help others.

Had the Templars been active in times of Columbus, they would have done the appropriate thing to conquer and colonize the Americas. This was unfortunate. There were only traces of the Templars' intentions with the arrival of Christopher Columbus. Maybe Columbus was a Templar, but just one with very little authority, and almost powerless to do anything significant for the Indians. It's possible that several Templars came with the Conquistadors and marched with the Spanish soldiers, but no longer as monk-warriors, but just as plain monks, and not enough of them to make a difference. Their presence in Paraguay may have been signaled by the Jesuits' missions, and so is their presence in New Mexico, Arizona, California, and Florida, with their missions, and the *encomienda* system that was never practiced as it was envisioned. In the USA and Canada, on the other hand, with the arrival of the Puritans, residuals of the Reformation, the native American culture was replaced with the Anglo-Saxon culture, and since then, a good number of their descendants hypocritically worship the God of Abraham, Isaac and Jacob.

The Knight Templars and War

In the life of the Templar the most difficult thing is to actively combat evil, because determining what is or is not evil requires more than good judgment. It also requires faith and a lot of intuition. Evil can take on many disguises, and it can fool us into making us believe that what we are confronting is not something bad, but rather something good. Perhaps this is the reason why Jesus never responded with violence against those who wanted to crucify him, because even acts of self-defensive violence are intrinsically evil. Contrary to what Niccolo Machiavelli argued to the effect that the "end justifies the means," on a more spiritual and ethical basis, if the end is good and the means are also good, both end and means would be justified by themselves, and would appear to justify each other. But the reality is that good ends justify themselves, while good means also justify themselves, and not necessarily each other. In this sense—and Jesus probably knew this better than anyone else—it is not morally correct to do something evil to achieve a good result (including self-defense), even if the positive end results surpass the bad effect of the evil means. Again, based on a similar argument to this one, the Catholic Church can never justify abortion, including therapeutic abortion—killing the fetus to save the life of the mother—because a bad deed is not an avenue to attain a good objective. The application of justice runs into the same dilemma: Doing something bad (punishment) in order to produce a good result (social order), reflects again Machiavelli's dictum, which is the reason why the administration of justice is left to the secular authorities. Jesus Himself was ever so reluctant to make judgments about peoples' actions or motives, because judging implies complete knowledge of the facts, including being able to differentiate between good and evil. Thus, perfect application of justice, within the parameters established by the *lex talionis*, is almost impossible to effect in actual judicial practice.

[Means and ends may seem to be connected in the physical, or material world, by a link of expeditiousness that would appear to justify the use of whatever means necessary, as long as we achieve a desired end that our ego labels as good, such that the good end completely overrides the evil means. But in the spiritual realm, of which the physical world is just but a faint reflection, means and ends stand by themselves, and each of them are intrinsically qualified by the ethics of the spirit as good or evil, so that there is no way of extending interconnections among these means and ends such that if one mean is evil, there is an end that by its own goodness cleanses the said mean evilness.]

Nevertheless, self-defense happens, and there is a sense in which self-defense is in accordance with the Principle of Preservation of Life—though this Principle still does not morally justifies it (certainly not on an ethical basis)—and we, the Templars, are going to withhold judgment in reference to self-defense—and also in reference to therapeutic abortion. In this context, we must remember that self-defense is a reaction of the ego and not a reaction of the anima, which makes it morally and spiritually unjustifiable, because self-defense is rooted in the flesh. Having said this, the fight for justice takes two forms: On the one hand, we can do it peacefully, and, on the other hand, we can do it forcefully. The place in the scale from peacefully fighting for justice to forcefully fighting for justice is determined by the participation of the ego. If there is no ego participation, and the anima leads the struggle, we fall on the peaceful end of the scale, but if the ego fully participates in the struggle, in addition to the anima, we fall on the forceful end of the scale. Since forcefully fighting for justice is a form of self-defense, we withhold any judgment for or against it.

This is a partial list of some of the people who have fought for justice:

Fray Bartolomé de las Casas, defender of the Indians;
Mahatma Ghandi, leader of the independence of India;
Martin Luther King, leader of the Civil Rights Movement in the USA;
Nelson Mandela, South African anti-Apartheid leader;
Karl Marx, founder of Communism;
Malcolm X, Black American leader;
John Brown and sons, US abolitionists (of slavery);
Simón Bolívar, Venezuelan leader of the fight for independence;
George Washington, US leader of the Revolutionary War;

The above list ranges from people who peacefully fought for humanity and for the sake of justice to people who forcefully fought for the same cause. There are others that should be included in this list, too numerous to mention, but who also deserve the honor of being called defenders of the human race. I use the term forcefulness instead of violence, because of the nature of the fight—the fight is for the sake of justice, not for other egotistic and evil purpose. The last three people mentioned above had the unfortunate fate of choosing armed struggle to fight for justice, which more often than not spills over into the commission of massacres, which is one reason why the Templars repudiate all kinds of violence, including self-defensive violence. Historical records are too blurry to determine whether or not George Washington and Simón Bolívar let massacres be committed under their command, but, like we said before, armed struggle always spills over into massacres and mass murder, often times without the knowledge of its commanders. We include George Washington in this list—though he led the fight for freedom of white people only—because slavery was beyond his capacity to oppose and combat, if not peacefully, certainly not forcefully, and for this, we give him the benefit of the doubt.

As for the inclusion of Karl Mark at the boundary of peaceful and forceful struggle, we can only say that the Marxist ideology is good in its intention, but ill-designed in its practical application. We have to judge Karl Marx in the light of the horrible injustices he witnessed in his time. He so passionately despised the capitalist system of production that he could not visualize any other way of transforming it than through violent revolution. Historically, I don't think Marx had any other alternative, since the bourgeoisie of his time was adamantly bent on accumulating capital by any means, rather than moralizing about the welfare of their workers, or conducting seminars on labor relations. Marx lived the crudest of all forms of capitalist exploitation—and yes, he did fight with the written word for human justice. Unfortunately, other well-intentioned people were led by Marxism to rise in arms against unjust social conditions, but morally speaking, good intentions are always better than wrongfully executed deeds.

Because the end does not justify the means, except when both ends and means are good, the so-called "wars of self-defense," "holy wars," and "just wars"—though the expressions sound grandiloquent, and yet sort of contradictory—cannot form part of the vocabulary of good ethics. The fact that from a spiritual point of view the achievement of a good end does not justify punitive means is a strong reason why the administration of justice is so very difficult to carry out—justice basically means inflicting pain for the better good of the social order—especially when it comes to imposing a punishment like the death penalty to those who committed a fault or a crime.

In fact, it is so difficult to bring about justice by actively confronting evil, and thus making the first move, or taking the initiative to fight evil, that we better wait for the command from Jesus Himself before we take any action against our enemies. We must make perfectly clear that the Templars will never resort to war to attain our goals, unless we are attacked (in which case we would be defending ourselves), or unless we get orders from high above (orders which may only come with Armageddon, or some other spiritual struggle), but never from human flesh. In short, the Templars will never take orders concerning spiritual matters from human flesh. In this sense, the Arab jihadists may be dead wrong with their methods of fighting evil.

Contrary to the modern interpretation of Saint Augustine's doctrine about just wars—later complemented by other interpretations of Saint Thomas Aquinas' thoughts about the same subject—we don't believe that war can ever be justifiable, not even as self-defense in the strictest sense of the word. In this regard, be aware that self-defense is just one kind of violence, and all violence is unjustified and unjustifiable. Even more, we believe that if somebody decides to wage war against us, it is only because they had a perception—right or wrong—that we represent a danger to them, or an obstacle to their goals, in which case every effort must be made to clarify misperceptions and misunderstandings before resorting to self-defense. Wars of conquest, on the other hand, are a different story. If we are targeted for conquest, be it with a noble purpose, or just for the sake of enslaving us, then, we will have to respond to external violence with aggression, without regards to the conquerors motives or intentions, which in no way sanctifies self-defense.

As we said before, we have to make perfectly clear that all violence is unjustified and unjustifiable, and self-defense is just another kind of violence—which means that even self-defense is unjustified and unjustifiable. We must remember that self-defense is an ego's reaction to preserve life, as a response to an ego's perception of danger, not a spiritual drive whose source is in the anima—in other words, the anima is not at the root of the need for self-defense. Therefore, there are no "just wars" or "holy wars," there are only wars of aggression and wars of self-defense (or forceful deterrence), and we will only add that true self-defense just happens, in which case we must withhold judgment in reference to self-defense, because its definition has been abused and it has even been misused as a disguise for wars of aggression.

The external contradiction of the terms that make the expressions 'holy war,' 'just war,' 'sacred war,' etc. is a reflection of the internal inconsistency of violence versus sanctity, which is why we say that we withhold judgment in reference to self-defense, since self-defense can never be judged *a priori*, but only *a posteriori*. Therefore, any propaganda for war, including wars of self-defense, is morally unjustified—precisely because, in the specific case of self-defense, it cannot be qualified as good *a priori*. And since nationalism, and other rhetorical talk relative to the defense of the country, or the nation, is intimately related to propaganda and indoctrination, they cannot be morally justified by reference to self-defense, or the so-called defense of the homeland. Thus, if we must go to war in order to defend the nation, we better get ready to confront the moral consequences of our actions, but only *a posteriori*, after the fact, which inhibits the qualification of any war as sacred or saint. And if even self-defense cannot be justified *a priori*, preemptive wars stand even a less chance of such an *a priori* justification.

This means that in the event we are forced to use violence in self-defense, we will be using an evil means to achieve a noble goal, mainly the preservation of our physical integrity. Therefore, the best strategy to fight evil is to retreat from evil and to avoid that which is evil at all costs, but if we have no other choice than to respond with violence to violent aggression, we must be aware that we are being forced to do something that is evil in order to combat evil, and this requires spiritual redemption, which comes in three facets: repentance, reparation, and forgiveness. So, contrary to what is said that St. Augustine and St. Thomas held in reference to just or holy wars, we say absolutely no to all wars, and absolutely no to any kind of war, including "just" or "holy" wars, unless they are ordered (required) by a supreme spiritual necessity, which is precisely the Church Fathers' criteria: first, authority; second, just cause; and third, limited intention (in retroaction and restoration), conditions dictated by profound spiritual necessities—for *authority* comes only from God, a *just cause* is good in and of itself (thus in conformity with

God's will), and *limited intention* conforms to natural law ("We do not seek peace in order to be at war, but we go to war that we may have peace"), and natural law is divine law, the will of God. Therefore, the apparent contradiction with Augustine and Aquinas disappears when tracing the profound spiritual root of their conditions for a justified violent response to aggression.

To digress a bit, we can mention Jesus' attitude towards violence in two different occasions. First, when He violently stroke the merchants at the Temple, he was responding to a spiritual necessity to use violence, which in this case must be swift, prompt, and fulminating, to clean the house of God of all human-directed worldliness. Second, when Jesus reprimanded Peter for using violence against the soldiers sent to apprehend Him, He was responding to a spiritual necessity to control the ego's automatic response of self-defense, manifested in Peter's aggressive behavior. In the first case, Jesus was taking orders from the Spirit to use violence against the desecration of a holy place; in the second case, Jesus was refusing to take orders from the flesh to use violence to preserve His and His disciples' physical integrity.

It follows from Augustine and Aquinas' theory of war that self-defense can only be justified as a collective endeavor. For self-defense, as an individual reaction to an attack, is untenable on moral grounds, as we showed before, since it is an automatic response of the ego (and thus, not of the anima) to a perceived danger or menace to the physical integrity of the individual—and this explains why we have the judicial system (and not the religious apparatus) to discern whether or not somebody acted in self-defense when injuring or killing his/her attacker. But self-defense as a collective response to an alien menace to the security of a nation or state, transcends the individual, and may become a spiritual compulsion to protect society—which, in any case, can only be determined *a posteriori*—with violence if necessary, against an external attack by another nation. And yet, every individual is still responsible for their personal actions, and must pay penance to attain redemption, even in the context of a genuine war of self-defense, which makes it even more crucial for the soldier to be able to fathom whether or not a given war may qualify as genuine self-defense. This dialectical contradiction—dialectical spirituality not contemplated by the Marxist philosophy—resolves itself into a spiritual justification of collective self-defense.

The followers of Saladin in the Arab world seem to be conducting their jihads as a self-defensive reaction to the Western World encroachment on their culture. But the same motivations that they may have to pursue war against the West would also be our motivations to fight our Western governments, and we are talking here about those aspects of Western politics, culture and economic policy that enslave and impoverish the people who are already poor, and yet we are not ready to go to war, precisely because we know that things can still be settled with persuasion and dialog.

The Templars' set of beliefs are very simple. We are Christians in the full sense of the word, and more, without rejecting other people from other religions, as long as those religions don't contradict the Axioms of Being. The Templars believe in one single God and in the Holy Trinity, and our goal is the protection of the weak and the powerless against all evil, earthly or spiritual. The book of Revelations establishes the role of the Templars as soldiers of God, such that the Templars must be prepared for the final battle against the forces of darkness. Next, we expand on why and how we oppose all wars without exceptions.

First, let's try to give a definition of a terrorist. A terrorist is a person who *intentionally* inflicts harm to *innocent people*. Terrorists usually justify their actions as self-defense against occupation, oppression, and control, often following a military invasion of the terrorists' country by an alien power, mainly an imperial nation expanding its sphere of influence.

Intention implies *knowledge* of the consequences of actions and *willingness* to carry them out in spite of those consequences.

The terrorists know that by planting bombs on a subway train, or bus, they are going to kill, maim, or injure *innocent* people, as well as those they feel are *surrogates* of their enemy. A surrogate is anyone who authorizes—through the popular vote, an institution called *democracy*—his/her elected leaders and officials to implement a government policy (which may be a policy of war) against the terrorists or the terrorists' nation. Since the terrorists *know* what's going to happen, and yet are *willing* to carry out their actions, then the terrorists *are intentionally* inflicting harm on innocent people.

The pilots who drop bombs on enemy positions *know* with great certainty (or at least envision the possibility) that they are going to kill or harm innocent people, as well as the enemy, in this case the terrorists. Nevertheless, they are *willing* to drop the bombs, as long as they kill some of the enemy. In military jargon, the dead innocents are labeled *collateral damages*. But these actions are never said to be *terrorist actions*. It is always argued that there was no *intention* to kill or harm the innocent, although there was *knowledge* of what was going to happen, and *willingness* to carry out the military operation (counter-insurgency), in spite of its possible consequences. The Templars' contention here is that it is difficult to separate what is good from what is evil, and since we don't fully understand the terrorists' murky intentions and motives, and since in this war on terror we don't have a clear-cut criteria to separate terrorists from non-terrorists—who may be acting in self-defense—we are going to withhold judgment and try to outline how, at the time of writing this book, we can deal with wars, specifically the war in Iraq. Suffices here to say that the Templars will never—and I emphasize, not ever—will justify wars, any kind of wars, *a priori*. The only thing we can do *a priori* with respect to wars is condemn them, repudiate them, and reject them all without exception. Wars of self-defense may eventually be justified, if ever, but only *a posteriori*.

But, in spite of what was explained above, and under the given definitions, the insurgents who use civilians as human shields are positively and definitively terrorists, and the pilots who know that the terrorists are using civilians as a shield, and still drop bombs to kill the terrorists (and their human shields), are also themselves terrorists.

Is it Time to Talk Peace Yet?

As we all know, a group of 19 terrorists kidnapped four passenger airplanes and crashed three of them against the Twin Towers in New York and against the Pentagon in Washington, killing themselves and 3000 people with them. The justification? To stop the USA from interfering in their world and in their affairs—that has always been the terrorists' contention ever since they started their attacks on the USA and its allies. Yet, our president and our government claim that the terrorists pursue the destruction of democracy, Western Civilization, and our way of life, in other words, the destruction of our traditional values—something hard to swallow and in need of more elaboration, since, according to the Hispanic saying, *we aren't children to be given 'atole' with the finger*. But, contrary to every gut feeling that tells me that this couldn't possibly be the case, let's give the president the benefit of the doubt, and say that the terrorists pursue the destruction of democracy, Western Civilization, and our way of life, as these Western values are encroaching on the Arabs' traditional culture of despotism, medieval civilization, and backward way of life, which amounts to the same thing as interfering in their world and in their affairs. Since this is a highly controversial theme and it's almost heresy to contradict our government about the terrorists' motives, we will leave it at that.

In order to bring the terrorists to justice, our government launched a massive offensive in their pursuit, resulting in a war in Afghanistan and a war in Iraq. As a consequence of both wars, thousands—surely, more people than those killed in New York—died and continue to die in the crossfire. The final result? Hundreds, if not thousands, of terrorists got killed, thousands of innocent people lost their lives and/or their properties, and terrorist activities stepped up all over the world. The president and our government claim that we are winning the war on terror, in spite of the fact that the causes of terrorism and the motivations that create terrorists are very much there, in the Middle East, as well as in the rest of the Arab world.

Furthermore, once Mr. Bush established the justification to fight the terrorists anywhere in the world, he found an additional one to fight them in Iraq, which is that *we have to fight them there, so that we won't have to fight them here (in the USA)*. Most of us know, or at least should know, that the latter is just an excuse to continue the war in Iraq, a ridiculous one if you ask me, since any amateur terrorist (or novice insurgent) also knows that a fundamental axiom of guerrilla fighting states that guerrillas choose where, and when, and under what circumstances to confront the enemy—axiom that translates into the guerrilla adage that says *"Let the elephant pass, and then shoot it in the ass."* Terrorists and insurgents also know that disregard of that basic guerrilla axiom results in catastrophic defeats like Hue for the Viet Cong, and Falluyah for the Iraqi insurgents. If terrorists can choose softer targets around the world, what makes Mr. Bush think that they are going to be lured into the fight in Iraq, at the expense of excluding all other planned operations anywhere else in the world, including America? Terrorists are fighting us in Iraq because we gave them the opportunity to do so—a bargain that they couldn't possibly turn down—and if terrorists are not attacking us in America, it must be for other reasons than because we keep them busy in Iraq. They would already be here in the USA, shooting us in the ass, if their operational environment were more favorable or appropriate, say, if they were Hispanic instead of Arabs—just picture yourself as an American terrorist fighting Arab troops in Egypt, or Syria, under extremely precarious circumstances!

No sooner had we started fighting the terrorists in Iraq, than something negative happened. A group of US soldiers—who, like the terrorists, are said to represent a tiny minority—are caught in the act of *abusing* (we prefer this euphemism instead of 'torturing' or 'terrorizing') a group of Iraqi prisoners. The justification? None is given, and the abusers reply that they were only following orders. Some other people claim that the detainees deserved it, and a few more would make comparisons between the US soldiers' deeds and the terrorists' deeds—the terrorists actually filmed the beheading of one Mr. Berg, an innocent civilian. Then numbers begin to crop up, and US government officials claim that there is no comparison between what Saddam Hussein did in the past and what the American soldiers did only recently, the argument underscoring that the alleged abuses had never been institutionalized, and that the Pentagon never officially sanctioned them. Whether or not the tiny minority of abusers and terrorists belong to the same species in the animal kingdom is something that will be debated for a long time to come.

This comes to show that the whole situation in Iraq requires a different approach, if we want to find a way out of such a colossal snare. It would be interesting to ascertain what Niccolo Machiavelli (1469-1537) would have thought about the quandary the US is in, and to do this, we have to put on our ego's hat. So, let's make a neo-Machiavellian analysis of the Iraq conundrum, placing ourselves in the position of the terrorists—if only as a mental exercise for political expediency—to try to find out what their motivations are. For that purpose we will use Machiavelli's dictum *"the end justifies the means."* Let's try to see how they justify their means to achieve their end—again, this is only a mental exercise to probe the inner workings of the terrorists' twisted minds. As a reminder, we will say that for the Templars, a good end can never morally justify bad or evil means.

There are two assumptions implied in the dictum mentioned above. First, the end is assumed to be *good*—or at least perceived to be good, irrespectively of whether or not the percipient is a hero or a villain—and, secondly, the end is assumed to be *greater* or *better* than the sum of the means. In the absence of these two assumptions, it would be irrational to apply the dictum to any real-life situation.

But before we continue with this analysis, let's first make a distinction between two kinds of terrorism: the terrorism of the wackos, the cultists, the so-called 'maras,' the neo-Nazis, the white supremacists, and the like; and the terrorism associated to movements of liberation (whatever that means to this kind of terrorists), anti-occupation by foreign powers (be it Jews or Americans), or just plain anti-imperialism (like in Chechnya, Mongolia, Sri Lanka), etc. The first kind of terrorism, which is nothing more than plain delinquency, is relatively easy to fight, because it always reaches a fixed number of followers, then it stops growing, or grows so slowly that once their members get killed or captured, the movement dwindles or disappears—remember the Shiny Path Guerrillas of Peru? The second kind of terrorism is more difficult to destroy, because every attempt to destroy it by sheer military force exacerbates its growth, and multiplies its membership. This is the kind of terrorism we would like to deal with in this chapter.

Let's now get into a terrorist's brain. Since the dawn of civilization, and once man invented war to subdue other men, there was a clear understanding that it was beneficial to send only soldiers to the battlefield—civilians, and the people who organized and created the armies, stayed behind, and the tacit agreement was that only armies would decide the outcome of the conflicts that led to wars. The rule that *civilians would not be unduly harmed by wars* was a fundamental rule of warfare, and breaking this rule is one of the maximum breaches of the military code of honor—which is why we adamantly refuse to talk peace with terrorists. Of course, things did not always work the way they were supposed to, and in more than one occasion, triumphant armies slaughtered opposing armies, as well as their corresponding civilian populations. But in general, soldiers (professional or not) were the only ones meant to fight wars, and civilians more or less stayed out of the armed conflicts. This tacit *contractual* agreement worked well as long as the conflicting parties were about the same size in numbers and strength.

Then the weaker party in the conflict—the underdogs, the would-be terrorists—decided that they couldn't fight against the army of the stronger party, and *guerrilla warfare* was invented. The weak would claim to represent his country, society, tribe, group, or whatever, while those 'represented,' in most cases would deny that representation, making it difficult to the bigger party to sort out the fighters from those civilians that didn't support them. And we know what the result of that ambiguity in the battlefield leads to—remember Viet Nam?

Even more, when the weaker party becomes extremely weak, and guerrilla fighting is not viable any more—modern techniques of anti-guerrilla warfare were invented and/or it was no longer practical to fight the enemy using the strategy of the little armies—terrorism is born, and terror would be considered by the terrorists the primary weapon of the weak—some would say of the coward. Terrorists would surely argue something like this: Since civilian enemies created the armies that represent them, and those armies are always ready to crush us, and since we don't have the means to fight those wars with a regular army, or even with the techniques of guerrilla warfare, we will attack the enemy, both civilians and their military, preferably civilians, and all of them become legitimate targets, and to our eyes, civilians and their soldiers are one and the same. The agreement of fighting armies only, in the event of a war, is scrapped unilaterally, and terrorists no longer will follow the long-established rules of war.

The problem is that the stronger party, the super-power—which is now at the vanguard of the nations of the world, and proclaims itself to be the leader of Western Civilization—has no appetite to destroy the terrorists together with their societies—especially if those societies have already surrendered in submission through war, or the threat of war, or through some other economic and diplomatic coercion—and, for the reasons mentioned before, and for other reasons, not least of all international pressure, the super-power has to appear cool and magnanimous. Furthermore, to compound the problem of the super-power, terrorists don't seem to be openly supported by their own people, which may very well be a false perception—all over the Arab world you will find people condemning terrorism, and yet when terrorists do something spectacular, more than a few take to the streets to celebrate their deeds, which means that deep down in their subconscious (and perhaps even in their conscious minds) a sizable number of Arabs do support the terrorists. So, how do you fight this kind of war? Terrorists have all the advantages in the world: the element of surprise, trickery, surreptitiousness, secrecy, and extreme fanaticism—and this is enormously important, since they are even ready to commit suicide, as long as they kill at least one of their perceived enemies.

The position of governments today has always been "no dialog with terrorists," let's hit them hard, let's finish them off, let's annihilate them; let's follow them wherever they hide, hole them up, and destroy them. This is a kind of 'negative' reinforcement that makes terrorists *change* their behavior. And here is where the mistake lies: this 'negative' reinforcement is really 'positive' for the terrorists— terrorists adapt to what they already anticipated, change their strategies, convince themselves and their followers that the fight must go on, and get an uplift to continue the struggle. Coming back to Machiavelli, what is needed is a 'positive' reinforcement to make them *stop* their terrorist acts—and 'positive' in the context of terrorism, can only mean talking to them, trying to find out whether or not their grievances are real or imaginary, digging into the causes of their frustration, removing the obstacles that make them angry—and doing all this while fighting them at the same time. We obviously would never use this kind of approach with common criminals, because their motivations are neither social nor political, and their objectives are "legally irrational." We must remember that there was a time during the Viet Nam war when talking to the Viet Cong was unthinkable. We must also remember that the guerrilla wars in Guatemala, Nicaragua, and El Salvador, among others, were impossible to win militarily—as it is still the case with the Colombian guerrillas—and that dialogues had to get started to pacify the region—although many right-wing politicians thought it was preposterous to open a dialogue with 'terrorists'—as the guerrilla fighters were then called. Even the British government granted the IRA, a terrorist organization, the opportunity to participate in peace talks over the Irish problem.

But again, the argument will be made that giving in to terrorist pressures is an incentive for the terrorists to continue, or increase, their terrorist activities, and a dialogue with terrorists will be interpreted as a weakness, a sign of defeat—and there is nothing more dreadful for a super-power than to be thought of as a 'paper tiger.' See, the super-power has the Word and the use of the Word, and the rest of the world can only listen and obey the Word. No super-power that respects itself is going to talk to terrorists—and here is where Machiavelli would say, if he was alive, that the "end surely justifies the means." If you want to stop the death and destruction brought about by terrorism, you must do the unthinkable, you must do what will be called political sacrilege—you must open a dialogue with terrorists, while at the same time confronting them in the battlefield. After all, president Bush has already given the first step towards this dialogue: he officially recognized that terrorists have us at war, and that we are fighting a *war on terror*, and it is very well-known that wars are sometimes settled in the negotiating table.

The implication that the military machine, once in a forward motion, cannot be stopped, or set in reverse—lest you recognize wrongdoing, or even worse, lest you acknowledge defeat—more than a military doctrine, is an emotional anxiety rooted in the vainglory, superciliousness, and arrogance of those who consider themselves infallible and invincible. It's just an expression of the *super-power syndrome*, clearly manifested in the expression 'we must stay the course,' even if staying the course leads to the abyss of real defeat.

In short, we need a panel of sober political scientists and world personalities, people who are real Machiavellians—in the good sense of the word, if ever a good sense can be found—who can look at the war on terror with dispassionate eyes, to see if they can come up with a solution to this new plague afflicting the whole of humanity. In the meantime, the generals and all those people who glorify and revere modern warfare—with all its technological advancements, like smart bombs and unmanned drones—must recognize, once and for all, that guerrilla warfare is difficult to defeat militarily, and that terrorism is still more difficult to deal with by the sheer use of military firepower. The only way to defeat terrorism is to *kill it before it's born*, to kill it while it's in gestation in the womb of social injustice bred by dictatorial regimes—like the one of Saddam Hussein, which thanks to Mr. Bush is already history, and the many others who are still in the heartland of the Arab nation. Treating terrorists like rabid dogs that must be wiped out of the face of the earth would be a great 'solution,' though an extremely simplistic one—once the rabid dogs are dead, the problem of rabies would be no more, except that, in the case of terrorists, for every 'rabid dog' that gets killed, dozens more seem to come to life with a much stronger strain of rabies. The other alternative is war on terror forever. This last alternative would force us to typify terrorism as a common crime, in which case we better get ready for yet another social endemic malaise that, like drug trafficking, money laundering, and other international crimes, will stay with us indefinitely, because terrorists are not going to destroy Western Civilization and Western values, just like Al Capone was never even close to develop a capability to take over the US government.

Things never happen in a vacuum or for no reason at all. Even common criminals pursue a given objective. A Colombian drug lord goes through all the problem of farming and purchasing the coca leaves, processing and refining the coca paste, fighting the law enforcement agents of several countries, and risking his life, his freedom, and his investment, with the purpose of obtaining some profits for the sale of the drug. A terrorist also has motivations, rational or irrational, and it is up to us to determine what causes their behavior, and how we can stop it. If their motivations are rooted in social injustice, then we must tackle those motivations accordingly; if their motivations are rooted in common criminal behavior, then we must intensify our national and international police work, and reinforce our law enforcement agencies to fight the problem. Of course, terrorists can get an atomic bomb and make it explode in New York, but Pablo Escobar Gavidia could also have had the chance to do the same, and we never used this rationale to invade Colombia, or any other country. If a terrorist simply has no motivations for being a terrorist, and we cannot establish a dialog with him, then we might as well be at the brink of the end of the world, and things wouldn't get better by invading other countries. In such an extreme situation, where nothing can be done, then perhaps we should get "the-end-of-the-world-is-near" banners and picket the streets of Washington with them. But we know that this isn't the case, and a responsible thing to do is to gather all our resources and deal with terrorism accordingly, either as a problem rooted in social injustice, or as a social malady to be treated by strong law enforcement. Going berserk invading other countries is not an option.

The Shameful Glorification of War

The notion of a suicide bomber strapped with explosives is so alien to our Latin American culture that it's almost incomprehensible. I kept asking myself, how can a man consciously decide to kill himself with the purpose of killing others? What drives an individual to carry out such an action? Trying to understand why there are suicide bombers gets even more complex when you try to explain also why there are so many of them, to the point of becoming a culture, the culture of suicide-bombing, within another culture, the Muslim culture. Then I realized that in our Western world, as well as in any other culture of the world, we have the notion of the hero. What the suicide bomber and the hero have in common is that both have managed to suppress the instinct of preservation of life in order to achieve their objectives: For the suicide bomber, killing himself to kill others he perceives as the enemy; for the hero, killing himself to save his comrades in arms, so that they may continue fighting (and killing) the enemy.

Irrespectively of the nobility or ignobility of their objectives, the core of the motivation to do what they do is so strong that both the bomber (Jihadists call them martyrs) and the hero have managed to suppress their instinct to preserve life. How do they do that? What makes a US soldier jump over, and cover a grenade with his body, so that his comrades survive? What makes the suicide bomber ignite the explosives hidden in his body, so that he kills himself and others? If it is a premeditated (as against a reflexive) action, and not the result of a split-second decision, the answer is indoctrination, indoctrination, and more indoctrination. It takes a lot of indoctrination to make a suicide bomber; this indoctrination must be intense, constant, personal, unrelenting and lasting, so that the individual gets to a point that he no longer can hold a sense of love of life, his or anybody else's. Indoctrination also has to be started early in life. When I was a child, I was constantly assailed in school with the concept of the national hero. In our cultural environment we had lots of heroes, both real and invented. (I think one invented heroine was Rafaela Herrera, a fifteen-year-old girl, whose father, a commander of a Spanish outpost over the San Juan River in Nicaragua, had just died, when the British ships were coming up the river; the Spanish troop got so cowed without a commander that the girl had to take control of the situation, and defeated the British naval ships!) As much as I tried to be a hero—and I honestly would have died for my country when I was young—I never had the opportunity to put in practice what I was indoctrinated to do.

But, how do we explain the actions of somebody going on a rampage shooting, killing innocent people indiscriminately for no apparent reason at all? The answer is the same, indoctrination that backfires, or self-indoctrination via blaming one's frustrations on others (on everybody else for that matter), to the point of becoming misanthropes. Rampage killers either misidentify their enemies, or resent society to the point of making people in general, or their peers in particular, their enemies—and this is a reflection of the lack of indoctrination of love, on both those who let loners ruminate in isolation their frustrations, and on those who reach the peak of loneliness for absence of incoming love and lack of outgoing love towards their fellow men. For there is nothing wrong with indoctrination itself, but with both the object and the subject of indoctrination. We wouldn't have the problems related with indoctrination of the sort discussed before, if we were to indoctrinate our children to love our fellow human beings, irrespectively of race, color, ethnic origin, religion, etc. Indoctrination of love would still produce our martyrs and heroes, like firefighters, emergency rescuers, and policemen, and even indiscriminate good-doers going on a rampage of good deeds for other people, because love of humanity is not selective, and thus, will not let you discriminate among individuals—it embraces the whole human race—and we would require an invasion of aliens from another planet to go back to the sort of problems of negative indoctrination we mentioned above.

It seems that human beings are genetically wired to glorify war. We talk of soldiers as heroes, and behold those heroes not as common men, but as demigods. And this cult of the hero is very much the same for every race, culture, and nationality of men, ever since we learned the art of making war—the "art" of getting together to gang-up on other human beings that compete for "our" territory and "our" resources. Having said this, in our present day and time, it may be necessary that some countries have armies and professional soldiers—given that the other alternative is for none of the countries of the world to have standing armies, which, for now, seems to be an impossibility. As far as I know, only Costa Rica is the only country in the world said not to have an army. One thing is for sure, defending ourselves is not a necessary evil, but an evil imposed on us by the ego's perceived necessity to preserve life. This is the reason why patriotism is rooted in nationalism: Some countries fear other countries, and they are all ever so ready to defend their territory against any foreign aggression that they need to boost their patriotism. But the world is coming to a point when one country, the USA, is so powerful, both economically and militarily, that no other country would be willing to attack us without getting badly battered—let's face it, we have nothing to fear from other countries, but we are always beating the drums of war with the pretext that we have to defend our freedom, and this is precisely what makes other countries and other people nervous, sometimes forcing them to act aggressively against us, since their patriotism makes them fear any possible aggression coming from the USA. If we could only project an image of being a peaceful country the world stage would be much more different, and less dangerous than what it is now. If we could only think in terms of humanity . . .

War is detestable and despicable, no matter who conducts it. Soldiers, warriors, liberators, or whatever you want to call them, are men trained to kill in the name of a country, or in the name of an ideal. They are transformed, through military training, from simple, peaceful, and perhaps good individuals, into brutal, merciless killers. And some men want to be soldiers, so they may have the chance to participate in the shrill of the killing game. Most of those men that choose to be soldiers don't do it on their own accord—not if they have been brainwashed to sanctify and glorify war. They have been bombarded mercilessly from early childhood (both at home and at school) with propaganda saturated with nationalism. The heinous crime committed against the common soldier is that he gets to believe that killing others in defense of the nation is not only good, but even sacred, so that if he dies fighting the enemy, he instantly becomes a hero, closer to a god than to a common human being—and the sad thing is that the rest of society also believes it, and makes of the fallen soldiers national heroes, when they are victims of a nationalist world-trend bigotry, and should be considered martyrs instead. Common, non-professional (volunteer or conscripted) soldiers, more than heroes, should be considered martyrs indeed. Martyrs, because they are either victims of the circumstances that may force them to kill, or victims of the enemy that may kill them. Either way, they are still martyrs, and we should respect them, and feel sorry for them, because most likely they may have been victimized by the society they love so much, and most definitively they are or will be victimized by war itself. This is true of every nation and every society that fosters national pride and nationalist aggrandizements.

There is something wrong with a society that doesn't blink at the sight of a journalist reporting about a soldier that the journalist met in Iraq, while the soldier was proudly standing by the corpse of an insurgent, like if it was a hunt trophy. The journalist goes on to say that, at first, he was shocked, but that he later understood the attitude of the soldier, who had been toughened by the cruelty of war and seasoned by the daily circumstances of the battle for Iraq. Obviously, there is something wrong with the soldier, there is something even more wrong with the journalist who unequivocally glorifies war, and there is something wrong with a society that doesn't see anything wrong with this kind of reporting.

When an US Army general claims that a homosexual should not be a soldier, because homosexuality is immoral, and society rebuts that this is unfair, not because being a soldier is questionable, but because there is nothing bad about homosexuality, we know (or at least ought to know) that there is something wrong with the morality of the general and with the moral values of a society that qualifies as immoral the rejection of homosexuality, while accepting as perfectly good that anybody (including a homosexual) be a soldier. Dragging corpses of US soldiers killed by a mob in the cities of Iraq, or on the streets of Mogadishu, is as immoral as proudly standing by a dead terrorist. There must be something wrong with a society that tolerates an atheist that curses God, while threatening to hurt (or kill) a person who dares question the heroism of being a soldier. But breaking up with society's taboos is difficult, and doing it publicly may even be dangerous. Our moral values drift away from genuine Christianity every time we praise a human being for joining the army—who could become a victim of our own enshrinement of the ego—and despise as coward somebody who refuses to be a soldier and, thus, a killer (even if an unwilling killer). But the reality of today's world is that we are told that we need soldiers to defend our freedom—in other words, we need somebody else to do what we don't dare to do, either because we are indeed cowards, or because we don't really believe that our freedom is at risk, which is not only immoral, but profoundly heinous.

Nevertheless, some of those soldiers (ours and from other countries) eventually feel the effect of society's deceit and treachery, once they return home from war, and yet they don't quite understand what's wrong with them, and fall into deep depression and hopelessness—veterans of Viet Nam and other cruel, senseless wars bear the physical and psychological scars of what their country did to them—even worse, if the war was lost, the said veterans don't get the treatment of heroes that the winners of other wars get. They feel they were used for an unjust cause, especially if the wars they fought were not really in self-defense, and they resent their country and the society that made them commit, or witness the commission of terrible crimes. They may even hate themselves for inflicting suffering on other people and on themselves in the name of a lie. The tragedy of war is that, even if we must participate in wars of self-defense, if we are true *Homo spiritualis*, war makes us lose a great deal of our humanity. We should tell those people who are going to defend our freedom that war is bad, and that there is no heroism in killing others. We should tell them that they may die, instead of us, because we are not willing, ready, or able to defend our own freedom—if indeed our freedom is at stake. We should tell them that our lack of willingness to fight our wars is because we are cowards, or because we don't need to make sacrifices when we can make others redeem our very lack of courage.

Most soldiers are just plain naïve young men, but a few others (at the highest rank level) thirst for blood and revenge—since there is not ever, nor has ever been a war in which killing the enemy is not something to enjoy, or not done with the purpose of taking revenge. The professional soldier (the one who makes of soldiering a way of life), like the professional preacher, is often a man with a weird mentality, no better than a mercenary—just imagine the two of them, one placing death on sale, and the other placing spiritual salvation also on sale. Non-imperial nations don't need professional soldiers to fight their wars of self-defense—peaceful nations nowadays may just need well-trained soldiers ready to reluctantly fight wars that may be justified on the basis of self-defense. Yet, the professional soldier of imperial nations is also a hero. He is a hired gun to give "protection" (when in reality he is his contractor's conquering *alter ego*), and hence, we glorify him, we shamefully make him our savior, our marvelous rescuer. The Templars will decide when and where we will defend ourselves, and we don't need others to do what the meaning of the expression *self-defense* would force each one of us to do individually and collectively. That's why every Templar must also be a soldier—ever hoping never to have to use the skills of a soldier—and if we, as Templars, are forced to fight wars to defend ourselves, we must do it with deep sadness in our hearts and with the knowledge that we will eventually pay for our transgressions—not before requesting God's indulgence—with heavy spiritual and physical penance.

Of course, you might still argue that wars conducted with the purpose of self-defense should be justified. Not so. Even a war of self-defense is degrading of the condition of being a human. Killing another person in self-defense may be something necessary, but not something that should make us proud. To begin with, how did it happen that another human being is willing to take our lives? How did we let things go so far as to produce in another person this desire to kill us? Even if we are absolutely innocent of the causes that make other humans wish to hurt us—killing that individual in order to preserve our physical integrity is something that should make us sad and ashamed. Because, deep down in our hearts, we know that something in our humanity failed us, something went extremely wrong if we had no other choice than to fight our enemy. We feel that we could have done something else before we were forced to fight, and yet we were led to kill to preserve our life that has been already diminished with the death of yet another human being. This is why the best self-defense is to avoid evil altogether, to run away from evil, to keep evil as far from us as possible. [When I was a kid, I never regretted avoiding, and even running away from a bully—meaning that I never lost a running battle—but sometimes I was forced to fight the bully at a disadvantage—thus, many times I lost a fighting contest.]

Unfortunately, to reiterate what I said before, countries sometimes need armies, and armies are made up of soldiers, both volunteer and professional, and we can only hope that those who are in command will be wise never to use those armies, if not for self-defense, with the knowledge that even in self-defense a war is the worst tragedy that can happen to a civilized society. Countries without armies carry the implication of a world without countries, a world without boundaries, where men don't see the necessity to defend what they call their turf, their nation, or their tribe. Not that human conflict is ever going to be completely eradicated, but at least we can expect in the future to deal with conflict without killing each other.

Are the Jihadists like the Knight Templars?

Pat Buchanan wrote on June 23, 2006—AN IDEA WHOSE TIME HAS COME?:

> ". . . [The Muslims] believe there is but one God, Allah, that Muhammad
> is his prophet, that Islam, or submission to the Quram is the only path
> to paradise and that a Godly society should be governed according to
> Sharia, the law of Islam."

If that quote wasn't making reference to the Muslims, it would sound like it was making reference to the Knight Templars. We believe in one God, and we believe in the son of God, Jesus Christ. We also believe that there is no need to separate church and state, that, as a matter of fact, it would probably be better if we were governed by a theocracy of wise men. But, there is a difference: we don't impose anything by force, and we don't believe that the advent of the City of God can be brought about by the power of the sword, but by the power of the word.

We understand why the Arab world is shaken by the intervention of Western powers in their internal affairs—especially Afghanistan, Iraq, and most probably in the immediate future, Iran. It should be something they should be very much concerned about, mainly because they are not doing enough to stop the actions of jihadist fanatics that take upon themselves the task of halting this modern Crusade, as if they were engaged in their own "crusade" to destroy Christianity and Western Civilization—at least that's how their actions are interpreted, right or wrong, by leaders of the Western World. It is unlikely that either Islam or Christianity will impose the one over the other; that's not going to happen. Therefore, the only way out of this conflict is to disengage and draw lines of respect for each other's beliefs.

Pat Buchanan continues:

> "What is the appeal of militant Islam? It is, first, its message: As all else has failed us, why not live the faith and law God gave us?"

> "... Islamic militants are gaining credibility because they show a willingness to share the poverty of the poor and fight the Americans."

The Knight Templars are willing to live the faith and law God gave us, and except for the reference to fight the Americans, we are willing to share, not the poverty of the poor, but the wealth of the rich, if and always the rich can be persuaded to share it with us. But there is one thing Mr. Buchanan is missing in his analysis: The followers of Islam should be very worried about the encroachment of Western Civilization on their turf, because Muslims have two great disadvantages. The first and most important disadvantage is technology and the capitalist system of production. Arab countries don't have advanced technology that compares to the West, and they rely by necessity on capitalism. The second big disadvantage is that Islam is a very forceful religion that negates the freedom of others to practice their own religious beliefs—anyone who is not a Muslim is an infidel, and the Koran is not very friendly to infidels. These last claims, if false, should be perfectly clarified by Muslims.

Furthermore, critics and dissidents, lumped together with the enemies of Western Civilization (if there be any), are vilified in extreme by our media, and even if they are not terrorists, they are denounced as such. The enemies of freedom, democracy, liberty and Christianity, the Muslim terrorists, are always trying to take away our freedom, our liberties, our money, our culture; they are constantly plotting to destroy Western Civilization. These conclusions, true or false, have been held unchallenged, because terrorists never state their principles, their objectives, and their cause—not that doing so would justify terrorism, but at least it would set the parameters for trying to understand their struggle. For the truth may be different. The Arabs—whom also have the dog's gene deeply implanted in their psyche, especially the ones that govern the rich oil-producing countries—are unaware, or perhaps don't care that much, that their culture is being threatened by these modern Crusaders (like Bush and Co.) who would like to bring them the same freedom and democracy we "enjoy" in the Western World. The majority of them don't suspect that once they accept the decadent values of Western Civilization—especially those that accompany capitalism, like greed and avarice—the "Christian" values, not of the televangelists, but of the extreme liberal left, will follow.

The problem is that in the Christian world it is easier to accept gambling, homosexuality, bestiality, hip-hop and rock-and-roll music, nudity, pornography, and other vices that the Muslim world finds very much repugnant. The positive aspects of Western Civilization and Christianity, including freedom (in the real sense of the word), sober liberalism, moderate conservatism, tolerance of beliefs and ideas, art, culture and science, etc. are shun by the negative ones. We go to church every Sunday to talk about love and read the Bible in the community of "believers," pray for whatever we pray, hear the preacher's sermon, collect the tithes and offerings, greet our friends (to let them know that we are Christians and never miss going to church), talk for a while with the priest or pastor (if we get a chance), and go back to our homes filled with empty love for our fellow human beings, and hypnotized by the power of "faith." In the meantime, and while we were at church, hundreds, perhaps thousands of children died of hunger and disease. In other words, we came out of the religious services exactly as we went in: empty of any real love for humanity. And we want to share this with the Muslim world.

In fact, the Muslim world is the very last bastion of moral integrity that impedes the white man from having a complete control over the world. This perspective of things to come to the Muslim world drives some of their jihadists nuts, especially when they sense that a great proportion of the Arab population is more than willing to embrace the corrupted brand of Western Civilization disguised with high-sounding words like freedom, liberty, openness, and democracy. The problem of the jihadists is compounded by the Arab masters of capitalism corrupted by the super-abundance of money from the sale of petroleum to the rest of the world. They know that capitalism drowns religion, even a tough religion like Islam, they know that with the appropriate philosophical maneuvering Islam will become like the classical Christianity of Western Civilization—a mourning Harlot (to paraphrase the Book of Revelations), softly complaining about the excesses and the moral degradation of its people, but eventually acquiescing to their vices. Spiritual people see this tidal wave of corruption coming, and get ready to deal with it. The only chance Muslims have to stop this invasion from the West is to create their own version of our Fraternity of the Templars, because the culture of hatred spread among suicide bombers and other violent jihadists is never going to work, and on the contrary, is going to exacerbate once more the conflict between Christians and Muslims.

To be able to understand why a terrorist (a suicide bomber) is willing to kill himself in order to kill others, we have to put on our spiritual glasses and see that they are willing to suppress their ego, even at the expense of their anima, in order to stop the destructive egos of those who want to contaminate Islam; this is a purely desperate move. If we, truly spiritual Christians were in the same situation of the Muslim jihadists, we would probably take the same steps they take in desperation to stop the mass of egos that would be threatening our world. Imagine a super-corrupted society of Arabs trying to impose their civilization on a weakened society of Christians (who would also happen to be corrupted by capitalism) and having the weapons and the firepower to crush it if necessary. Wouldn't we do the same, and I am talking here about non-Templars? Except that the perfect application of the Principle of Love, especially the part about fighting evil, is very difficult to comply with, and the Templars would not go to the extremes of conducting wholesale murder of people at the expense of our own lives. That's what makes the Templars different from the jihadists, plus the fact that the Templars don't believe in war as a means to achieve anything, and the Templars would never glorify war to the point of making it *holy*.

I couldn't believe my eyes when I read that Pat Buchanan could at least barely begin to understand the problem of the Arabs (within the context of their jihads), and as much as I disagree with Pat Buchanan's position on immigration in USA politics—he shows all the signs of the Irish dog's gene in a weird combination with the master's gene—he hit the nail right in the head with his analysis of the Arab world problems.

To end this chapter, we will say that the Chinese are already doomed with their marriage with capitalism. The Japanese learned that the capitalist system of production (the greed-ego combination) is better than their old way of life. The Russians are so humiliated with their failed communist system that they have no other choice than align themselves so very much reluctantly with the Western World. And Africa is in such a dismal social and economic disaster that only the Muslim world is left to be conquered by the West. Once the world is totally controlled by the "democracy" and "freedom" of the white man, then humanity is free to spiral down into a reverse evolution back to the animal kingdom. Sooner or later we will find some ways of liberalizing sex, marriage, and sexual relations with children, and the church will become a closer accomplice of the white dominators, and the world will finally become the city of man where the city of God will have no chance.

But if this ever happens, then there is no alternative than Armageddon first, and the final intervention of God who would bring the Apocalypse at last.

The End of the Testosterone Era

No other hormone—that in reality is a natural drug, almost a hallucinogen—has wrought so much death and destruction throughout the history of mankind than testosterone. In the Spanish-speaking countries we have a cult for testosterone, whose street name is "huevos," "bolas," or sometimes "cojones." We raise the *macho* man to a level of superiority far above the valiant or courageous individual. All Latin American countries raise their children to be *machos*, constantly encouraging them to feel their "cojones" and to hold them in place. In English-speaking countries people talk about the "balls" in a similar fashion that Latin Americans do about the "huevos" or "cojones." All these expressions make reference to the testicles, the place where people believe "machismo" resides, and the place where testosterone is synthesized by the human body.

Testosterone has a necessary natural function in the human organism, especially for reproductive purposes; but given the fact that we belong to the animal kingdom we couldn't help but develop the secondary effects of testosterone, which is the capacity to raise up the level of aggressiveness when confronted with danger or competition for females. This was nature's way of making sure that the species of men and other animals would survive. Once the danger brought by competition subsided, the secondary function of testosterone was no longer necessary, but as it usually happens in nature every time we acquire (through evolution) a given trait as a response to environmental changes, it is passed from one generation to another, long after the environmental threat ceases to exist.

The source of man's aggressiveness is rooted in testosterone, in addition to other negative human traits like selfishness and avarice, and they all have been the origin of the wars that have ravaged humanity up to our present times. It is a fact that because of aggressiveness fired up by testosterone, society followed the path of the patriarchy rather than matriarchy, but given the failure of the male leadership, we should give women a try, and let women take a stronger lead in society. But, of course, the fact that women may be more temperate than men when confronting a menace to their nation doesn't mean that they cannot be as aggressive as the worst of men. Take for example Margaret Thatcher and Olga Meier, who seemed to be men disguised as women, given their eagerness to resolve international problems by taking aggressive postures, including war.

Thus, it is the Templars' belief that giving women a wider participation in the affairs of society, we may sometime in the future be able to end the testosterone era of humanity that has been an affliction to society far worse than all earthquakes, volcanic eruptions, floods, and other natural disasters put together.

5

JOHN OF JERUSALEM

One of the most interesting stories indirectly related to the Order of the Templars is the one about a monk named John of Jerusalem. Nevertheless, this name refers to a number of people, making it difficult to pinpoint who exactly wrote the prophecies mentioned below.

It was in 1991 that the book The Secret Rituals of the Templars was published in Spain, whose author, occult under the name of Frater Iacobus, for the first time revealed publicly the secrets of the enigmatic Order founded during the First Crusade, one of whose founders being the prophet John of Jerusalem.

Originally founded with the purpose of helping the pilgrims that went to the Holy Land, the Order obtained papal approval on January, 1128, in the Council of Troyes, with the spiritual backing of Bernard de Clairvaux, although it wasn't definitively recognized until the year 1163. The nine kingths that founded the Order were great initiated people who followed the instructions of the Universal Tradition named the Unknown Superiors, whom the great occultist and magician L. McGregor Mathers would mention later. Among the goals of the Templars, whose name came from the Temple of Solomon, was the defense of the holy places and the Christian faith, to establish occult contacts with initiated Muslim and sourcerers, and gather all the people under one Universal Republic, where fraternity would rule and we would go back to the occult mysteries of antiquity. Also, they had as their goal the search of holy relics, mainly the Ark of the Covenant and the Tablets of the Mosaic Law. Their members had to take a vow of poverty, obedience and chastity, and to be admitted they had to comply with a series of difficult rituals of initiation.

According to Frater Iacobus, the 22 grand masters that directed the destiny of the Order through almost 200 years correspond to the Major Arcane of the Tarot, the 22 letters being the sacred letters of the Hebrew alphabet, and the 22 letters of the magic alphabet of the Rosicrucians.

Among the charges presented to suppress the Order of the Templars (one of the greatest injustices in the tenebrous history of the Catholic Church, according to the theosophist C. W. Leadbeater in his book *Old Mystic Rituals*) we found: that they didn't care about committing sins and injustices; that they practiced sexual orgies; that in the ceremonies of initiation they kissed their derrieres; that their rituals were conducted at night; that they denied and cursed Jesus kicking and trampling a crucifix; that they prayed and kissed the anus of a diabolic idol called Baphomet; that their seal (of the Templars) two knights on the same horse meant that they enjoyed sodomy; etc. The two knights on the horse really represent the duality of the Knight Templars: monks and warriors, body and spirit, the anima and the ego, dualities that lead the self to the proper course of action when their directions and actions are balanced by the anima.

Were the Templars guilty of any crime? Asks Frater Iacobus. Spiritually speaking no, they were not guilty of any crime. But for the church of their time the answer is yes, totally guilty as charged. The Templars wanted to go back to primitive Christianity and to the initiation mysteries of antiquity, within a universal religion, tolerant and evolutionary. They were, even within the Occult Temple, *Initiated*, but also men. Nevertheless, the Templars were far ahead of their time and didn't respect the religious precepts of a petrified religious era like the medieval times.

These are the historical facts more or less well-known. What is perhaps not so well-known, due to the fact that the discovery of the text of John is relatively recent, is that his secret book of prophecies was one of the elements used against the Templars. There were seven copies of the text, three of which were given to the Order's Grand Master who sent them to Bernard of Clairvaux. M Galvieski, who popularized the text of John of Jerusalem, tries to reconstruct the history of these books: one was taken to Rome, and according to him there is evidence that they are still in the Vatican Archives. Another was donated by St. Bernard to the Vezelay Monastery, and disappeared in the epoch of the process against the Templars. A third copy was supposedly in the hands of the jurists of the court of France. Another one fell in the hands of Nostradamus. In recent years, one more copy of the book reached the Russian Bolsheviks, who destroyed it because they considered it a counter-revolutionary document. Some researchers suppose that it is probable that besides the document found in the Zagorsk Monastery, there is another one in Mount Athos, Greece, kept securely in its inaccessible libraries.

When in 1307 the Grand Master Jacques de Molay and sixty knights of God were arrested, writes Galvieski, they took the manuscripts as elements to indict them, so that the Secret Protocols of the Prophecies was presented as something dictated by Lucifer himself, thus proving that the Templars were in connivance with the forces of evil. It didn't matter to the accusers that the text of John of Jerusalem was talking about the Third Millennium. According to them, it described the future as a hell; this way, they had given away men to the will of the evil one. Among all the monstrous crimes the Templars were accused of, it was repeated that they were soldiers of the devil, the knights of evil, the protocol being the proof of their evil alliances.

Prophecies

John of Jerusalem was born near Vezelay, France, around the year 1040 or 1042 AD. He was one of the founders of the Order of the Knight Templars (1118), and died one or two years later, around 1119 or 1120 AD at the age of 77.

His book of prophecies called the Secret Protocol of the Prophecies may have been known by Nostradamus who used it as a guide for his own prophetic visions.

One manuscript discovered in Zagorsk, near Moscow, dated to the XIV Century, refers to John of Jerusalem as prudent among the prudent, saint among the saint, and that he knew how to read and listen to heavens. It also mentions that John used to retire very frequently to the desert to pray and meditate and that he was at the border between earth and heavens.

While he stayed in Jerusalem, in the year 1099, he met several rabbis, wise Muslim scholars, initiated novices, mystics and cabalists, people who practiced the art of divination, astrology and numerology.

These prophecies were hidden for several years until during World War II in 1941 were found by the SS in a synagogue of Warsaw. After the defeat of Nazi Germany they again disappeared until they were rediscovered recently in the archives of the soviet KGB.

The prophecies seem to have been written specifically for the end of this millennium, as if this was the time that they should be known. All of them begin with the phrase "At the start of the millennium that follows the millennium . . ." In spite of its crudeness (especially in relation to HIV and contamination of the environment) they have great poetic beauty, which makes it different to other prophetic texts.

"I see and I know," wrote John of Jerusalem. "My eyes discover in heavens what will be, and I traverse time with one single step. A hand guides me to what neither you can see, nor can you know . . . I see and know what will happen. I am the scribe."

[Tomado de LO INEXPLICABLE, Martes, 01 de Febrero de 2005 (LOS TEMPLARIOS) Publicado por jcap @ 23:27 y traducido al Inglés por Manuel S. Marín.]

The cataclysmic confrontation of good and evil will fuse, give origin, and synthesize a new reality completely different to the reality of good and evil that we currently hold. This new higher level reality will be fundamentally dissimilar from ours, and yet far superior to it. It is God's absolute beatitude of Heavenly contemplation, which can only be intuited by the Anima. Those Anima that 'live' this superior reality, are in Paradise; those that only wish to 'live' it, are in Hell. Therefore Hell is only a profound nostalgia or melancholy of what could have been and wasn't, and whether or not this is worse than burning in a Hell of fire—as presented by most religions—only those bound to Hell will be able to experience.

"When the millennium that follows this millennium ends, Men will have finally opened their eyes.

They will no longer be imprisoned in their heads and cities, but will be able to see from one end of the Earth to another, and understand each other.

They will know what makes one suffer hurts another.

Men will form one huge body of which each will be a tiny part.

Together they will form the heart of this body.

There will be a common language spoken by everybody, and thus, finally, a glorious humanity will come into existence . . .

Because Woman will arrive to reign supreme;

She will govern the future and decree Her philosophy to Man.

She will be the Mother of the millennium that follows the millennium.

She will, after the days of the devil, radiate the gentle sweetness of a mother.

She will, after the days of barbarity, embody beauty.

The millennium that follows the millennium will metamorphose into an age of lightness:

Men will love each other, sharing everything, dream, and dreams will turn into Reality.

Thus Man will have his second birth.

Spirit will possess the mass of men, who will be united in brotherhood.

So an end will be proclaimed to barbarity.

It will be an era of a new strength of belief.

The dark days at the beginning of the millennium that follows the millennium, will be ensued by days of jubilation:

Men will once more find the righteous path of humanity, and Earth will find harmony once more . . . .

There will be roads that connect one end of earth and the sky to the other;

The woods will once more be dense, the desert will once more be irrigated, and the water will once more be pure.

The Earth will be like a garden:

Men will take care of every living thing, and he will clean everything he dirtied, he will understand that the whole of Earth is his home, and he will think with wisdom of the morrow.

Man will know everything on Earth and his own body.

Diseases will be cured before they are manifested, and everybody will cure themselves and each other.

Man will have understood that he has to help himself to stay upright; and after the days of reticence and avarice,

Man will open his heart and his purse to the poor;

He will define himself curator of human species,

And so, finally, a New Era will begin.

When Man has learnt to give and share, the bitter days of solitude will be at an end.

He will once more believe in the Spirit, and barbarians will once more be unheard of . . .

But all this will happen after the wars and the fires.

And this will arise from the ashes of the burnt Towers of Babel.

And a strong hand will be needed to bring order to chaos, and to put Man on the right path.

Man will learn that all creatures are bringers of light, and all creatures must be respected.

Man, in his lifetime, will live more than one life, and will learn that the Light never goes out."

[John of Jerusalem, *The Book of Prophecies.*]

* * *

As much as I tried to check the originality of this poem, I couldn't, leading me to believe that it is the creation of a recent or contemporary sympathizer of humanity. Nevertheless, the poem reflects accurately what we, the Templars, would like the world to be: A world of brotherhood and of human understanding, a world where the poor, the miserable, and the wretched will be no more.

One more thing that makes the poem suspect is its reference to mother deities, avatars, or rulers of the world, when the Templars of the 12th century, and even those religious leaders of the 3rd or 4th century, don't appear to believe in a specific feminine gender for the Creator, except the always implicit (and many times explicit) references to one single male God. Still, it would be interesting to consider the idea that perhaps the world should be led by women, instead of men. In any case, women should be assigned a stronger role in the fight for a better society. The problem we have in this world is not sexism proper as reflected in feminism or anti-feminism, but an excess of testosterone. Perhaps a return to a matriarchal system would benefit humanity, especially since this patriarchal age has been such a dismal failure. Given the history of humanity, we may very well say that males had their chance to change the world for the better, and they failed. It is time to give women a stronger role in the leadership of society, but always being careful not to follow the lead of male-women like Margaret Thatcher, Jean Kirkpatrick, Golda Meier, or Hillary Clinton, who appears to be a testosterone-intoxicated woman. We need women like Indira Gandhi, Benazir Bhutto, Evita Peron, Violeta Chamorro, or Corazon Aquino of the Philippines.

John of Jerusalem was purported to be a Benedictine monk who, depending on the version you encounter, could be John of Jerusalem of the 12th century or the bishop of the same name of the 3rd/4th century.

A text of *"The Secret Register of Prophecies"* in modern French was translated by a Russian professor, M. Galvieski, and published in France in 1994 by Editions Jean-Claude Lattes. There is some controversy as to the existence of original text, even the authenticity of *The Secret Register of Prophecies.* Is this prophecy of the Mother of the Millennium linked to and intertwined with other biblical prophecies? Is there sufficient evidence to suggest that it is a prophecy after all?

The prophecies seem to be written specifically for the end of the second millennium and the beginning of the third as if this is the appropriate time when they should be known. All of them begin with the phrase: "At the start of the millennium that follows the millennium . . ."

"I see and I know—wrote John of Jerusalem more than one thousand years ago—I see and I know."

"My eyes discover in heavens what will be, and I traverse time with one single step. A hand guides me towards what neither you can see nor know. One thousand years will pass and Jerusalem no longer will be the city of the Crusaders of Christ. The sand will have buried the walls of our castles, our armors and our bones. It will have quieted our voices and our prayers."

"Christians that came from afar on a pilgrimage, there where they had their rights and their laws, will not dare to get close to the sepulcher and to the relics, if not escorted by the Knight Jews, that will have here, as if Christ had never suffered in the cross, their Kingdom and their Temple."

"The infidels will make an innumerable multitude extended everywhere, and their faith will resound like a drum from one end of the earth to the other."

"I can see the earth immense; continents that Herodotus never mentioned, except in dreams, will get added far beyond the huge forests talked about by Tacit, and in the afar end of unlimited seas that begin beyond the columns of Hercules."

"One thousand years will have passed from the time we now live, and the funds of the whole world will accumulate in great kingdoms and vast empires. Numerous wars, like the chain maille worn by the knights of the order intertwine, will destroy kingdoms, and the empires will spindle others. And the servants, village dwellers, the homeless poor, will rise in anger one thousand times, will burn the crops, castles and villages, until they be burned alive, and the survivors return to their shacks. They thought they were kings."

"One thousand years will have passed and man will have conquered the depth of the seas and the skies, and he will be like a star in heavens. He will have acquired the power of the sun and feel like God, building one thousand Babel towers over the immensity of the earth. He will have raised walls over the ruins of those that the Roman emperors built, and these will separate once more the legions of the barbarian tribes."

"Beyond the huge forests there will be an empire. When the walls fall, the empire will be no more than swampy water. People will mix once more. Then it will be the beginning of the year one thousand that follows the year one thousand."

"I see and know what will be. I am the scribe."

"At the start of the millennium that follows the millennium man will be in front of the somber entrance of a dark labyrinth. And down deep in the night in which man will walk, I see the eyes of the Minotaur. Beware of its cruel furor, you that will live in the millennium that follows the millennium."

"At the start of the millennium that follows the millennium . . ."

"Gold will be in the blood. He who contemplates heavens will count dinars; he who enters the temple will find merchants; the leaders will be money exchangers and usurers. The sword will defend the serpent. But fire will be latent, all cities will be Sodom and Gomorrah, and the sons of the sons will transform into the ardent cloud; they will reach the old banners."

"At the start of the millennium that follows the millennium, man will have populated land and the skies and the seas with his creatures; he will give orders, pretending to have God's powers. He will know no limits. But everything will revolt; he will stagger like a drunken king; he will horse ride like a blind knight and will spur his horse into the forest; at the end of the way there will be the abyss."

"At the start of the millennium that follows the millennium, Babel towers will be built in all corners of earth, in Rome and in Byzantium; the fields will be emptied; there will be no more law than to care for ourselves and our own. But the barbarians will be in the city; there will not be enough bread for all and the games will not be enough; then the futureless people will provoke enormous fires."

"At the start of the millennium that follows the millennium, hunger will press the guts of so many people and cold will wither away the hands that they will want to see another world and will come merchants of illusions that will offer the poison. But this will destroy the bodies and will rot the souls; and those that mix the poison with their blood will become like savage beasts caught in a trap, and will kill and rape and rob and life will be a daily apocalypse."

"At the start of the millennium that follows the millennium, everybody will try to enjoy pleasures as much as they can; man will repudiate his wife as many times as he will get married and the woman will take the easy way out taking whom she pleases, giving birth without carrying the father's name. But no teacher will guide the child and each one will be alone among the others; tradition will get lost; the law will be forgotten as if it had never been announced and man will become a savage again."

"At the start of the millennium that follows the millennium, the father will seek pleasure in his daughter, man with man, woman with woman, the old with the young child, and this will happen at the sight of everyone. But the blood will become contaminated; the illness will propagate from bed to bed; the body will assimilate all the rot of the earth, faces will lose their luster, the members of the body will lose the flesh; love will be a menace for those that meet in the flesh."

"At the start of the millennium that follows the millennium, he who talks of promises and law will not be heard; he who preaches faith in Christ will lose his voice in the desert. But everywhere the powerful forces of the infidel religions will spread and extend; false messiahs will gather blind men. The armed infidel will be like never had been before; he will talk of justice and right, but his faith will be of blood and fire; he will take vengeance on the crusade."

"At the start of the millennium that follows the millennium, the heat of provoked death will advance like a storm over the earth; barbarians will infiltrate the soldiers of the last legions; the infidels will live in the heart of the holy cities; all in turn will be barbarians, infidels and savages. There will not be orders and norms, hatred will spread like fire on a dry forest, barbarians will massacre soldiers, and infidels will cut the throat of believers. Savagery will be something of each and all, and cities will die."

"At the start of the millennium that follows the millennium, men will judge each other in accordance with their blood and their faith; no one will listen the aching heart of children; they will be thrown out of the nest like birds do with their hatchlings; and no one will protect them from the iron-gloved armed hand. Hatred will inundate the lands believed to have been pacified. No one will feel free, neither old people nor the wounded; homes will be robbed or destroyed; some will usurp the place of others; none will open the eyes to see the raped women."

"At the start of the millennium that follows the millennium, everyone will know what's happening on the other side of the earth; the child with just the skin covering his bones and flies roaming on his eyes will be seen; they will be hunted like if they were rats. But the man witnessing the hunt will turn his head away, worried only about himself; he will give away a fistful of grain, while he sleeps over bags full of the wheat, and what he gives with one hand will pick up with the other."

"At the start of the millennium that follows the millennium, man will commercialize everything; everything will have a price: the tree, water and animal; nothing will be voluntarily given, unless sold. But man will be no more worth than his weight in flesh; his body will be traded like cattle in feet; they will take his eye and his heart; nothing will be sacred, not even life itself or the soul; his remains and his blood will be disputed as if his body was no more than carrion."

"At the start of the millennium that follows the millennium, man will have changed the face of the earth; he will proclaim himself sovereign lord of the forests and the herds; he will have gone through the sun and the skies and will trace paths on rivers and seas. But the earth will remain naked and will be unproductive, sterile, the wind will burn the skin and water will stink; life will wither away because man will deplete the riches of the world. And man will be all alone like a wolf with the hatred of himself."

"At the start of the millennium that follows the millennium, children will also be sold; some will use them like rag dolls to enjoy their soft skin; others will treat them like servile animals. The holy innocence and weakness of the child will be forgotten as well as their ministry; it will be like breaking a horse, bleeding and sacrificing a lamb. And man will become nothing less than a barbarian."

"At the start of the millennium that follows the millennium, the vision and spirit of man will be prisoners; they will be unknowingly drunk; they will interpret images and reflections as the truth of the world; it will be done to them what's done with a lamb. Then the butchers will show up; the rapacious creatures will place them in groups and guide them to the abyss and incite one against the other; they will be killed for their wool and skin, and those that survive will be dispossessed of their soul."

"At the start of the millennium that follows the millennium, the faithless sovereigns will reign; they will command over multitudes of passive and innocent humans; they will hide their face and keep in secret their names and their fortresses will be lost in the forests. But they will decide the future of everything and everybody; no one will participate in the assemblies of their order; only those from the savage and heretical cities will rise in protest, but they will also be defeated and burned alive."

"At the start of the millennium that follows the millennium, men will be so numerous on earth that they will be like ant nests that somebody stirred with a stick; they will move restless, and death will crush them like crazed insects with its heal. Great social movements will confront them one against the other; the dark skins will intermingle with the white skins; the faith of Christ with the faith of the infidel; some will preach concerted peace, but all over the world there will be tribal wars among enemies."

"At the start of the millennium that follows the millennium, men will want to jump over the walls; the mother's hair will grey like if she was old; the way of nature will be abandoned, and families will be like separated grains that nobody will be able to join again. It will be, hence, another world; all people will wander aimlessly like unbridled horses running in all directions, with nothing to guide them; damned the knights riding those horses with no stirrups—they will fall through the ditch."

"At the start of the millennium that follows the millennium, men will not trust God's law, and, to the contrary, will guide their lives like a mounted horse; they will choose their children in the mother's womb, and kill those they don't want. But, what will be of these men who think they are God? The most powerful will take the best land and the most beautiful women; the poor and the weak will be like cattle; the drunken ones will become like strong fortresses (strongholds); fear will invade hearts like poison."

"At the start of the millennium that follows the millennium, there will surge a dark and secret order; its law will be hatred and its weapon will be poison; it will seek more gold and its kingdom will extend all over the earth, and its servants will be united by a kiss of blood. The weak and the just men will accept its rule. The powerful men will voluntarily serve it. The only law will be that dictated in the shadow; poison will even come to the churches. And the world will advance with that scorpion under its foot."

"At the start of the millennium that follows the millennium, many men will remain seated with their crossed arms on their chests, will go to unknown places with empty eyes, for they will have no forge where they could melt the metal, nor any field for cultivation. They will be like seed that will never root. Wanderers and impoverished, the older ones and the younger ones often homeless. Their only salvation will be war, and will combat against each other and will hate their lives."

"At the start of the millennium that follows the millennium, diseases of the water, the sky, and of the land will attack man and will threaten him; he will want to rebuild what he destroyed, and protect its surroundings; he will be scared of the future days. But it will be too late; the dessert will devour the earth and, water will be found deeper and deeper, and some days it will overflow, dragging everything in its way, like a deluge, and the next day the earth will lack it, and the fledgling will perish."

"At the start of the millennium that follows the millennium, the earth will shake in many places and the cities will sink; all that was built without consulting the sages will be threatened and destroyed; mud will sink the towns and the soil will crack open under the palaces. Man will obfuscate because pride is his insanity; he won't listen the repeated warnings of earth and fire will destroy the new Romes, and among accumulated ruins, the poor and the barbarian—in spite of the legions—will loot the abandoned riches."

"At the start of the millennium that follows the millennium, the sun will scorch the earth; the air will no longer be like a veil that protects from heat. It will not be more than a ragged veil, and the burning fire will consume the skin and the eyes. The sea will rise like furious water; cities and river valleys will be inundated and whole continents will disappear; men will find refuge in the high places, and forgetting what happened, will begin reconstruction."

"At the start of the millennium that follows the millennium, men will bring mirages into reality; senses will be deceived and will touch what doesn't exist; they will follow paths that only eyes will see and dreams will come into reality. But man will no longer be able to distinguish between what is and what is not. He will be lost in false labyrinths; those who give life to mirages will mock the naïve, cheating him. And countless men will become servile dogs."

"At the start of the millennium that follows the millennium, the animals that Noah embarked in his Ark will no longer be in man's hands more than beasts transformed to man's will; and who will care of their vital sufferings? Man will have made of each animal what he pleases and will have destroyed several species. What would be of the man who changed the laws of life, who made the live animal a piece of clay? Will he be equal to God, or the devil's son?"

"At the start of the millennium that follows the millennium, we must fear for the son of man; poison and desperation will stalk him; he will not be desired more than for ourselves, not for him or for the world; he will be accosted by lewdness and sometimes will sell his body. But even those protected by their peers will run the risk of spiritual death; he will live in games and mirages. Who will guide him when lacking a teacher? No one will have taught him to wait and act."

"At the start of the millennium that follows the millennium, man will think he's God, though his progress since birth is null. He will attack overwhelmed by ire and jealousy. And his arm will be armed with the power that he misappropriated; blinded Prometheus will be able to destroy all around him. He will be soul-dwarfed but will have the strength of a giant; he will advance with long leaps but will not know where he's going. His head will be loaded with knowledge, but will not know why he lives or why he dies; he will be as always the fool that gesticulates or the child that mourns."

"At the start of the millennium that follows the millennium; entire regions will become looted by war. Beyond the Roman limits, and even within the limits of the old empire, men of the same cities will cut each other's throat; here there will be wars among tribes and over there wars among believers. The Jews and Allah's children will not stop warring, and Christ's land will be their battleground; but the faithful will want to defend all over the world the purity of their faith, and, before them, there will be nothing more than doubt and power; then death will advance all over the earth like the banner of the new times."

"At the start of the millennium that follows the millennium, great multitudes of men will be excluded from human life; they will lack their rights, a roof over their heads, and bread to eat; they will be naked and will have nothing but their bodies to sell; they will be expelled far from the Babel towers of opulence. They will agitate like remorse or threat; they will occupy entire regions and will proliferate; they will listen to the preaching of vengeance and will launch the assault of the proud towers; this will be the times of the barbarian invasions."

"At the start of the millennium that follows the millennium, man will have entered the obscure labyrinths; he will be afraid and will close his eyes, for he will no longer know how to see; he will mistrust everything and will fear each step taken, but he will be pushed forwards, and will not be allowed to stop. Cassandra's voice will be, nevertheless, clear and potent. But he will not hear anything, for he will seek more and more each day that passes and his head will be lost in fantasies; his teachers will deceive him and he will only have bad counsel."

"At the millennium that follows the millennium, men at last will open their eyes; they will no longer be locked in their heads and in their cities; they will see and hear from one end of earth to the other; they will know that what hurts them will injure others. Men will form one single body, and each one of them will be a tiny part of this body, and together will build the heart, and there will be a language spoken by all, and this way, the great human (humanity) will have been born."

"At the millennium that follows the millennium, man will have conquered the sky; he will create stars in the somber great blue sea, and will navigate in that shiny ship, new Ulysses, companion of the sun, towards the celestial odyssey. But he will also be sovereign of the waters; he will have built great nautical cities whose nutrients will be harvested at the sea; he will live, thus, in every corner of his great domain, and nothing will be forbidden."

"At the millennium that follows the millennium, men will be able to reach the depth of the waters; their body will be renewed and they will be fish, and some will fly higher than birds, as if the stones would not fall. They will communicate among themselves, for their spirits will be so wide open that will be able to pick up all messages, and their dreams will be shared among themselves, and they will live so long as the oldest of all men, that whom the sacred books talk about."

"At the millennium that follows the millennium, man will know the spirit of everything, the stone or water, the animal's body or the looks of other; he will have discovered the secrets that the old gods knew, and he will push one door after the other in the labyrinth of the new life. He will create with the force of a new fountain; teaching his knowledge to the multitude of men, and children will know the earth and sky better than any one before them. And man's body will be larger and abler. And his spirit will have encompassed every thing possessing them."

"At the millennium that follows the millennium, man will no longer be the only sovereign, since woman will grab the scepter; she will be the great teacher of future times, and whatever she thinks will be imposed on men; she will be the mother of the year one thousand that follows the year one thousand. She will spread the tender sweetness of the mother after the days of the devil; she will be beauty after the ugliness of the times of the barbarians; the year on thousand that follows the year one thousand will change in a short time; people will love and share, dream and give life to dreams."

"At the millennium that follows the millennium, man will know a second birth; the spirit will possess the people that will live in fraternal communion; then it will be announced the end of the time of the barbarians. It will be a time of a new invigorating faith; after the beginning of the dark days of the year one thousand that follows the year one thousand, we will see happier days; man will recognize the way of men and earth will be reorganized."

"At the millennium that follows the millennium, roads will go from one point of the earth and the sky to the next point; forests will again be lush and desserts will have been irrigated; the waters will again be pure. Earth will be a garden; man will care again for everything that lives; he will purify what he contaminated; this way he will sense that the whole earth is his home and he will be wise and think about tomorrow."

"At the millennium that follows the millennium, all will be like ordered movements, everything about the world and about the body will be known; sickness will be dreamt before it manifests; everyone will cure himself and others. It will be understood that it is necessary to help to maintain us, and men, after the shutting and avarice will open their heart and their purse to the dispossessed; he will feel like a knight of the human order, and at last a new era will commence."

"At the millennium that follows the millennium, man will have learned to give and share; the bitter days of solitude will have passed; he will believe again in the Spirit and the barbarians will acquire their right to citizenship. But this will come after the wars and the fires; this will sprout from the blackened ruins of the Babel towers. And an iron fist will have been necessary for disorder to turn into order and so that man finds his way."

"At the millennium that follows the millennium, man will know that all living beings are carriers of light and that they are creatures to be respected; he will have built the new cities in the sky, over the earth and in the sea. He will keep memory of what was and will know what will be; he will no longer be afraid of his own death, because in his life will have lived several lives and will know that the light will never wither."

NOTE: The above is a translation, originally published in Spanish, taken from **Buena Siembra : La Revista de Acuario ::**
Argentina-Buenos Aires
2001-2006

Additional Bibliography

Addison, Charles G.: *The History of the knights templars.* 1997 Adventures Unlimited Press, U.S.A; First published in London, 1842.

Atienza, Juan G.: *Los enclaves templarios.* Martínez Roca, 1995, Barcelona.

Charpentier, Louis: *Los misterios templarios.* Apóstrofe, 1995, Barcelona.

Fluguerto Martí, Fernando. : *Expediciones al Golfo de San Matías, Patagonia Argentina.* Comunicación personal y en la WEB: www.delphos.com.ar

Melville, Marion: *Nosotros los templarios.* Tikal, 1995, Girona, España.

Walker, Martin: *El misterio de los Templarios.* Edicomunicación, 1993, Barcelona.

Arroyo Durán, Fernando y Fernández Palacio, Jorge L. : *Historia Secreta del Temple, La Mano que Meció Europa.* Artículo publicado en la revista MÁS ALLÁ DE LA CIENCIA No. 138 de Agosto de 2000 (TEMPLESPAÑA).

Knights Templar. From Wikipedia, the free encyclopedia.

Juan de Jerusalén (Lo Inexplicable). De Los Templarios, Martes, 01 de Febrero de 2005.

Della Torre, Horacio A.: *Los Caballeros Templarios—Hechos, Supuestos y Misterios.*

Nicolas Martin y Mateo: *Los Templarios, sus Claves Históricas y Misterios.* Editado por las Revistas Esfinge y Rosacruz.

Abramsen, Elías: *El Poder Actual de los Templarios.* Traducción de un artículo publicado en Malasia sobre los templarios y sus acciones en el Vaticano (Del Malasian Financial News, 25 de Julio 2003).

Gittins, Jonathan A.: *The Rule of the Templars and the Monastic Vows of Poverty, Chastity, and Obedience* (Copyright by Jonathan Gittins, 2003).

6

CAPITALISM AND THE PHILOSOPHER'S STONE

The concepts presented in this section of the book represent just a summary of what the Templars' economic system epitomizes. It is just a blueprint for what I call the advent of the City of God in the city of man. The exposition of these ideas will be expanded accordingly with the region considered and the stage of development of the countries involved. This is a task for each individual chapter of the Orbis Unum party to work on.

Before I touch summarily about the capitalist system of production, I would like to make some comments about the term *exploitation*. The word exploitation inevitably brings memories of the past hard-core Marxist era of the 19th and 20th Centuries; it is associated with ideological fanatics and Revolutionaries. And yet, it is a word that more than describes the plight of the modern worker, but under changed circumstances. Nowadays we feel we are not exploited when we hold a given job, because we voluntarily applied for the job, and we agreed to the terms of employment; we accepted the rate of pay for the given job. If you ever make the comment that you are being exploited doing certain work, your interlocutor most likely will respond that you are free to walk away from the job, that we live in a free society, and that, therefore, you don't have to accept the terms of employment from your current employer. There is a sense of aloofness from the employer and from the population at large when we talk about freedom in general, including freedom to work or not to work, freedom to choose where you are going to work, freedom to employ or be employed, freedom to complain about the conditions of employment, and even freedom to be poor if you choose to be poor. This "freedom" nonsense is even reflected in the labor practices in the state of Texas, where employment is legally characterized as "at will," meaning that your employer can terminate you for no reason at all, and the employee can leave an employment anytime he/she wishes. This "at will" characterization of employment practices appears to be fair, when in reality is an avenue for the employers to get rid of their employees any time they deem it necessary and expedient to do so, since it's hard for an employee to arrogantly switch employment "at will."

Thus something is not right; something tells me that the employer, the boss, the *patrón*, somehow has the upper hand. There is something of unfairness when a human being has the freedom to terminate your employment, and you somehow don't have that much freedom to tell him/her: "Here, take your job and shove it!" Why is it that another individual that is no different than what you are, that may not be more intelligent than you are, that may not be even intellectually or spiritually fit to manage a business, can choose whether or not he can keep you working for your livelihood? The unfairness stems from the fact that he can decide about your life, about your immediate future, and about the livelihood of your children, and yet, he is no different than you. It's all because he is the owner of the means of production; it's all because of some past or present unjust circumstances that made him rich or to become rich. It's because he happens to have been born with an advantage, and you happen to have been born poor. But this last statement is not true; I was not born poor, I was *made* to be born poor. The capitalist, in most cases, was not born rich; he was *made* rich by a capitalist system that holds an unfair system of wealth distribution. This general air of unfairness makes the capitalist an *exploiter*, and makes you an *exploited* individual, which is why I am not going to apologize for using the term *exploitation*.

The fact of life that we were born poor or rich gets even unfairer—to the point of being almost criminal—when we talk about royal families and the aristocracy and nobility that still flourishes in many parts of today's world. Countries like England, Spain, Norway, Japan, Jordan, Saudi Arabia, etc. maintain this offensive unfairness in the name of culture and tradition. They feed, grow, revere, and feel deeply proud of keeping families that never worked and will never work, families turned into objects of their sycophantism, and who hold the privilege of birthing children raised to "live for free." You can barely fail to pick up a popular magazine that doesn't mention some queen or king, prince or princess, or other member of a royal family, praising their frivolities or talking about some aspect of their meaningless lives. Some countries even equate their cultural identity with their tradition of raising these spiritual orphans, and elevate their national pride by promoting the respect and veneration of them who are no more than social parasites. And yet these social parasites are not to be blamed, if not because they participate and acquiesce to perpetuate the charade, since their narcissism and hedonism is too strong to reject such an easy life of privileges—and because peoples, countries, and cultures are free to do as they wish, even if harmful to themselves . . . long live democracy! If it hadn't been for the French Revolution, the French would also be guilty of the practice of growing a class of aristocrats and charlatans—this, by the way, doesn't justify the way the French and Russian Revolutionaries got rid of their own high-class outcasts in the name of freedom and justice. And talking about outcasts, just as there are those who literally live like kings, there are those who are despised by every other social group in a given country, and we are referring to the so-called pariahs in India, Pakistan, and maybe in other parts of the world—like the gypsies in Central Europe—whose only crime is to have been born within a certain group of people with different customs and a negative historical hurdle imposed by tradition. These are truly people born to be poor, born to remain at the fringe of society, and to be socially outcasts for no fault of their own, but as the result of some stupid social custom or social convention.

That's as far as holding a job, or being a member of a social group is concerned. The same story is true when I buy things in the marketplace. If I want to fly from Houston to Mexico City, I pay more or less, depending on the time of the year. Around Christmas-time, and in the summer-time, the ticket is almost twice as expensive as if I buy it "out of season." Now, if I choose to purchase the ticket very close to the date I will be traveling—say within five days of the time of my scheduled trip—I always end up paying more than if I buy the ticket with one month of anticipation. And yet it doesn't help me to buy the ticket one year in advance, because it would be almost as expensive as if I buy it within three days of my trip. Of course, if I make any changes to my schedule once I purchased the ticket, then I have to pay more. Airline companies bend the rules in such a way that the customer always loses, and this is exploitation. Nevertheless, you never hear anybody complaining, because they have been led to believe that prices are set by supply and demand in a free-market economic system. And this is also true of gasoline prices. If the price of oil goes up, gas prices almost immediately go up; but if oil prices go down, gas prices take some time to go down. Economists are always finding reasons that explain why prices behave that way. It is supply vs. demand, they end up saying; they tell us that capitalists cannot do anything against the market forces.

This is exploitation, and yet people believe the crap of "economic forces." The truth is that producers decide what the price of products is going to be, based on costs of production, and scarcity may force people to be willing to pay a higher price for a product, which they wouldn't do, if the seller didn't agree to raise prices, and that's exploitation. If economics were indeed a true science, it would be a branch of psychology—this one a genuine social science—for we have to explain why the merchant, or owner of a product, raises the price of his/her product, as the need for the product increases. The answer being because of selfishness, avarice, and greed, and not because of some obscure market forces, or "invisible hand" at work. Physical laws, and any other laws of science, operate with a sense of inevitability (like in classical mechanics), or at least with a sense of statistical probability (like in quantum and statistical mechanics). The "science" of Economics wants us to believe that the increase in price of a given product follows *inevitably* the increase in demand of the said product, which is false, if the producer *decides* not to increase the price of the product, or the consumer *decides* not to pay more for the said product, or both.

The OPEC cartel sets the international prices of oil by reducing or incrementing production, but this is just posturing and playing the phony supply/demand game, because they may very well decide not to sell (without reducing production), in which case oil prices would go up, or else fully satiate the world demand (they have the capacity to pump enough oil) by adjusting down the oil prices, and they can do this whenever they feel like doing so, because one way or another, *the world already consumes the oil that it needs and it now produces*, and consumption is not going to substantially increase/decrease just because we can get our gas at a cheaper or more expensive price, if and always the price increase/decrease is kept within a certain margin of tolerance. In essence, even if I could get gas for free, there is a limit to the amount of free gas that I would be willing to burn; conversely, if gas were far more expensive than it now is, I would still be willing to consume the absolutely necessary amount to barely satisfy my mobility needs. Of course, the tendency is for prices to go up, because that's how the mammoth oil companies extort money from the gas consumers, but prices may sometimes go down as well, because that's how the same mammoth oil companies extort money from the stock market gamblers who decide to play the same phony supply/demand game, but this time with oil stocks.

If the myth of supply vs. demand were true, why is it that the Mexican Metro, or the New York subway, or the London and Paris Metro systems are not more expensive at rush hours? Why is the price of my book the same whether I sell one or a million units? What makes a fisherman at an open South American market sell his fish at the same price, even if he is surrounded by eager buyers? Why would the fisherman be so anxious to sell his fish as soon as possible, at the same price he fixed from the very beginning? Of course, he could make his product more expensive at the sight of the eager buyers crowding his stall, in which case people would complain that he is a thief, and he would indeed be an exploiter, because his original price was based on cost of production, not on speculative calculations. The same is true for the capitalist system in general: If the production of goods matches the consumption of those goods, prices remain stable based mainly on costs of production. But if consumption increases ahead of production, somebody decides to ask for a higher price—market forces don't operate automatically by themselves, and they don't make decisions about prices; those decisions are made by human beings. The fisherman above will finish his product and tell those who didn't get a chance to buy to come over the next day, when he will have more fish to sell. Again, he might also decide to increase the price of the fish the next day, and that's exploitation. The differential price at movie theaters, based on day and night presentations is exploitation. Charging more for dinner, as against lunch, for the same food is exploitation if the cost of production of the food remains the same. Setting a limit to the production and sale of video games to a single place and a single day to keep the price artificially high is exploitation. Making changes to MS Windows so that older programs cannot work with it to force people to buy newer versions of the programs is exploitation. Does it matter if I am perfectly happy with my new version of MS Windows? Can it still be said that I was exploited? Of course I was exploited, except that, just as with the dog's gene, the fact that I don't feel pain for being subservient to my master (the capitalist system) doesn't make me less of a victim.

Contrary to what Marx and Engels held, the capitalist system of production was not born at the turn of the 19th Century, and is not the offshoot of the steam-engine and the invention of the locomotive and the automobile. The capitalist system of production was born with the first man who decided to use another man as an instrument, or means of production. In fact, as long as men used animals to help them in the process of production, we could not talk of capitalism. It was only when some men decided to snatch the freedom of other men to make them work to create riches for the benefit of the oppressor that capitalism came into being. Hence, the transition from slavery to the feudal system, to capitalism proper, is only the transition from forced labor without pay, to (semi-free) labor with or without retribution, to voluntary labor with monetary retribution, within the same system of production, the capitalist system. The difference between slavery, feudalism and the capitalist system is only a difference of semantics—the capitalist is the owner of the means of production, including labor, even if the laborer is forced by sheer physical coercion to work for his master, or if by a semblance of voluntarism, or if by the circumstances where the capitalist controls the labor market and the price of labor.

We have to revise Karl Mark and Frederick Engels' Historical Materialism, if only in a very summarily way. We will begin with the following axiom:

> *The value of every product manufactured by man is given by the price of labor to manufacture the given product.*

Nothing that is made by man contains in its value anything that is not the value of human labor—both physical and mental human labor. From a pound of sea-salt to an airplane, whatever the price of the salt is, and whatever the price of the airplane is, that price is given by the cost of labor, and by no other cost, because land is free, and natural resources—which include land and its sub-soil, water and air—are given by nature for free. Whatever else is added to the cost of manufactured products is redundant value that is appropriated by the usurper of that value, in most cases the capitalist. If you pick up a pebble with certain characteristics that I value, you are entitled to sell me the pebble for the value of the effort you invested in picking it up and keeping it. If you add to that value a proportional marginal price of the land where you found the pebble, you become an usurper, and you are exploiting me. And since the money I pay you for your pebble was obtained as a result of labor, for which I was paid, you are effectively an usurper of human labor, a capitalist exploiter.

How is it then, that works of art from painters like Van Gogh and Picasso are so expensive? It's because of the fantasy that money imbues in the minds of rich people. Works of Van Gogh, Picasso, and Michelangelo are priceless works of art, whose value cannot be measured with money, whose price go beyond the work of the men and the material they invested in them, because the artists imprinted their soul in their work, and that cannot be labeled with a price sticker. Paying 60 million dollars for a Van Gogh is like weighing his spirit in units of pounds or kilograms. And yet, capitalists pay that much for a painting, because they have the money to buy it, which doesn't make them worthy of privately owning it.

The Capitalist system of production consists basically of the following main components:

a. The concept of free enterprise and free participation in the capitalist system of production, also called the *free market system*. This means that anybody is free to participate, that anybody is free to compete in the process of production, distribution and sale of the products and services offered by the capitalist system. But this can only be accomplished by those that have money, land, and assets—in other words, capital. Therefore, this free market system is a chimera, a dream never to be realized for the poor and the penniless. In this sense the capitalist system of production is a club in which only the rich can participate. Of course, there are also those meager and small businesses that keep a great portion of society occupied in the process of production, but these have a minimal participation in the macro-economic activity of the capitalist world.

b. The concept of free enterprise presupposes the concept of *private property*. The capitalist system of production cannot be without the protection the legal system must give to the individual ownership of property. Property must be able to be transferred from one individual to another, especially from parents to their children or other close relatives, hence, the concept of inheritance. Property, thus, must be able to be inherited.

c. The concept of the free action of the market forces of *supply and demand*. The capitalist produces products and services, and thus sets the price of those products and services based on their cost of production, plus what capitalists call profits. Those who do not produce, i.e. those who are not capitalists, buy the products and services they need compelled by the supply of those products offered by the producers (the members of the capitalist club). The pseudo-scientific argument is that prices are set by the law of supply and demand, and that this law is fair because it is symmetric, which is not true because this law is, if anything, asymmetric. Consumers are compelled to buy their products at the 'market price,' and depending on the product, they will be compelled to buy almost at any price. Producers, on the other hand, may not be so compelled to sell their products at the 'market price,' and depending on how precarious their need to sell is, they can hold to their products almost indefinitely. Capitalists want us to believe that the harm a consumer suffers for paying higher prices is the same as the harm the producer suffers for selling at lower prices. This is not true. In fact, whenever a capitalist goes bankrupt because it can no longer compete in the marketplace, the people most benefited from this are the other capitalists—companies that go bankrupt are absorbed by their creditors, and very little passes on to consumers. On the contrary, consumers are bound to pay higher prices for the products and services they need as the "market forces" accommodate to the new situation of one less competitor in the production side of the marketplace.

d. The concept of *money and currency*. This is such an important part of the production and exchange of consumer products that neither capitalism, nor even the strongest form of communism that we have ever known, could get away without the circulation of money. Money is the greatest single economic invention in the history of mankind that expedites the free exchange of the products of human labor. Money represents an abstract, standardized value of the labor invested in the production of something, and it also represents the exchange value of that something. With money or currency, we can transfer, transport, and convert wealth into consumer products and/or assets.

But in spite of its great economic utility, money represents a terrible tool of exploitation as well, because it facilitates the rationalization of the concept of profit, which is in reality, on the one hand (from the worker's point of view), minus-value of labor, and on the other hand (from the capitalist's point of view), plus-value of labor. Without money there could hardly be exploitation, interest rates, and inflation. In an ideal, closed society with no scarcity, no excessive production of products, and with absolute free exchange and access to the consumer products needed in life, there would be no need for an abstract vehicle of exchange of products called money. Money paid to the worker for his labor, terminates any *de facto* claim on the residual value of human labor for the production of something; when I get more money than the value of labor invested in the production of a thing, and make a profit, I am in fact cutting the ties of labor to the value of the thing produced, and appropriating the plus-value (the worker's minus-value) for myself.

When money itself becomes merchandise, like in the case of the dollar as an international currency, it produces the same effect of loss-gain that it produces in the normal process of production. Weaker currencies fall victim to this appropriation of value, and those economically weaker countries that have their own currency, will suffer the fall of their currency value in addition to the internal inflation of their own economies—and this represents an internationalization of exploitation. The best thing to do for those countries with economies that depend on richer nations (like the USA) is to adopt the currency of the stronger country. But this does not bode well with the local capitalists, who save or export their earnings in the form of hard currency (dollars, euros, or yens) to national or international banks, respectively.

The way capitalists use money to mask the exploitation of human labor can be exemplified with, let's say an owner of a cotton plantation, or sugar mill producing facility, operated by slave labor. If the master owner can produce anything he needs to feed, clothe, and shelter his slaves, in addition to the cotton or sugar itself, he doesn't need money to run the closed operation of his business. All the cotton or sugar produced, nevertheless, represents human labor transformed into the products that the owner commercializes as his. This kind of human exploitation is too crude not to be open to criticism, and we are going to suppose that the slave owner has a change of heart, plus he knows that this situation can't last for long. Because of questions of increased productivity, and for other commercial reasons, like product quality, etc. the owner of the business may decide to pay his former slaves for the work they do, and let them loose as free men and women, changing their status from slaves to labor workers. He will claim that he pays fair wages to his workers for the work performed, and in this way, money helps him mask the exploitation of human labor the former slave owner still performs. And if he sells cotton or sugar to his ex-slaves transformed into labor workers—at a fair price, so he says—our entrepreneur makes still some more additional profits.

In essence, to be a capitalist you need capital and an idea for investment—an idea for investment may go from a simple useful invention to improve the quality of life of human beings to a chance on profiteering on drugs, gambling, prostitution or any other fringe human activity. Most capitalists invest because they expect a return on their investment, or a reward for taking the risk of investing, or a profit, or payback for the effort of doing something 'useful' for humanity, or in simple crude terms, capitalists invest because they are greedy, they want more profits, more money than what they already have. If they are already rich, they want to get richer.

Now, with money you can buy land, machinery, and materials for what you want to invest on. But in addition to things, the capitalist must buy labor, human labor—both physical and mental human labor—if he is going to produce anything. Products are produced by mediation of land, material, and labor. In its origin, land is free and it doesn't belong to anybody; material things come from the earth, which is free, and doesn't belong to anybody either; labor used to be free (in times of slavery), though it belonged to the laborer, and yet nowadays is only partially paid for, since the capitalist appropriates some of that labor, through the payment of wages that, most often than not, are below the real value of labor. The question is, then, if land is free, and material things only have matter (whatever the matter) invested on them, plus labor to transform that matter, why is it appropriated by somebody called the capitalist, when this capitalist only partially made a payment for labor? It is the concept of private property that comes here into play. The capitalist has lots of property, assets, or capital because he appropriated this capital through the capitalist system of production, or because he inherited this capital. Because capital is not free, and it doesn't grow on trees, if my cost of production of a hamburger is $2.00, and I sell it for $3.00, the $1.00 dollar that I, as a capitalist made as a profit, must have been lost by somebody else in the form of wages, or simple appropriation of money, or property, in the process of selling the hamburger. Profits are at the heart of the capitalist accumulation of wealth, not to mention inflation, an invention of a system that never fills its bag of avarice.

There is absolutely no reason why there should be inflation that grows at a faster pace than the price of labor. Inflation is just a form of taxation invented by the capitalist system of production in order to crop some more profits from the workers. Of course, the capitalist never has control over inflation, but he has to consider it in his cost of production. Similarly, if he borrows money from a bank, he has to pay interests, which increases his cost of production by that much—and if he doesn't borrow money from a bank, the capitalist still increases the cost of production by that much, which translates into additional profits that go to his pockets. It is true that this inflationary process is not controlled by one individual, not even by a group of individuals, but by the system as a whole, which, in the final analysis, makes the worker pay more for the products he consumes, leaving the capitalist producer unaffected by inflation. Have you ever wondered why inflation is unstoppable? Wonder no more, because inflation is a form of taxation that benefits the capitalist, at the expense of the consumer (usually the worker), and when the worker can no longer deal with the inflationary trend, the capital gives in. Charged with generosity the capitalist allows an increase in wages, and from time to time, the government increases the legal minimum wage to compensate for the workers' losses and to get him ready for the next train of inflationary increases in consumer prices.

When capital in the form of cash concentrates among the very few who are rich, barely any inflation at all ensues. But when cash concentrates on the great percentage of the population who are poor, inflation triggers up uncontrollably, sometimes becoming what has been called hyper-inflation. As long as there is idle capital that doesn't purchase anything, or is not invested in productive ventures, inflation remains basically constant, but as soon as the purchasing power of the masses increases, then inflation fires up in such a way that it requires in many cases government intervention. Why is that? Because with the influx of eager buyers, capitalists envision the possibility of snatching the extra cash of those empowered buyers without increasing production, so capitalists increase the price of their products beyond what the additional injection of circulating money among the masses required, which is pure speculation.

This has been a difficult problem for socialist economies where the government effectively controls only certain aspects of the economy. The increase in circulation of money should not make products more expensive, but it just happens that people are desperate to buy, giving the capitalist speculators the opportunity to increase their profits. This would not happen if people did not offer more for the consumption products they need than what their current price is, buying just what the market offers. In this case, the capitalist would have no other option than to sell what they have, and try to produce more to satisfy the increased demand. At the end, hyper-inflation doesn't benefit the consumers or the producers, because the impressive accumulation of capital washes out the profits of the capitalists, given that the price of everything increases at a faster rate than the normal inflationary trend would require. Effectively, then, inflation, just like hyper-inflation, is triggered by avarice and the need to crop the cash that circulates among the poor. One way to fight inflation of this sort is to open cash accounts for the poor in the form of benefits to be had in the future, rather than flooding the population with extra cash to spend. On the higher end, idle capital should be punished with a negative interest rate, so that capitalists are forced to invest their cash—giving, at the same time, some incentives to new capital investments.

The great mistake of socialist and communist governments has always been trying to empower the poor with an increase in the cash flow, so that people can buy more. If and always the capitalist system is still in place, this measure is going to produce inflation and even hyper-inflation. A different approach would be something similar to the social security fund. The money from social security is not there to cover the immediate necessities of the individual and should be invested in productive ventures—for once I agree with president Bush, except that his objective is to loose some capital to benefit the rich, while I would free that capital for investments that would benefit the poor. Social-security-like funds that would cover the whole conglomerate of individuals are some of the main objectives of a government in the hands of the Orbis Unum party. The cash reserves in the Central Banks are another source of money that could be used to invest in productive ventures. These bank reserves should appropriately be made to belong to the people in the form of bonds, or security stocks, to create new enterprises that effectively would belong to the poor. This is very much what president Hugo Chavez has been trying to do with his Communal Counsels in Venezuela. These organizations propose investment projects, and the government funds them. But be mindful that private, individual investment is crucial, because people must feel that they are working for what belongs to them—a company that "belongs" to the government kills the incentive the worker may have for it.

The Orbis Unum Party's objective is to try to gain the presidency and most seats in the congress, assembly, or parliament of any given country, to be able to make meaningful economic reforms. There are no more important investment funds than the government budget, and we are not talking here about the creation of state companies; that doesn't work. We are talking here about the creation of people's companies: The government may supply some of the funds—in some cases, preferably the majority of those funds—but the people must also invest their savings and personal capital to promote their business ventures and common ideas. Hence, the importance of the so-called Communal Counsels, or whatever you want to call them, which are mainly associations of people with similar interests to promote a given venture or a common project that would be beneficial to the community. This doesn't discard the creation of purely national or state enterprises that would control certain resources too vital or strategic to the nation to be left in the hands of private enterprises (petroleum exploration and exploitation, utility projects, communications, massive public projects, strategic scientific investigations, etc.) In the meantime, the capitalist system of production would continue in its traditional form. Those capitalists who wish to invest in the creation of other business enterprises are welcome to do it, except that they will be operating in a slightly tougher environment, with the participation of the workers in their own productive enterprises.

The government in this kind of political system will be more than a provider of the necessary infrastructure that capital development requires, and becomes a participant in the economic growth of the nation. The government controlled by the Orbis Unum Party would be effectively combating poverty and unemployment. Of course, there are a myriad of other things that the government needs to implement to bring about the beginnings of the advent of the City of God in the city of man, but nothing is more important than eradicating poverty. One of those other government tasks is the creation of capital reserves that would empower with financial resources every child since his/her birth—something similar to the social security funds for the workers, except that these funds would originate in inheritance taxation and/or taxation of idle capital. These children, once they become adults, can use these funds to invest and participate in the economic game of the country, given the proper training in the use of those funds. We propose that every child should be born with a bank account that he/she can use in the future.

Before we give, or create the perception that we are against human creativity, we must emphasize here, and onwards, that human genius and ingenuity are characteristics that must be cultivated and cherished. People who invented the locomotive, the telephone, the internal combustion engine, the radio and TV, the personal computer, and all those who advance social progress with their creativity, must reap the rewards of their efforts in monetary terms. In this sense we radically depart from classic communism, since we give our wholehearted support to those brilliant minds that create new and easier ways of doing things, and should, by all means, enjoy their monetary gains without government interference. It is greed and avarice that we are against. On the other hand, we welcome the technological advances generated mainly by the capitalist system of production. The positive part of greed is that it also generates an incentive to produce new things; the need to make money fast has driven a lot of people to invent things, or create new ways of creating things. The vast number of technological advances in medicine, electronics, space technology, pharmacology, chemistry, industrial production, mechanization and modernization of agriculture could only be had thanks to the capitalist system of production that inherently promotes productivity and innovation.

Thus, it must be made perfectly clear that the incentive for the production of goods and services may not necessarily be identified with greed and avarice as such. People who create, invent, innovate and facilitate a productive process, must be rewarded with incentives for their ingenious efforts, which classic communism failed to do, therefore, bringing onto itself doom and failure. Innovators like Henry Ford, Bill Gates, and so many other tycoons that have populated the imagination of Americans and have filled the history of the United States, certainly deserved to keep the riches they created with their new products. It's only when their successors inherit those riches that the problems begin, because we are concerned here with leveling the field of competitive participation in the capitalist game, more than with preserving privileges that didn't result from ingenuity and innovation.

I am not saying that there is anything wrong with a father making it easier for the son to make a living. It's only that society has to balance the needs of the people, even at the expense of the abundance accrued to the successor of the original innovator. Hence, the concept of the inheritance tax, or the tax on idle capital, makes sense in this context, especially when there is no reason why the people's assets should remain in the hands of someone who does not merit them as a reward for making most everyone's life easier through creative production techniques and product invention and innovation. The capitalist system would not be so bad if capitalists had never invented the concept of inheritance, the privilege of being able to transfer riches to our offspring—the new rule would state that you deserve what your ideas, ingenuity and managerial capacity generated, but your children must forfeit some of what you gained by your lawful efforts, so that others should have a chance to prove their worth.

Incentives in this new sense of the word are both a carrot and a stick: you gain if you make an effort to create, and you create by the lure of the gain. In other words, we are not in favor of dispossessing the children of the inventor or innovator, but in favor of returning some of the inventor's or innovator's gains back to those who produced them in the first place. Of course, willfully forfeiting those gains would facilitate the process, which is the idea behind God Enterprises (GEnte). Making profits by other "legal" or illegal means is a far different story. Fringe activities and quasi-legal operations, like gambling and pornography, should be heavily taxed, if allowed at all.

Financial companies that lend money to businesses and individuals charge interest for the use of money and to compensate for the risk of losing it, should the borrower default repayment, and this is at the root of inflation—and not only at the root of inflation, but also as a means of plain outright legalized theft, and if you want one example of this, just take a look at your contract agreement with credit card companies. (I always tell my friends to get a good credit, obtain as many credit cards as you can, spend their money, and then file for bankruptcy; it's the easiest way of getting even with those thieves).

In a total economy, not driven by greed, but controlled by the need to increase productivity to the benefit of society, capital investments would be interest free, since the price of risk is already vested in the magnitude of the expected profits, and in the monetary value of the investment returns to the public as an added bonus to society. This is why God Enterprises (GEnte) would be confident to invest in the formation of other companies that would generate more jobs and cheaper products, as long as they are part of the corporation, or are willing to participate in the goals and objectives of the corporation. Internal investments, like in a multiple-operations corporation, should be encouraged, as well as investments that follow a straight line, from production to distribution to consumption, covering all aspects of the production process—clearing the land for the coffee plantation, harvesting the crop, processing it, packaging the product, transporting it to the distribution centers (supermarkets), and selling the final product, say coffee. The problem with free capital investment is availability of the funds, and this drives people to pay for the use of money in exactly the same fashion that scarcity drives people to pay more for products with an increased demand, caused by a low output supply of the said products. Therefore, to facilitate the acquisition of free capital investment, it is necessary that the state intervenes through reimbursable taxation of idle bank accounts to finance feasible and realistic investment ventures—the state taking the position of guarantor of the "loan" repayments. This, of course, would enrage those people with money to spare. Another alternative would be to force these money-holders to participate in the investment process as partners.

Insurance is another form of taxation imposed on the consumer—and I am referring here to what individual families pay for auto insurance, health insurance, and other property insurance. Why is it that the government doesn't provide insurance, or even regulates it—and I mean regulate? There is nothing that private companies are doing that could not be done by a good government that represents the interests of the people. In fact, by just leaving the insurance providers as they actually are, functioning as they are actually functioning, a GEnte-like corporation would be able to re-invest the so-called profits left by the insurance business into other productive endeavors, or onto services to benefit society as a whole. The argument that government is not a good administrator stems from the fact that government-controlled agencies "belong to everyone, and don't belong to anyone in particular," which is the cause of the massive failure of the concept of collective property promulgated by communism. God Enterprises are business ventures that have a tangible owner, the people working for each of the companies—just like public corporations are owned by investors—they are not government offices operated by bureaucrats interested in earning a salary. The interest in the efficient operation of the businesses is not for the benefit of abstract realities called the "nation," the "people," or the "government," but for a tangible, real, physical presence of each one of the workers of the company, imbued with love of humanity, which is the spiritual motivation to help others deal with the daily necessities of life, this in addition to the fact that they will be earning a decent salary.

Providing health care insurance for all is not just a business, but an obligation of society. Health provision for the poor in the richest country of the world is absolutely dismal, and I can talk by experience. Why is that? Because health, just like education and religion, for the capitalist system of production is just another business. Doctors, nurses, hospitals, clinics, pharmaceutical companies, and all the businesses and industries related to health care are interested in making profits, more than in taking care of people.

When the dictator Somoza was president of Nicaragua, we had a good health care system—nonetheless the Sandinistas, in their senseless drive to socialize poverty, wiped it out in less than ten years—divided in three branches: the public health care system, the private health care system, and the health care system provided by Social Security. The public health care for the general population of Somoza's Nicaragua of the 1970's, was not so good in terms of quality and technological advancement, but very good in terms of attention, and I bet it provided much better services to the public than those services to the uninsured provided in the USA today, in the year 2007. I remember that in the clinics of the Social Security system, people would raise hell if they had to wait for more than half an hour to be seen by a doctor. In the public hospitals of Nicaragua people would go wild if they had to wait in the ER for more than two hours. Here, in the United States of America, if you don't have insurance, you can clock waiting times of 12 hours or more. I know this by personal experience: It happened to me twice in the Ben Taub Hospital of Houston, TX, as well as in another hospital of Los Angeles, CA.

The USA is probably the only country of the industrialized world where a person dies while waiting to be attended in the emergency halls of a hospital, even after the dying person calls 911 asking for help. A Hispanic woman laid on the floor, vomiting blood and dying in an L.A. hospital, and she actually died before anybody would pay attention to her, even after she called 911, and this happened in May of 2007, in the United States of America. And all because she couldn't afford health care insurance. This is what the news commented about this case: ". . . Last month [May, 2007], a woman died after writhing untreated for 45 minutes on the floor of the emergency room lobby. In February, a brain tumor patient allegedly languished in the ER for four days before his family drove him to another hospital for emergency surgery." Compassion is an unknown word in the capitalist system, even when dealing with health care. Nor is loyalty a trademark of the capitalist system, which in fact is an advantage for the process of globalization of man.

Modern capitalism in the USA has several great contradictions to grapple with. One of them is its desperate need for cheap labor, mostly from immigration (especially illegal immigration), which is adamantly opposed by most American people. Another one has to do with production costs trimmings that is causing manufacture to emigrate to other countries where labor is cheap, like China, Mexico, India, Malaysia, the Philippines, Indonesia, Singapore, and other Southeast Asian countries. Thanks to the Internet, with its virtually instantaneous global communications, some skilled labor is also being outsourced to countries like India, Russia, Ireland, Pakistan, Mexico, the Philippines, and Brazil, where it is much cheaper than in the USA. And, as we mentioned before, the capitalist system knows no loyalty and it certainly cares little about patriotism, which goes in favor of globalization. The conservative forces within the USA that would like to keep cheap laborers outside the country (including agricultural workers, restaurant workers, gardeners, maids, nannies, construction workers, and others that cannot be outsourced) become rabidly nationalistic, and thus, oppose legal or illegal immigration. But countries like Mexico, and others in Central and South America, can only export their surplus cheap labor to the North—cheap labor that in no way forces wages down in the mainstream American labor market—while their skilled laborers, professionals and technicians, stay where they are, in their native countries. This means that in the USA, semi-skilled and skilled laborers, scientists, CEO's, and highly skilled technicians are barely feeling the pressure of job instability due to immigration, free trade, outsourcing and globalization. Only the low-skilled and unskilled sectors of the labor market of this country have been affected by this new capitalist phenomenon: globalization of the world economy. But those who oppose immigration, free trade, and outsourcing, are fighting a losing battle against capitalism, and the preferential status that American workers have enjoyed with the unbridled growth of capitalism is beginning to spill over to other countries, in spite of the stiff opposition of those who for so long benefited from the pre-Internet capitalist expansion. It almost seems that globalization is the nemesis of nationalism and isolationism.

To see how the modern capitalist system of production evolved, we have to take a quick historical tour of the discovery, conquest and colonization of the Americas, since the expansion of modern capitalism had a tremendous impulse with the discoveries of the 15th and 16th Centuries.

When the Spanish sailors set foot on American soil, the only investment they had made was in the ships and other *vituallas* that the Spanish Crown provided, plus the effort of the men who sailed in the ships. The next steps from discovery to conquest to colonization was a process of open plunder, confiscation, misappropriation of land, natural resources and labor. Never mind the Conquistadors own labor, misappropriated by their bosses and masters—which is also part of the capitalist process of production—what is important is that in addition to land and natural resources, they found great amounts of free Indian labor. With the English and French conquest and colonization of the American Continent, something very similar happened to what the Spanish did, except that in the case of the English colonies, and because of the particular characteristics of the English colonization, the British never saw the necessity of tapping, or could never tap the free abundant Indian labor they found. This condition may also have been prompted by the characteristics of the North American Indians, which were not as badly infested with the dog's gene as the Central and South American Indians, a fact that made them more difficult to enslave. This vacuum was filled by black African slaves. In essence, all misappropriation of the products that results from the capitalist system of production boils down to robbery and plunder of human labor that belongs to the laborer, and violent appropriation of natural resources that belong to all, including the natives of the land. It doesn't really matter if after several centuries of unshackled exploitation, this confiscation of labor and property creates its own legal system that regulates the transition, transmission, inheritance and use of these resources, giving the appearance of honesty, civility and order to the process of production. The capitalist system used in this fashion is plain and simple robbery. The argument that more than 500 hundred years have passed doesn't erase the debt that the white man has with the dark-skinned people of the American continent, which is why inheritance must be taxed in order to help pay this bulky debt that the white man has with the native peoples of the American continent.

The fundamental difference between the Spanish conquest of America and the Anglo-Saxon conquest of North America is a difference of style, rather than content. While the Spaniards had the fixation (inherited probably from the Knight Templars) with the idea of the spread of Christianity and the eradication of evil, goals that went awry because of the choice of people to conduct the conquest and colonization of the continent, the British and the French were mainly renegade, so-called pilgrims who were nothing but a bunch of bigots being persecuted by another bunch of bigots, the Roman Catholic Church and other religious reformers. The British pilgrims came to America with the purpose of forcing their way into the new world by imposing and substituting, if necessary, one race of people and one set of cultural traits by another, primarily by the Anglo-Saxon culture and the protestant religions, including Anglicanism and Presbyterianism. They were in no way interested in converting the Indians. This is one of the reasons why America, south of the border with the United States, is mainly a heterogeneous mixture of peoples from Indian, black and Spanish descent. The egotistic self-centeredness of the North American culture, plus the idolatry of individualism is a product of Protestantism, Puritanism, and anti-Catholic backlash, a mixture of extreme religious bigotry and racism. The Spanish, on their part, were led by a thirst for gold, riches and the search of the mythical fountain of youth, which were powerful antidotes against any moral quibbles in their drive to conquer what they considered inferior races of people. Slavery is another story, though one very much related with what we said above.

Slavery and the annihilation of the natives of America is the result of both ventures. What was meant to be an avenue for the spread of Christianity became a rapacious venture, a free for all misappropriation of what belonged to the peoples of America. And this is one of the profound reasons why the descendants of slaves must be paid, if the concept of inheritance is going to make any sense. For how can people inherit riches, but not the debts owed to the descendants of those slaves that were forced to work for free, unpaid labor they reluctantly contributed to the white, free society of masters? And yet, in spite of the Spanish and Anglo-Saxon invasion with its consequent plunder of the native's land and natural resources, the capitalist system of production that the white man imported, expanded, and "improved," turned out to be so monstrously efficient that it will eventually feed the world. This is why we, members of the Fraternity of the Templars, consider the capitalist system of production the Holy Grail (and the Ark of the Covenant as well) rediscovered by these, the pious monk-warriors of the 21st Century, system of production that will soon develop into the socialism of the 21st Century, much publicized by president Hugo Chavez of Venezuela.

7

GREED AND THE INSATIABLE EGO

Every economic system, including capitalism—with the exception (in principle, at any rate) of socialism—that has ever existed is based on greed and avarice. We can call the difference between revenues and costs investment profits, gains, returns, dividends, interests, yields, earnings, incentives, surplus, etc. but in the end, it amounts to nothing else than an ingenious product of the works of greed and avarice.

A short review of Marx's analysis of capitalism displays in full view the ravenous nature of the most powerful tool to produce wealth that ever existed, called the capitalist system of production, which through centuries was (and still is) monopolized and misappropriated by selfish individuals for their own personal interests. Marx's criticism of the capitalist system of production is unfair, nevertheless, given that the system itself is not what's at fault, but the way it was put to use by some people enslaved by an insatiable ego. Nothing that covers man necessities come from outside the world, and nothing that man transforms into useful objects or tools are anything else but matter and the product of human labor. And the world does not belong to anyone in particular. The division of the world into nations is mainly a product of the ethnical and cultural affinities of groups of individuals, and in some cases a product of the selfishness of those who hold common interests and decided to set limits to portions of the world's land to attend to their egotistic ambitions. That's also why, within a nation, we have political parties.

Marx's dictum that "religion is the opium of the people" is almost an axiom. Religion has always been used as a tool of appeasement against the unhappiness of the dispossessed. It has always been a way out for those who refuse to share their riches with the poor—a clearance house with a pinch of cosmic injustice

143

that forces religionists to affirm that there will always be poor and rich people in this world. If not, just try to review the Bible, or other religious books, and see if you can find whether they mention profit—or whatever its equivalent was called in past times—in positive terms. Just try to find out whether or not the incentive to produce is anywhere criticized by the great religious books of humanity, except as a manifestation of usury, or mistreatment and underpayment of laborers. Nevertheless, the great religious writings of humanity view the possession and accumulation of riches as something given by God—while at the same time stressing that "the given" must also be shared with the poor.

In modern times the search for a profit is almost treated as a virtue. Capitalists consider this drive to produce and accumulate riches anything but greed. There is not even one commandment in the Decalogue that makes reference to greed, and yet it commands that we should not desire somebody else's espouse. Greed is a vice par with robbery, not a minor human deviation from righteous behavior. It is often the cause of murder and theft, since people would rarely murder or steal if not for greed. Modern economic doctrine—which is mostly pseudo-science, together with political "science"—justifies greed on the basis of entrepreneurial reward for those capitalists that invest in productive ventures that "benefit" humanity, and they call it earnings, profits, or investment returns. The promoters of the notion of the capital even invented the so-called law of supply and demand to justify despoiling whenever they raise prices in response to an increased demand. The true basis, the core of the capitalist system of production is the reaping of benefits for those who invest in the capitalist enterprise, with little or no consideration for either workers or buyers. There is absolutely nothing that moves men to produce if not for making a gain, reaping a profit, earning something, or obtaining some kind of personal advantage.

But making a profit implies producing something, building something, providing a service to somebody, or to something, and production requires the concept of property. And property needs protection, people who produce need to rely on the security and continuity of their assets and of the things they produce—they need a legal basis for the concept of private property. The capitalist system requires that some people permanently possess (and keep) the means of production as an incentive to produce. The means of production are those things, tools, or materials needed to produce; they can be just a material substance, or made of some material; they can be something already given by nature (like land) or they can be ideas, or human labor. The only two things that legitimately belong to a person are his or her ideas, and his or her labor force. Everything else is either given by nature, or transformed into final or intermediate products by human labor. In order to make products, the capitalist needs the means of production that he appropriated as his own, the ideas or mental effort to conduct the production process, and human labor. The capitalist's wealth has its origin in inheritance, sheer appropriation of property, and/or accumulation of capital through the process of production (which amounts to appropriation of property), because the capitalist is never going to pay a fair price for the labor invested in the production of goods and services. So far, we are with Marx, and nothing in this analysis is new to Marxism, except when it comes to the Marxist historical classification of the different economic systems that humanity has known, what Marx and Engels calls Historical Materialism.

The new argument in this book is that primitive communism, slavery, feudalism, classical capitalism, and modern imperialism are not different at the core of the process of production from capitalism proper, except in their external form. It's always the same story, the master, the capitalist, the entrepreneur, etc. appropriates some of the labor of the worker, the slave, the servant, or whatever we care to call them. The story always follows the same sequence: Somebody appropriates the means of production, and accumulates riches at the expense of others. The modern notion of capitalism rests on another "economic" concept, mainly free enterprise, which is freedom to produce and to be used as a means of production. The producer needs to justify his operation by affirming that the capitalist society is a free society, and anybody who wants to be a producer is free to be so—those who can't be producers, or capitalists, necessarily are going to be used as manual, or intellectual laborers, for the production process.

Furthermore, the capitalist has to protect his right to produce with the appropriate legislation, and the same is true for the right of property, protected in such a way as to make it sacrosanct. Therefore, the thread to exploitation and to the capitalist system of production is clear: First there is greed, next the right to private property, the right of inheritance, the right to accumulate property or wealth, all within the economic laws of the free enterprise economic system, supply and demand, and free competition. But this world is such that, if somebody gains something, somebody else loses in exactly the same amount as the gain of the other, because objects, natural or man-made, as we said before, only possess two things: matter and the labor, or human ideas, that transformed them into useful objects. Matter is free, labor is not free, and has to be compensated, the same way ideas are not free, and the originator of such ideas has to be compensated. So, nothing, in principle, would be left for the individual that claims that the material and the means of productions are his—if he pays the laborer and the inventor whatever fairness determines to be the price of their physical or mental effort, and if he sells the product at a price that reflects the cost of the inputs to its manufacturing. But he is a capitalist, he is the owner of the means of production, and he imposes on others his price—always, God forbids, dictated by the free market forces, and by the law of supply and demand.

Take for example the production of a bushel of corn. The land where the corn grows is free. The seed to plant the corn is also free, if obtained from a previous harvest and labor of the farmer-owner. But work must be done to prepare the soil, plant the seed, and take care of the process of production. At harvest time labor is used to gather the corn, clean it, and place it in storage. So, the final product is corn, plus labor invested in its production. If the corn is sold at cost, and labor is paid in a fair manner, nothing is left for the capitalist who claims the land to be his, and who contracted the labor to grow the corn. And yet, the producer also must benefit from his effort. But in addition to the producer's efforts, there is greed and the object of greed—the material things we want to possess, and in order to possess them, we must invent the concept of private property, which may be acquired by our own effort, or by force that usurps the efforts others invested in the production of the material object. To possess property, you must have worked to obtain it, or you must have inherited it, and be able to pass it on to your progeny. The protection of property requires force, and force is created by capital in order to protect that which may have been acquired by force, and the state becomes a tool of the rich, of the ones who yield power. The system must be justified, and the propaganda is intense until the exploited feels that he must also work to protect the system. This is total indoctrination (performed in a very subtle way), no different than brainwashing in communist societies—the capital controls the means of communication (the media), the means of imposing order (the army and police), the means of production (the industry), and the means of moralizing about the system (the media and religious freedom). And all this thanks to greed—the capitalist knows that the workers must be kept happy, and creates the illusion that everyone can become rich, hence freedom and democracy. And indeed, some people will become rich, the black, the poor, the Indian, etc. and the propaganda machinery will grow noisier, until the underdogs, under such manipulation, accept their total control and submission to the system. There is only a small amount of troublemakers, the communists and anarchists, the ones who proclaim that instead of greed, the fuel that should move the capitalist machinery should be love, but these can always be discredited, or taken care of by other means.

In the animal kingdom we can see that greed, as described here, doesn't exist. There are no animals that would take the food from other animals of their own species to hoard it. There are no animals that will exploit other animals of their own species to hoard food or property. There are no animals that will legally claim a given territory as their own to the total exclusion of other animals of the same or different species—the territorial defense, so common among animals, is not a claim of property, but a claim of "living space," so that territorial animals chase others out of the territory that is an extension of their life, but they cannot lay a legal claim to that territory, nor can they inherit it to their progeny. Furthermore, among herbivorous species of animals there is almost no claim at all to territorial ownership—this territorial claim is more prevalent among those animals that feed on other animals (carnivorous). In essence, exploitation of one group of animals by others with the purpose of accumulating material things is not seen among animal species other than man. Therefore, greed, accumulation of material things, exploitation of the work of others, and the right to inheritance that are so prevalent in the capitalist system of production are not a product of *natural right*. The capitalist system, thus, is a product of the right of force, or the violence of the powerful, which is not *natural right*, not among rational beings.

We may, thus, speculate that at the dawn of humanity, people supplied for their own needs either individually or collectively, and all that was obtained either way was consumed either individually or collectively. There was no exploitation of man by man. But eventually, someone must have learned that it was more convenient to appropriate the work of others than to do the work themselves. This is the origin of greed. Of course, this acceptance of greed must have come naturally, something akin to the original sin, which means that man is naturally prone to evil, that man has an inclination to do what is evil. Yet, it is not easy to take someone else's property, or product of their hard work, without giving some kind of justification. At first, the only justification must have been force. The strong reigned and became the chief, the commander, and finally the king.

Humanity may be on the road to failure, but there is still a chance to change direction. Our failure stems from following the dictates of our ego. Our ego wants money and the things of this world, preferably without having to work for them. Our ego wants sex, pleasure, satisfaction, enjoyment, the good life, and more, and there is nothing wrong with this, as long as we get them by our own effort, or pay for them at our own expense. But our ego has no boundaries for what it wants, knows no limits to what it needs, and will do anything to get it. The capitalist system caters to our ego. The capitalist system is in a race to get it all, no matter what, even if we leave the dead corpses of other people behind. Morality appeases and restrains a little our actions, which otherwise would go overboard, but it doesn't stop us from doing what will lead to hoarding goods and pleasures. Western Civilization lost its way ever since the birth, and beyond the fall of the Roman Empire, and in spite of Jesus and the Christian doctrine. Can we change this trend?

We may, but we have to subdue our ego. And the only thing up to this job is the anima, if and only if the anima is armed with a strong spiritual shield. Ever since Buddha and Zoroaster, Muhammad and Jesus Christ, humanity had the opportunity to take the route of the anima instead of the route of the ego. If we continue to fail spiritually, then Armageddon is the only option left. The apocalyptic view of the end of the world is the result of our failure to correct our ways. If we don't straighten our path, apocalypse will signal the end of man. And yet, it doesn't have to happen that way. We can and should bring the City of God to the city of man. It all means that our efforts must be directed to produce what society needs, so that we may bring an end to poverty and suffering. To do this, we must derail our ego in its path to unlimited accumulation of riches, and use these riches to alleviate the suffering of the weak and the poor and the forlorn. This is the path of the spirit, the way of our anima that leads to a full implementation of the Principle of Love.

Therefore, the struggle is going to be almost insurmountable, because this world is populated by gigantic egos. The enormous egos of the religious authorities, of the secular authorities (presidents, leaders, princes, kings, governors), of the capitalists and potentates, of the people who yield power, of the military, are so blinding that it's going to take great efforts to control and combat them—even the power of the sword may be necessary to stop those egos from continuing to do harm, because they will continue to fight for their riches, for their privileges, for what they think they deserve.

After those people who lived in primitive communism learned to domesticate animals to help them produce their products of consumption, they later also learned to domesticate other men, and we will talk about this when we discuss the dog's gene. The result of the domestication of other men was more appropriation of the riches by a few who had claim to the means of production, mainly land. The final objects that we consume have nothing else in them that give them value, other than labor, human, animal or machine-aided labor. Intellectual labor is also part of the value, but not a tangible part. The capitalist system, the Holy Grail, was misused throughout centuries to enrich a few, in detriment of the most. Modern communism could not deal with capitalism, because it also had a rapacious nature. It is about time now that the rich give back what God meant to belong to everybody, and this has to be done with persuasion, not force.

As our topic here is greed, we will say that the difference between the British conquest and the Spanish conquest of America marked the difference between a venture led by greed, selfishness and inhumanity, and another venture led also by greed, and by a corrupted and bizarre humanism—the sincere, but utopian goal of Christianizing the New World envisioned by the Catholic Sovereigns of Spain. The result is the difference between the Anglos and the Latinos, and this makes the latter more prone to spirituality, rather than materiality. It doesn't make us more intelligent, but it takes us closer to *Homo spiritualis*, and thus, by an historic accident of illegal conquest, the Latinos have become the modern super-race of *mestizo* people. A super-race, but just potentially, and in the spiritual sense of the word.

8

ATHEIST MARXISM VERSUS THEIST MARXISM

Just when Karl Marx was thought to be history, his specter rises over the horizon of the rich nations to reclaim the past and present authenticity of contemporary Marxism. Communism is not dead; what's dead is the Soviet Communist model, which got lost in the interplay with the modern capitalist system of production. The two fatal errors of the Marxist theory are its atheism and its advocacy of violence to attain its objectives; in other words, its absence of love. The Dictatorship of the Proletariat became exactly what it is called, a nefarious dictatorship of the populace. The truth of the dictum "religion is the opium of the people" was transformed into a slogan of the uncontrolled masses in their way towards an authoritarian reign of terror. In the absence of love, hatred was its substitute, and hatred can never be the engine of social progress, nor can it be the ultimate criterion of justice. Love and hatred cannot dwell in the same individual without distorting everything he/she encounters, people and objects. Love of the people, the workers, the masses, the proletariat, is not love of humanity, because an important part of the human race is left out to be nurtured by and with hatred, mainly the so-called bourgeoisie, which in their turn manifest hatred for what they call the populace, the irrational, stupid and ignorant masses, the scum of social perversion, the communists.

Once Marxism is devoid of its atheist and violent elements, all the negative aspects of it also disappear. Since there is nobody to hate or to be hated by, there is no need to control people through a police state and censorship of the media, and since we all know what is good for the people, for humanity, there is no need to impose things and ordinances on anybody, except for the normal state apparatus to control delinquency and crime. Of course, there is always going to be dissidents, people who claim things for themselves that may be unreasonable, but we have been able to deal with these circumstances without the need to annihilate or destroy others. The forum for the resolution of issues is going to be the dialogue, and not the theatre of war. If this seems too simplistic, just picture a capitalist system without the need to exploit other people, or the sense of being exploited—in fact, these other people will long to be "exploited," because it all goes to the benefit of society. This non-violent theist Marxism blends into a capitalism with no capitalists in total control of the means of production—instead we will have able managers doing all they can to the benefit of the company—where all members of society will willingly be "exploited" so that others who cannot reap the fruits of human work and effort, for whatever reason, except a delinquent mentality, can have a loaf of bread to eat.

It's not the same thing to have a state company where the sense of proprietorship is lost than to have a company that we feel is ours because we know that some of the benefits of the company in the form of profits will go towards the betterment of the workers themselves, or to a directed social program that will benefit the poor and the disadvantaged. Marxism, especially as it was implemented in Cuba and Nicaragua, did not fail exclusively because of the errors of the Marxist ideology—and we mentioned before violence, atheism and imposition of the will of others on the general population—but because of the enormous and merciless economic blockade of the most powerful capitalist nation in the world, the United States of America. This blockade was nothing but economic aggression. We will never know how far the Cuban model would have gone (advanced) in its progress towards socialism without the US pressure on the Cuban government and economy, as we will never know whether or not the Nicaraguan communist example would ever have succeeded without the pressure of the *contras* and the pressure of the US Empire. As for the Soviet model, it failed because it lacked the necessary incentives to increase productivity to a level that only a capitalist system can raise. In other words, destroying the capitalist machinery of production to substitute it for a slow and inefficient and impersonal machinery of the state was a terrible blunder of the Marxist ideology that led to the demise of the Soviet Empire. The Chinese managed to avoid the mistakes of the Soviets, and have made of their economy one of the fastest growing economies of the world, and not precisely because it is a communist economy, but because it is capitalism in the works with state control and supervision. In essence, we can say that Marxism is well and kicking, and the time has come to transform the ugly face of Marxism—the true ugly face, and the one created by the capitalist propaganda—into the face of a humanitarian system in which basically the "owner" of the company is interested in making it produce for the benefit of the other "owners"—the workers—who will feel compelled to give all of themselves so that the profits get reinvested in other capitalist ventures managed by, say, God Enterprises.

The Marxist analysis of the capitalist system is still valid, because it is a dissection of the misuse of one of the most powerful engines of production. It is not capitalism in itself what's evil, but the misappropriation of the surplus value of the work of men to the benefit of the capitalist. What is needed now is to make the system work for the people, for the proletariat, for the workers, for the scum of the social matrix, not by snatching the property of those who misappropriated wealth, but by turning the little wealth we have into more and vaster sources of wealth. This in turn will leave the capitalist without the steam to increment his riches, and in the gambit of the capitalist system of production, it will eventually bankrupt him, or else will force him to join God Enterprises, submitting to the new rules of the game. And all this for humanity, for the benefit of humanity, including the populace and the capitalist, who, will eventually understand that his ego misled him into believing that accumulation of riches was the source of his earthly salvation.

Therefore, any new communist society must work hard to avoid the common mistakes of the old brand of communism: violence, atheism, totalitarianism, control of both society and the economy, and control of the press. Violence and confrontation impedes growth, since some of the resources of society must be invested in the army and police, while they could have been invested in other social programs. Society cannot afford to be squabbling with dissidents at every level and every corner of the nation. What's going to drown capitalism is not confiscation of their assets, but free and unbridled competition, and I don't think the capitalist can survive a competitive economic fight against those enterprises—like God Enterprises—that would be managed in perfect harmony by both their owners and their workers.

9

GOD ENTERPRISES AND THE HEAVENLY ORDER

Thus, the heavenly order will be found in the workings of God Enterprises and the Orbis Unum Party, both of which are visible entities of the social order that quiver and pulsate in the midst of the *continuum*. The Fraternity of the Templars is somewhat more diffused in its consistency as a link between these organizations and the society envisioned by the Templars, which stands to be protected by them. You may think this is old utopia, but it's not, because it has been brought into reality before, in more or less similar terms, although not as a result of the Templars' idea of a heavenly—and thus, spiritually charged—social order. As I said in the introduction to this book, the heavenly order works the material world through the *continuum*, and it never matters how good or bad we view the results of the work of the *continuum*—for we always look at them as a partial and limited work of God, or *Opus Dei*—because the real picture, the ample view of what's going on in the *continuum* follows and obeys the purposes and intentions of God, which are always good. We are limited to visualize just a tiny fraction of the workings of the *continuum*, and the work of God will only be seen and understood in its totality by superior spiritual beings, perhaps other than *Homo spiritualis*.

We will describe here how the City of God fits in the city of man. In order to do that we must recall Saint Augustine's concept of the City of God as a spiritual entity embedded in the city of man. In other words, Saint Augustine's City of God is in the realm of the spirit and, thus, invisible in the environment in which we live, which is the realm of matter and the physical world. But let's visualize a little bit the City of God by giving to Augustine's spiritual vision of a heavenly order a more earthly form, that is, by adding to the spiritual city the characteristics of a human social and economic order. We will say that the City of God is just like any of our big metropolis, except that in our ideal city there is no crime, and there is no poverty like we experience in our earthly cities. The City of God is a city where people are completely ignorant of negative human passions like greed, ambition, selfishness, and the pursuit of profits or earnings. It's a city filled with love, and if there is love, there is no sin, and without sin, there can't be hell—in other words, it's a mansion of the spirits (angels) both in heaven and in earth, and this last part is not contradictory, because in the world of the spirit there are no contradictions. It is, then, a city where there is no currency, because people can willingly take all they need from the supermarkets and grocery stores, and there is no need to pay for the things they require for the sustenance of life. And since there is no currency, there are no banks. Every human necessity is duly covered in the City of God, including education, health, food and shelter. But people still have to work in order to produce the things they consume, because there is going to be no manna from heaven in the City of God. Since we said that the population of the City of God is completely devoid of selfishness and greed, everyone does his forty hours a week of productive and efficient work, and even more, and there is no salary to be paid, because there is no need for money, given that everyone can stop at a grocery store, or gas station, and get what they need "for free."

In this the City of God, human labor is valued by what everyone can get to cover their basic human necessities, which means that the work of the laborer and the work of the NASA space engineer are valued the same. Let's not forget that in this society there is no selfishness, and the NASA engineer is not going to be offended if his work is valued the same as the work of a construction worker. This concept was to Karl Marx the ultimate principle of communism, since society gets "From each according to their ability," and it gives "to each according to their needs." Marx was such an idealist, and yet he claimed to be a tough materialist.

The next step for us is to envision this City of God where companies get the things they need from other companies, and nobody pays for anything. The products they make are shipped to other companies, so they can be distributed to the consumer, and still they don't get paid for the services they provide. This is an ideal city where everyone knows what to do, and everyone does their work without the intervention of money. It is a city just like our cities, except that we never get to see the money transactions, because there is no need for money to transact operations, or to assemble the material for the production of goods. Something similar happens with the provision of services. If we get sick, all we have to do is to walk into a clinic and get medical help, without paying anything for the services rendered; next, we go to the pharmacy, get our medicine, and expect to get well soon so that we can return to be productive human beings as soon as possible. Since this is a snapshot of an ideal city, we will not talk about how things got built, and where everything to build them was obtained. Just think of a modern city and delete from your vision of this modern city everything that has to do with money transactions, in such a way that the complete formal operation of the city never stops. Extending this ideal society beyond our borders, and spreading its modus operandi around the world, the execution of all the economic transactions in the world would be made in a similar fashion. We would send cars to other countries, and they would give us back coffee and sugar. One more thing, in the City of God the counterparts of Bill Gates, Warren Buffet, Carlos Slim, Ingvar Kamprad, Lakshmi Mittal and other multi-billionaires, would be the archangels of efficient production and accumulation of capital (in the form of physical assets), except that they would be owners of nothing, wouldn't have a penny in the bank, or own any stocks, because in the City of God there is no money, banks or stocks. Their selfless contribution to this ideal society would be in the form of ideas, inventions, and proficient, effective, and productive new ways of making things, or providing services.

But there are going to be a few more things absent from the City of God, in addition to money and currency. There will be no banks and financial institutions, and there would be no need for insurance companies, and no stock markets. Inflation would be unknown, because things don't have a monetary price, and because there are no banks to loan/borrow money. If there is a need to build a new factory, no problem, we don't need the banks for a loan; all we have to do is order the things we need to build the factory and bring new workers from the pool of labor that would be constantly changing. The concept of private property doesn't exist in the City of God, except perhaps personal property like clothing, shoes, toiletry, etc. And since there is no property, there is nothing to be inherited to our children. I don't need to own a house, because if I must move to a new job, I also have to move to a house closer to my job. I may need a car if the City of God lacks efficient public transportation, but even a car doesn't need to be "mine." The government in the City of God would operate exactly as any private company. It would just order the things it needs, and it would provide the government services free of charge—come to think of it, there may even be no need of government as such.

In essence, the City of God is a complete and total utopia. Given that the City of God resembles so much the Marxist view of communism, Marxism was and is also an utopia, especially because Marxism promotes violence as the mover towards the ideal society; it also promotes the forceful seizure of private property, henceforth declaring it common property of a socialist society. Another assumption that turned out to be wrong in Marxism is that the new society was going to be populated by unselfish workers eager to build the ultimate egalitarian society, and those persons with the ideas to produce, invent, and innovate (the capitalists) would be well buried under seven feet of dirt.

We now come back to the real world. The City of God is a model, an ideal, and as a model, blueprint, or ideal of things to come, it is an utopia. But even if our social objectives are utopian, we can move our present social order towards that utopist dream without making our actual efforts towards the utopia an utopia itself. And this is why The Fraternity of the Templars, God Enterprises and the Orbis Unum Party will continue its work of bringing to fruition the City of God in the city of man, though we know it is going to take long for the city of man to morph into what would be a caricature of what we envision the heavenly order to be. But there is also the other model, the one we actually follow in our present days. This other model presses on with the concept of private property, with the continuous production of goods following the capitalist system as such, so that in a future, we will be so efficient and productive, that even the least-paid workers will be able to cover their basic necessities of life. Society then would be bipolar in the sense that on the one hand, we will have the very few millionaires and billionaires, and on the other hand, we will have the "poor," more accurately described as non-millionaires—that in the ideal capitalist world, in the pure capitalist system envisioned by its economists, will be made mainly of the middle class. The perfect utopian capitalist system of production will have no impoverished, miserable workers, just a vast middle class living a comfortable life, and a tiny number of privileged businessmen and entrepreneurs living the perfect life. This capitalist system is promoted by the two political parties we already know in the United States. The Democrats, being a little bit lenient, will go for more social programs and social aid, better wages for the workers, and for a bit more equalitarian society, while the Republicans will continue pressing on with capital, the sanctity of the private property, self-sufficiency, non-intervention of the state in the process of production, total absence of taxes (if at all possible), etc. But, whether Republican or Democrat, the trend will be the same, the march of society towards more and stronger capitalism. In this capitalist system, the essence of greed will probably be the highest of virtues, but the word 'greed'—soon to be replaced by the 'g-word'—will be erased of the realm of business and production, where profit margins, capital earnings, or investment profits represent a better terminology for the ever constant search of labor plus-value, which represents the same thing as the harvest of greed.

Before we go to the next section, we may ask whether or not it is possible to live in a money-less society, meaning a society that can do away with cash transactions, thus making of currency and the circulation of money an anachronism. If you think that's impossible, think again. I, for my part, have been able to care for my basic necessities almost without carrying in my pocket any cash at all. My paycheck is deposited in my bank account, I can pay almost all my bills online using the Internet, and I can also buy a lot of things I need, again, using the Internet. I can buy gas, groceries, clothing, etc. using my bankcard, and there is barely anything I wouldn't do without using the so-called 'plastic money.' If we imagine a society where every business and commercial transaction is done through bank accounts, and credit or debit cards, you are imagining the embryo of the City of God in the city of man I mentioned before. In fact, even the IRS in the United States collects most of the government revenues (mostly income tax) through online transactions and bank account transfers that reflect money figures (basically numbers) without the use of actual currency. Now, if we can further imagine a society with abundant production of goods and services, and salaries that cover (for all of us) more than the basic necessities of life—we can even throw in some moderately expensive luxury items—we are getting closer and closer to the City of God, because then, if we can always spend less than what we generate in the production process, there is no need to keep an account of our revenues and expenses, there is also no need for us to use currency to cover our needs, and society could very well do away without currency, without money, and without banks. We may be one millennium away from such a society, but as of today, we can see the rudimentary workings of it in the myriad of money-less transfers and transactions kept by banks, especially through the use of the Internet.

Next, we examine how there have been some very rough sketches or experiments on the formation of microscopic companies that approximately resemble God Enterprises' companies. These are part of my own life experience.

Carlos Pasos and the PAYCO Textile Factory

Something that worked and functioned like one of God Enterprises was already operated in the 1940's by a rich Nicaraguan entrepreneur called Carlos Pasos. Mr. Pasos built a textile factory in the Western outskirts of the city of Managua, and with the factory he also built housing for his workers. I know this, because I was born and lived in one of those houses, house number 10 at the Colonia Pasos. My mother and my uncles used to work for Mr. Pasos' textile company, and they were assigned housing at subsidized rent; they also got subsidized water and electricity. These houses were exceedingly good by the Nicaraguan standards of the forties, since they had plumbing, electricity, running water and sewage system. They also had bedroom areas, a kitchen area and a living room, in addition to an ample backyard where we used to raise chickens. And anybody who worked for Mr. Pasos could rent a house like this at subsidized prices. This was a nice small community where all people knew each other, since we were all members of the Pasos family.

The Pasos factory-housing complex also had a medical clinic for the workers and their families, a *comisariato*, or consumer cooperative to buy retail products of first necessity at wholesale prices, an elementary school, and a sports field, so that people would play baseball in the evenings and over the weekends.

I don't think Mr. Pasos knew anything like God Enterprises, Marxism or any other ideology. His idea came spontaneously out of his *de facto* willingness to help people. At the end, Mr. Pasos went into exile to Costa Rica for his opposition to the Somoza regime, and the project Payco disappeared, but it left a blueprint in my mind of what a productive company can do for its workers—especially since Mr. Pasos proved that it could also be good for him as a capitalist and investor. Mr. Pasos was far from being a philanthropist, he just did what he thought was fair for his workers, and good for his business. He did what the *continuum* made him to do.

The Fabretto Foundation

Before touching on the Fabretto Foundation, let me briefly talk about the company I work for at the time of writing this book. It's not anything close to a GEnte company, but it has a nice little feature that makes it interesting. It is said that Mr. James D. Pitcock, the owner of Williams Brothers Construction Co., plans to give 45% of its assets to the workers in the form of a profit sharing and retirement plan. This, in fact, makes some of the workers who have been long enough with this company, owners of a good percentage of its assets. The workers like very much the profit sharing program, and they feel and act as if they are in fact co-owners of the company. In the Introduction to this book I explained how I met Mr. Robert Jones, and how I assimilated from him the concept of the *continuum*.

A quasi-religious corporation worth mentioning is the Fabretto Foundation, based in Nicaragua. This Foundation is a true God Enterprise. Father Rafael María Fabretto was an Italian priest who moved to Nicaragua with the purpose of opening and managing an orphanage. I lived in 1955 in Father Fabretto's orphanage called Oratorio Festivo San Juan Bosco, located in Somoto, Nicaragua. It was a catastrophic failure. Father Fabretto's experiment almost killed me, together with other kids who were rescued at the brink of starvation. Ironically, it was Anastasio Somoza (the father, the first member of the Somoza dynasty) who saved our lives, thanks to an invitation to visit the Oratorio given to him by Father Fabretto. When Somoza saw the dismal conditions of the children in the school, he panicked and ordered the removal of most of the children, mainly the ones who were not orphans, in less than 24 hours. The *continuum* works in marvelous ways; just picture a hated, soft-hearted tyrant being impacted by the sight of more than 300 children starving to death. I bet his conscience screamed to his inner ears that he was going to be blamed if some of those children were to die, especially since Somoza himself had donated the "school" grounds of the Oratorio, which were actually the remnants of a concentration camp that his government had reserved for the Germans living in Nicaragua during World War II, and which was never used for that purpose. Somoza was moved by the *continuum* to do what is atypical of dictators, an act of love.

I remember one day at the Oratorio—and this was always the same struggle every day—that the claw of hunger was clutching my stomach, when another kid gave me a secret: "Go upstairs, knock on the door, and tell Father Fabretto that you are hungry. He will give you some food." I did as the child told me, Father Fabretto's sister opened the door and I said: "I'm hungry." From inside the living room, the Father told his sister to let me in, and give me some food. She gave me a plate of steamed rice with butter and a tortilla, and went back to the kitchen. I was busy eating at a corner table, when I heard Father Fabretto sobbing uncontrollably. I was eating to my heart's content, so my semblance must have changed from terribly sad to somewhat satisfied. Father Fabretto was at the dinner table with both of his hands covering his face, I walked up to him, tapped on his shoulder, and asked: "Why are you crying, Father?"—my mouth must have been smeared with grains of rice and butter, and who knows, maybe I even had the looks of a surprised, but content child. He looked up at me, and said: "I don't know. Don't mind me, son. Perhaps I am a wussy priest"—"No lo sé. No me hagas caso, hijo. Tal vez soy un cura llorón." His faith was crumbling, and now I know that the *continuum* sent him a message . . . and he got it. Like in the film "Quo vadis?," when St. Peter was fleeing Rome, the child suddenly stops and tells him "Where are you going?," and St. Peter immediately understands the meaning of the question, turns around and returns to Rome, the *continuum* had told Father Fabretto to get busy and go to work. Shortly after that incident, there was much food in the Oratorio: fruits, vegetables, cookies and candies, and even meat, but for those of us who were not orphans, we were getting close to go home, since Somoza was scheduled to visit the school within a few days.

Almost 30 years later, around 1984, when the Sandinistas were in power, I had an encounter with an old man, the same Father Fabretto I had known in my childhood—he was always perspiring due to the unforgiving climate of Nicaragua, unshaven, wearing an old faded black robe that hung down to his ankles, worn-out shoes—except that this time he was missing almost all his front teeth, and was much older. But things were different this time, his beloved orphans looked very well-fed and decently dressed (they even wore an uniform), he was driving a fairly good, almost brand new, 4-wheel drive Toyota pick-up, and was supervising the unloading, at the local government coffee purchasing depot, of the coffee bean bags that they had picked up that day—I was also in the business of growing coffee, and I was selling the pick of coffee beans of the day. Ironically, the government of Daniel Ortega had granted the Fabretto Foundation a coffee plantation that had been owned by the Somoza family. Father Fabretto devised the idea that his children would work the coffee plantation, and the money collected from the sale of the product would be used to buy food, and to pay for the cost of maintaining a school in the farm, where Father Fabretto had included the idea of also caring for landless peasants. Even more, Father Fabretto had been the founder of the town of San José de Cusmapa in Northern Nicaragua, a town wholly set up on the basis of cooperative peasant work, rather than charity donations. Just like I said before, the *continuum* works in strange, marvelous and miraculous ways. Even the Sandinistas got shaken by the works of the *continuum*.

The Continuum and Rationality

We have connected above several situations (that otherwise would appear disconnected) by making reference to the *continuum*, and this requires talking a little bit about human rationality. Anything that cannot be explained within the bounds of human reason is deemed to be irrational. Therefore, the universe of phenomena that requires explanation can be divided into three spheres of possible investigation: the sphere of rational things, the sphere of irrational things, and the sphere of supra-rational things (for all practical purposes, this last sphere is also irrational to scientific endeavor). Science deals with rational things, and whatever doesn't fit the world of reasonable behavior is considered to be irrational, which is why animals would do things that humans wouldn't do. Spirituality deals with things supra-rational that for science are beyond the limits of rationality, and are, therefore, irrational. That's why faith and the practice of meditation are irrational to science. In essence, to a rational mind, whoever oversteps the upper limits of rationality is irrational, just like whoever oversteps the lower bounds of rationality is also thought to be irrational. But this division of the world into three spheres of possible (rational) investigation is dictated by human whim on the basis of human reason, and may be totally artificial, which means that the world may be supra-rational in its entirety (in its totality)—that is, as if viewed or considered as a total entity—and this supra-rationality that I call the *continuum* (and very often is irrationality to us) would require a subject, an actor or a doer, mainly God.

In the examples given above, I have seen purpose where there seems to be no purpose-er (where there seems to be no subject of the stated purpose). This is something we frequently see in scientific investigations. It is said that an octopus mimics the environment for two purposes (not *purposes in mind*, because we have determined that octopuses don't think rationally): One is to appear invisible to predators, and the other is to appear invisible to pray. Science goes on to explain that this is a product of evolution, that this is a biological process developed over thousands, probably millions of years; that this is the work of Nature. In other words, science tells us that there is an insensitive (non-feeling), non-conscious, irrational, non-thinking purpose-er, i.e. Nature, that does things purposely. This scientific explanation of biological phenomena breaks down all rationality, because we are pairing a purpose with a non-thinking purpose-er, which is Nature, and axiomatically, we know that where there is a purpose, there must be a conscious, thinking purpose-er. Other non-scientific minds would argue that since there is a purpose, there must be a purpose-er that thought everything out perfectly, and this thinking, feeling, conscious purpose-er is God, and, therefore, there is Intelligent Design at work in Nature. The problem with this last argument is that this purpose-er, which is God, is invisible to us, and thus, non-acceptable to scientific explanation. Also, the justification of the purpose by the "presence" of an invisible, living, thinking purpose-er, presents an additional problem, we are extrapolating our rationality to include in our explanations what ought to explain our own existence—we are giving *existence* to a spiritual entity that really *is*, and we are doing this by transposing our rationality to God who may not have an attribute of rationality, not anything as lowly as human rationality, anyway. In Other words, we are overstepping the boundaries of our reason by giving reason, or the capacity to think rationally—just like we do—to God, and this is anthropomorphism. Hence, the only thing that we can reasonably do (and I am using here the word reasonably, not rationally) is to talk metaphorically, and say that the mind of God is manifested in the *continuum*. And, unlike God, the *continuum* can be named, and we can use as one of its names the word Nexus.

[And since we touched on this subject, we might as well digress a little bit. It does not matter what we name the *continuum*, as long as we invoke it with its name. Christians use the name of Jesus to connect with God, but non-Christians can very well use the word Nexus. Now, bear in mind that it is important to invoke the name, and at the same time perform an action to stir the *continuum* into the process of complying with our request. This is called ritual. Again, some Christians will make the sign of the cross to either request a miracle, or ask for protection against evil; others will just raise their hands towards heavens. The Knights Templars in the past used the name Baphomet to invoke the *continuum*, because they thought the name of Jesus was too holy to be used for mundane purposes. They did use the name of Jesus, but only for extreme requests, or under extreme circumstances. Modern Templars cannot use the name Baphomet, because it was soiled and contaminated during the trial processes held against the Templars, so following the Templars' costume, we will invoke the *continuum* with the word Nexus, and under extreme circumstances, with the name of Jesus our Lord, followed by the sign of the cross.]

The problem with anthropomorphic assignment of attributes to God is that we run into difficulties when trying to explain why something irrational (something that our human reasoning deems irrational) happens to us. If a flood kills 200,000 people in Indonesia, we immediately think that God did something irrational, and begin to think that perhaps God is not as good as we think. Otherwise we reason that the flood must have been caused by the devil, in which case God could not stop the works of the devil, and God is not that all-powerful after all. We may even think that God doesn't care what happens to humanity, and thus, lets natural disasters happen at the will of Nature, or else is punishing the Indonesians for whatever bad deeds may be attributable to the victims of the flood. Anthropomorphism assigns the same weaknesses of humans to God, and weakens our faith in spiritual things. Therefore, we should opt for the concept of the *continuum* to explain God's deeds, and keep in mind that our rationality is not always in synch with God's supra-rationality, which means that what we see as God's purpose may not have the same moral qualifier that it has for us humans. Again, speaking metaphorically, God's purposes and intentions, manifested in the workings of the *continuum*, may have different (though higher) moral qualifiers than what we see in our limited view of even the smallest chunk of God's actions in the *continuum*.

We sometimes wonder why we can't communicate directly with God, especially when the Christian doctrine explicitly recommends doing it through Jesus Christ, who is our intermediary with God the Father. We cannot talk to God, because God is a spiritual being whom we can't even name, less communicate with Him; but we can do it through Jesus Christ, who is and was a physical manifestation of God, and thus, is God; or we can do it through the Nexus, which is the Holy Ghost, the active manifestation of the works of God in the *continuum*.

Just as we assign human attributes to God, we must be careful with assigning non-human, or rather inhuman, attributes to other living beings. When we observe the irrational acts of a monkey, we measure the animal's intelligence against our own, which we narcissistically deem to be better, or of a higher quality. But we don't know that. We don't know if the monkey is the result of an evolutionary process that has passed through something similar to what we are, and the monkey is in reality an animal better suited to cope with changes in nature than we are. We measure the rationality of other living creatures as if what the world filters through our sense perceptions represents the standard of good or better. We don't really know if ants live a happier (to use yet another anthropomorphism) more civilized life than humans, and we probably will never know—even if they are sometimes sprayed with insecticide, as we sometimes are hit by storms, earthquakes, and other natural catastrophes. We tend to forget that the *continuum* works in very compartmentalized ways, and it doesn't ever tell us what it doesn't want us to know. The secrets of the *continuum* are called mysteries, and we don't have the capacity—because we were not given that capacity—to decode some of those mysteries.

This mirroring of human qualities towards the rest of the universe, which is very typical with the concept of human rationality, also happens with the Darwinian concept of evolution. We think of evolution as something that always goes forward, from bad to good to better. There is no devolution or retro-evolution. If an animal manages to get out of the sea and learns to crawl on the surface of the earth, is only because it evolved, and if it learns to fly, is only because it evolved further, always for the better. "Evolving" and "better" being anthropomorphic narcissisms that permit low forms of life to move up in the human scale of the (better) path to evolution, towards *Homo sapiens*, the apex of natural progression from bad to best. It never occurred to evolutionists that perhaps the better end-results of the sequential strings of life changes lead to some other form of animal life, and not precisely to the human species. We look for intelligent civilizations in outer space with the hope that we will communicate with them, and this is another anthropomorphic narcissistic idea, as if their "intelligence" will ever be in synch with our intelligence. How do we know that they are not going to look at us just like we look at cockroaches or microbes, or the other way around? How do we know that they (or we) will ever break the communication barrier that there is bound to be among species of animals so different from each other?

The Miracle of Miracles

In order to attain the City of God in the city of man, we have to spark the greatest of all collective miracles. We said before that in order to achieve an objective (worked in the realm of the spirit) we have to start the chain of actions that will lead to the miracle. We mention prayer as one avenue of stimulating God's will to perform the miracle, but in many instances it takes more than prayer; we have to "help ourselves, so that God can help us." What this means is that we have to lead the actions—which in any case will be minimal—that will spark the miracle. John's apocalyptic view of the final triumph of good over evil will be conducted in the spiritual realm, which is the substratum of our earthly triumph over evil in the material world. The miracle consists in making humanity start the actions (together with prayer) so that in the world of the spirit, good will prevail over evil, and this will be reflected in our reality, with good prevailing over evil in this our physical world. Once this miracle of miracles is produced, the transition of man from the world of the flesh to the world of the spirit will be smooth and painless, and we will have conquered death. This is the symbol of the ascension of Christ in soul and body to the heavenly quarters.

10

ORBIS UNUM, THE GLOBALIZATION OF MAN

The pre-history of humanity starts with an animal in the process of becoming *Homo sapiens*. Right at the brink of leaving behind the animal kingdom proper, men probably lived in small groups of individuals related by kinship or family ties. At this stage of human development, there must have been some sort of hierarchical organization among the members of the group, just as it happens with higher species of animals, but nobody is yet superior to anyone else. This pecking system is dictated by the need to survive as a species. Whatever the group of individuals obtains is distributed equally among the different members of the clan. In the meantime, the ego begins to develop naturally, and as the ego appears in some of the hominids, the anima also makes its debut. Conflict between the ego and the anima is inevitable, because the biological man continues to be an animal, and will try to satisfy his animal needs, while the spiritual man would relate his existence to the being of the tribe or the clan as a whole, and will create little by little a spiritual code of moral behavior (spiritual values for the benefit of the group). Man's ego will only care about the biological system that includes his immediate family, and will only care for himself and his immediate relatives as an extension of the individual. The father (patriarch) or the mother (matriarch) becomes the boss, and there is transmission and succession of command that goes from the top boss to other secondary foci of authority.

A clan looks to another clan as a source of free labor through the appropriation (stealing) of their property, or of the objects they make, and eventually through the appropriation of individuals of the foreign clan and the use of those individuals' forced labor for production or servitude, without paying for the extorted work obtained; this constitutes the beginnings of slavery. Wealth accumulates and the ego

---

163

grows. This development happens in all societies making the shift from irrational animals to *Homo sapiens*. The ego cannot sustain itself without the feeling of greed, and greed drives men to invent the concept of property, which must be inheritable if it is going to remain in the possession of an individual whose extension is his progeny. This involves also the invention of legislation to regulate the appropriation, transfer, use, and disposal of property. Civilization is born, and the system of production has to be justified philosophically with the help of religion and myth. The king becomes a god, or somebody imposed by the gods, and the priests and the aristocracy that surrounds the king become the perpetuators of the myth of the divine origin of authority and social control. The servant must obey the dictates of the ruler, no matter what the ruler orders. The greatest evil of humanity—which is also the greatest invention for the free exchange of products—money, begins to circulate, first as a necessary means of exchanging things, and eventually as a mask for robbery, extortion and exploitation.

The reign of the duality ego-greed in humanity makes its presence for the first time and will not subside even to our present days. The path to spirituality is only contemplated as a tool to bond man to the new society. This human bondage to the new order will be reinforced by culture, art, religion, myth, and other coercive social controls like the army, police, the judicial system, etc. Prophets may appear to attempt to rectify the situation, trying to make things right in the new social order. But the ego reigns, and the prophets are absorbed into the new system in such a way that they become useful to keep society under the bondage of the king, the rulers, or the group of rulers that control society (the oligarchy).

But there are prophets with a great vision to see what's going to happen, and predict that this city of man is eventually going to fall apart by itself, and give way to a new era ruled by the spirit or anima (the City of God) that will make humanity prosper indefinitely in time, or God will have to scrap his "experiment" with humanity through the apocalyptic destruction of the world, and the final judgment of men. Whenever this happens, and if it ever happens, we are admonished that the game for humanity will be certainly over. But man's ego is stubborn, it will remain deaf to all warnings, and it will continue its rampant search for newly invented pleasures that eventually will be transformed into necessities. And even if we manage to make things correctly, and open up an era of abundance for humanity, the process towards uprightness can only be advanced after a final spiritual battle against the forces of darkness in spiritual Armageddon, when the ego will be finally defeated, and the march of humankind headed for the city of God will continue, until we eventually see the beginnings of the system of the City of God in the city of man, which is the path to divinity and pure spirituality, ushering a time of happiness for everyone, but only after the final destruction of the forces of the ego. Mind you, there will be some irreducible egos that will march into the final battle and perish. This has been already contemplated by the prophets, and brings about the importance of the Knight Templar, or the monk-warrior, that will have to confront the forces of evil, represented by the system of the ego-greed that has dominated society up to our present times.

One of the most important aspects of the process of globalization (or humanization) of man consists in giving to each individual the respect that we all deserve as members of the family of *Homo sapiens*, a necessary step for the transition from being members of the animal kingdom to being members of the spiritual kingdom, so that we can be akin to the great spiritual minds of humankind, like Jesus Christ, Moses, Buddha, the Saints of the Catholic Church, the prophets, if not akin to heavenly beings, like angels, spirit guides, and sages. Contemporary man is just like any other animal, except that he has been able to acquire a better knowledge of the world, discovered and invented science, and thus deserves to be classified as *Homo sapiens*. And yet, spiritually, he is closer to *Homo neanderthalis* than to *Homo spiritualis*. We constantly display all the traits we see in other species of animals, among others: territoriality, aggressiveness, selfishness, rapaciousness, implacability, cruelty, lasciviousness, and other negative characteristics. It's only within our closest social conglomerate that we sometimes display feelings of love, but these sparks of human sanity are obscured by the immense night of human avarice in our further relations with other human beings outside our circle of family and friends.

To say that it is in the nature of man to display territoriality, and thus, that it is a drive justified by *natural law*, because we observe the same behavior in animals, is to try to justify, or rationalize, a conscious regression to the animal kingdom. Nationalism and national pride, and its associated relatives: chauvinism, racism, Zionism and Messianism—the belief that a group of people, a race, an ethnia, are chosen by God (or by natural selection) to dominate or to lead the world by means of physical force, or to be set apart from the rest of humanity by a higher intellect, higher set of moral values, or by some other lofty characteristics—are at the root of the wars among different groups of people within a country, or among different groups of countries within a region. This primitive appetite for territory, or its proxy, the so-called "sphere of influence," is what divides the world into countries, confronts one country against another for disputed chunks of land, and is partially responsible for the imperialist domination of the one country that grows stronger than others, and forcefully extends its boundaries to include the territory of smaller or weaker countries. It makes one nation enslave other nations and their peoples. All this dominance is accompanied with violence, aggressiveness, cruelty, and the desire to destroy others, leading to the practice of genocide. There are also some small groups of people who try to change the life of the poor through charity, but their efforts, though commendable and important, get shadowed by the more powerful forces of those who want to conquer and subdue humanity by force.

And whenever we are not occupied with war, the instrument to create wealth, the capitalist system of production, is misused to the detriment of the majority of the people of the world. We know the consequences brought about by avarice, selfishness, and rapaciousness. We know what the richest and most powerful country of the world can do to protect its "national interests," which necessarily include "national security," and this is ultimately the interest and security of one nation, disregarding, disrespecting, and dismissing the interest and security of other nations. *Homo sapiens* has ruled that might and force makes right; in Spanish we call this principle "la ley del más fuerte," i.e. "the law of the strongest," often justified on the basis of natural or divine law—*lex naturalis* or *lex divinitas*—when there is nothing in the nature of man that comes from God establishing that the strongest should rule over the weak. Much to the contrary, in the book of Genesis we are told that man will rule and have dominion over the living and non-living creatures of the world—man, meaning every man, not just one particular man, or one particular group of men. The said book doesn't say anything about men having dominion over other men, which rules out slavery and oppression of one group of people over others. Let's next make a brief historical outline of how man came to be an enemy of man.

It is said that the first modern men originated in east-central Africa and spread all over the world in about some 50,000 years. We are talking here about *Homo sapiens*. On his way to populate the world, and after hundreds of generations followed one another, *Homo sapiens* differentiated and changed in response to the diverse climates and geophysical conditions encountered in his way around the globe, in a process of adaptation that gave origin to the multiple human races. Strangely enough, it was in the Americas, mainly in Mexico, Central and South America, that the different races of men mingled together, thanks to what happened in Europe at the end of the 15th century—immediately before and during the Spanish conquest—mainly the re-conquest of the Spanish peninsula from the hands of the Moors. The Spaniards that came to America had already inherited a mixture of the different race components inhabiting the Iberian Peninsula, including the Spanish people proper, Arabs, and Jews, and when they came to the newly discovered continent, they also intermingled with the Indians and the blacks, enriching their blood lineage in the so-called native *mestizos* of America. Something tells me that the mestizo gene-brew is more favorable than the genes just coming from a pure blood lineage—but then, I may be wrong. This symbolically represented the integration of humanity in the peoples of America. We feel that by having these different gene configurations mixed into one gene-soup of American *mestizos*, man came back to his origin. This is what we want for all peoples of the world. We need to come back to our origins. We can say, then, that humanity originated in east-central Africa, enriched its gene pool as it spread all over the world, and had a first re-encounter in the American continent. We hope to have more re-encounters, but even if this isn't possible, there is no reason why humanity cannot make the entire world the place of its final gathering, if only in the sense of peacefully cohabiting the planet, with the implementation of an economic order based on the classical capitalist system, and modeled by God Enterprises and the Orbis Unum Party, under the leadership of the Fraternity of the Templars.

And yet the final human re-encounter is not enough. The dark-skinned people have to do a search of soul before we can heal our psychological wounds, and the white people also have to do a search of soul before they can be conscious of their past generational culpability that requires redemption. The meaning of this is that one group of people, the majority, must forgive, and the other group of people, the historical oppressors, a white minority, must repent. This implies that before we can reach any level of human integration, we first have to recognize the problems that human domination of one group of men over others have created, especially the unconscious scars that it left on the dark-skinned races, since it was the white man who dominated them for almost the whole of human history. I am talking here about racism, discrimination and its sequel, the exploitation of man by man. In the rest of this book I am forced to establish a conceptual separation between the white man and the dark-skinned man, and view them as historical oppressor and oppressed, respectively, which is going to be uncomfortable (and maybe even offensive) especially to the white man, who would like to see racial conflict as a problem already substantially resolved. Yet, we still suffer the consequences of past and present forceful domination of one group of people against another, and the dominators still happen to be mostly white, while the dominated still happen to be mostly dark-skinned.

The Dog's Gene

Here I use the expression the "dog's gene" to describe the behavior that reflects total submission and servile attitudes of one individual towards another individual, especially if there is no reason for such behavior. The "master's gene" is the dog's gene counterpart manifested as the tendency to control and enslave other people. If the dog's gene and the master's gene are not biological entities, they are at least psychological attitudes deeply implanted in the inner beings of certain groups of people: the master's gene, for the white people; the dog's gene, for the dark-skinned people. Granted that slavery was abolished long ago, the sequels and the consequences of such forceful domination are still fresh in both the oppressed and the oppressor for the related attitudes to disappear—we must remember that in the USA hardly six generations have passed since the abolition of slavery. The conquest of the American Indians started a bit more than five hundred years ago, but both slavery and conquest have been going on for millennia, so the rooting of both the dog's gene and the master's gene have had plenty of time to take hold of both the conquered and the conqueror, respectively. The dog's gene should not be confused with plain servility, given that the latter is practiced on the expectation of a reward or an advantage. The dog's gene implies total submissiveness without necessarily the expectation of a recompense or something in return.

If you think of this talk of the dog's gene and the master's gene preposterous, just read some current literature about the psychological problems some people go through under a situation of dominion/submission: The kidnapped eventually submits to and identifies with the kidnapper; torturers eventually overrule their moral upbringing, making them enjoy inflicting pain on others (if they didn't enjoy it before); torturers also eventually feel elated about their power and superiority over their victims. And these are very-well documented phenomena that occur within one generation. Just imagine how things may turn out over several generations of a relationship of dominion vs. submission among races.

I thought about using the expression "the slave's gene" as the counterpart of the "master's gene," but I decided to go against this idea because a slave may very well be oppressed, and yet he may be plotting on how to kill his master, or flee from slavery, and we have a multitude of instances of rebellions conducted by slaves that attest to the fact that some slaves were far from being infested with the "dog's gene"—case in point **Nat Turner** in the USA and **Toussaint Louverture** in Haiti—this one being an internal psychologically or biologically imprinted condition, not something externally imposed by sheer force, as it happened to many enslaved people. Thus, it wouldn't be fair to call this condition the slave's gene, because a good portion of the slave population never manifested the degrading condition of gladly accepting (and sometimes even volunteering) to be slaves. When you observe a black man complaining about discrimination, and doing it in such a way that it seems to indicate that he is not ruling out violence to end discrimination, and when you hear his white counterpart reposting that the black person is a racist, most people fail to see that the white man is still a racist, masking his own bigotry with an open accusation of racism against the black person, and the black person is still haunted by his feeling of inferiority, and doesn't even know it consciously. Dark-skinned people don't know how to tackle an inferiority complex, except through violence or total and unconditional submission. The only solution to racism is for the white man to accept that he is infested with the master's gene, and for the black man to recognize that he may still be in denial as to his infestation with the dog's gene, which gives him a subconscious feeling of inferiority.

The dog's gene behavior is abundantly found among black people, as well as among people of Indian descent, and is manifested as an excessive servility towards the white individuals who, on the other hand, seem to exhibit the counterpart of the dog's gene, what I call the master's gene, present in every domineering or paternalistic attitude towards the dark-skinned people. Whites are constantly trying to lecture dark-skinned people about democracy, liberty, respect of human rights, etc. if not pounding those who refuse to submit to their dictates with their powerful war machinery, or with economic pressures, sanctions, and/or blockades.

White people will only give in to white people, and this seems to be a different manifestation or strand of the dog's gene. The white dog's gene is mostly found among Spanish, Italians, Polish and Irish peoples, and, to a lesser degree, among the French, and other East Europeans. The white Anglo-Saxon or Caucasian and the Germans seem to be the all-dominant white people, the ones infested with the primeval master's gene. Now, since the dog's gene is almost universally found among dark-skinned people, white people—suffering from the master's gene—get to believe that they are somehow superior to darker folks, although most recently they will never openly manifest this belief, and yet it will be reflected in their paternalistic attitudes towards the "inferior races." There are also people who are neutral to the dog's gene or the master's gene—people who don't manifest one kind of infestation or the other. Russians and some people from central Europe and China seem to belong to this group, as well as perhaps the Hindus, and some "white regions" of South America and Canada.

The master's gene is as nefarious as the dog's gene. It makes white people claim—sometimes openly, sometimes privately, sometimes quietly (without ever saying it), and sometimes "scientifically"—that white people are more intelligent than dark-skinned people. I used to think that this conclusion was true, and told myself that it was enough to take a look at the map of the world to know that only white people are technologically advanced (except perhaps the Japanese, though they may also be considered white). Countries of the African, Asian, and American continent, where the dark population was high, were extremely backwards, and this observation reinforced my belief that Hitler, the Nazis, the British, the Germans, the white Americans, the Jews—although these people affirm it quietly, never openly, and for religious reasons—all of them with their stupid cancerous social growths like Zionism, the "rednecks," the skin-heads, and the KKK, were absolutely right. I used to think that our race of Indians (and I am a *mestizo*) were inferior beings, much less intelligent than white people (even as it was obvious that a neo-Nazi is a supremely stupid individual) which is the reason why we follow the lead of the white man. It never occurred to me that perhaps we are less intelligent (or at least we appear to be) because we are poor, and not the other way around—although some white people would want us to believe that we are poor because we are less intelligent.

With respect to the dog's gene, my own experience reflects what's going on in dark-skinned societies as a whole. At first, I believed without any shadow of a doubt that white people were superior to dark-skinned people, I even felt a bit proud about this because I was predominantly white, and this was a period in my life of open subconscious acceptance of the dog's gene, I was willing to be subservient to white people. It was until I came to the USA (and I was then barely nineteen years of age) that I realized that I was not white, that I was being discriminated by whites, just like they would do it with blacks and Indians. I tried very hard to mix with white people, making efforts to encounter my position in white society, but I was rejected.

It took a while for me to realize that being a *mestizo*, though a "white *mestizo*," meant the same as being an Indian. This made me feel very disappointed, and this was the beginning of the second phase of my race-awareness development, entering a period of denial, manifested as hatred for all white people. I should mention that it was hard for me to understand that for white Europeans the children of mixed races bore the race designation of the "inferior" race, which is why Collin Powell is black, rather than white, and I am an Indian (though I consider myself *mestizo*), rather than white—exactly the contrary happens in dark-skinned societies, where children of mixed races get the designation of the "superior" race, which is why in Nicaragua I was considered white, and some people used to call me 'chele,' which is a Spanish slang word for 'blondie'.

The second phase could be characterized as a process of accommodation, trying to find a position among the dark-skinned people, declaring open hostility for whites, and the sort, which betrayed the fact that I was still feeling inferior to the whites. It is at this time that I expressed sympathy for extreme ideologies like communism, and grew fondness of black leaders like Malcolm X and the Black Panthers. I profoundly despised black leaders like Martin Luther King, and felt almost apotheosis-like sympathy for Patrice Lumumba and Che Guevara. I was nothing less than a Revolutionary (though in attitude only, because I never took arms to fight it out, nor did I belong to any Revolutionary organization) and rejected all religions, especially Catholicism and Christianity in general. My inner being was fighting a battle between a sense of false superiority, versus a background of deep feelings of inferiority. The dog's gene was still in me. But I began to notice that something was wrong about my view of the linkage between intelligence and race: There were stupid white people, as well as stupid dark-skinned people; there were also intelligent dark-skinned people, as well as intelligent white people. I came to the conclusion that intelligence is measured individually, not collectively, or more specifically, intelligence is not an attribute of a race of humans, but of individual humans of any race. Intelligence is a characteristic of individuals, not of societies. Why is it, then, that there was an overwhelming number of white people that were famous for their contributions to philosophy, science and mathematics, as against "colored" contributors?

This question was a problem for my overall understanding of race and intelligence. I went through names like Newton, Einstein, Leibniz, Oppenheimer, Plank, Plato, Aristotle, St. Augustine, St. Thomas, Hume, Hobbes, Berkeley, Lavoisier, Curie, Edison, Galileo, Bohr, Pavlov, Darwin, Mendeleyev, etc. and didn't find any dark-skinned scientist or philosopher (except perhaps St. Augustine) famous enough to compare to those mentioned. What happened to the contribution to science from dark-skinned people? This was a killer question, since everywhere I looked, only white people's names popped up as major contributors to the advancement of science and technology. And then the answer hit me right in the face: I am linking intelligence to science, when science is a cultural manifestation of a particular race of people, the white people. And white people—with the advancement of science as a means of subjugation of other peoples and cultures—made of science the measure of intelligence. It's like if black people, who created jazz, had made of jazz music-composing a measure of intelligence. It's exactly like if Hindus were to make of transcendental meditation, "guruism" and "fakirism" a measure of intelligence. Intelligence is not just manipulating numbers and discovering chemical reactions or physical laws in nature, and it should be measured by the level of spirituality in individual human beings as manifested in culture—and culture is language, art, science, tradition, religion, human relationships, and environmental adaptation. It is only in this sense that some people are more intelligent than others—which explains why Jesus, Muhammad, Gandhi, Buddha, Marx, Atahualpa Yupanqui, St. Francis of Assisi, Mother Theresa, Picasso, Rivera, Goya, as well as other scientists and cultural innovators were more intelligent than the common man. Intelligence was not, then, an attribute of a particular race or ethnos, but an attribute of individuals of any race. As soon as I came to this conclusion, the grip of the dog's gene let me go. I freed myself from centuries of accumulated retro-bigotry that the white man had imposed on me, and my people, through generations of oppression and exploitation.

Similarly, what was said above about the dog's gene can be said about the master's gene. White people who treated slaves like if they were domestic animals, especially during the American conquest and colonization, to a certain degree cared for their "human animals," just the same they would care for their dogs, cattle and horses. But in the white man's mind these blacks were still animals, inferior beings that had to be fed, cared for, and put to work hard for their master. Of course, there were other systems of slavery, practiced in Rome and in the Eurasian continent of antiquity, which were a simple manifestation of the power of the conqueror over the conquered, so that although the vanquished were submitted to the brutality of slavery—black, whites, or people of any other color—they were still looked upon as human beings. No wonder masters would sometimes give the task of educating their children to slaves. And of course, just like some people mistreat their animals, especially when they are transported and distributed, slave traders and raiders would apply unimaginable punishments and would treat with extreme cruelty their slaves. But whether treated humanely or not, slaves were considered inferior beings, especially if we are talking about black or Indian slaves. The difference between the northerners and the southerners during the American Civil War was not that the first considered the slaves as equal to them, while the others rejected them as sub-human beings, but that the northerners visualized a different economic system where the freed slaves would be more productive as paid laborers. For Lincoln and others in the North, the blacks were still inferior human beings at best, if not animals. Just read the following passage.

In a letter to Horace Greeley of August 22, 1862, Lincoln said in response to an article of the *New York Tribune* the following:

> "I would save the Union. I would save it the shortest way under the Constitution. The sooner the national authority can be restored; the nearer the Union will be "the Union as it was." If there be those who would not save the Union, unless they could at the same time *save* slavery, I do not agree with them. If there be those who would not save the Union unless they could at the same time *destroy* slavery, I do not agree with them. My paramount object in this struggle *is* to save the Union, and is *not* either to save or to destroy slavery. If I could save the Union without freeing *any* slave I would do it, and if I could save it by freeing *all* the slaves I would do it; and if I could save it by freeing some and leaving others alone I would also do that. What I do about slavery, and the colored race, I do because I believe it helps to save the Union; and what I forbear, I forbear because I do *not* believe it would help to save the Union. I shall do *less* whenever I shall believe what I am doing hurts the cause, and I shall do *more* whenever I shall believe doing more will help the cause. I shall try to correct errors when shown to be errors; and I shall adopt new views so fast as they shall appear to be true views."

If anyone had any doubts about whether or not Lincoln was against slavery, but only as a political expedience, they should read the above paragraph again. If in doubt about whether or not Lincoln was a racist, read the following one. Neither the previous paragraph, nor the next one can be misinterpreted as being out of context, because I took care of citing enough of the original writings.

> "While I was at the hotel to-day, an elderly gentleman called upon me to know whether I was really in favor of producing perfect equality between the negroes and white people. While I had not proposed to myself on this occasion to say much on that subject, yet as the question was asked me, I thought I would occupy perhaps five minutes in saying something in regard to it. I will say then that I am not, nor ever have been, in favor of bringing about in any way the social and political equality of the white and black races, that I am not, nor ever have been, in favor of making voters or jurors of negroes, nor of qualifying them to hold office, nor to intermarry with white people; and I will say in addition to this that there is a physical difference between the white and black races which I believe will forever forbid the two races living together on terms of social and political equality. And inasmuch as they cannot so live, while they do remain together there must be the position of superior and inferior, and

I as much as any other man am in favor of having the superior position assigned to the white race. I say upon this occasion I do not perceive that because the white man is to have the superior position the negro should be denied everything. I do not understand that because I do not want a negro woman for a slave I must necessarily want her for a wife. My understanding is that I can just let her alone. I am now in my fiftieth year, and I certainly never had a black woman for either a slave or a wife. So it seems to me quite possible for us to get along without making either slaves or wives of negroes. I will add to this that I have never seen, to my knowledge, a man, woman, or child who was in favor of producing a perfect equality, social and political, between negroes and white men. I recollect of but one distinguished instance that I ever heard of so frequently as to be entirely satisfied of its correctness, and that is the case of Judge Douglas's old friend Col. Richard M. Johnson. I will also add to the remarks I have made (for I am not going to enter at large upon this subject), that I have never had the least apprehension that I or my friends would marry negroes if there was no law to keep them from it; but as Judge Douglas and his friends seem to be in great apprehension that they might, if there were no law to keep them from it, I give him the most solemn pledge that I will to the very last stand by the law of this State, which forbids the marrying of white people with negroes . . ."

Abraham Lincoln—Fourth Joint Debate at Charleston, Mr. Lincoln's Speech (September 18, 1858)

As for George Washington and some of the Founding Fathers, they were also slave owners, racists, and probably white supremacists, but we shouldn't hold these epithets too strongly upon them, because the slave system then was something like modern capitalism today with respect to labor exploitation, very hard to see to be almost invisible to the eyes of our conscience. But if still seems a blasphemy on my part to say these things about these "holy men," let me tell my critics that I am a Templar who owes complete loyalty only to my God, and not to any man, dead or alive, because men are imperfect beings.

If you think Liberia was created for the black people, just like Israel was created for the Jews, think again. The white man in the United States wanted to get rid of blacks, if not read what follows:

"The roots of the colonization movement date back to various plans first proposed in the eighteenth century. From the start, colonization of free blacks in Africa was an issue on which both whites and blacks were divided. Some blacks supported emigration because they thought that black Americans would never receive justice in the United States. Others believed African-Americans should remain in the United States to fight against slavery and for full legal rights as American citizens. Some whites saw colonization as a way of ridding the nation of blacks, while others believed black Americans would be happier in Africa, where they could live free of racial discrimination. Still others believed black American colonists could play a central role in Christianizing and civilizing Africa."

And the paragraph above was written in the 21st Century by somebody of the Library of Congress Resource Guide for the Study of Black History & Culture.

On the other hand, there were people like John Brown, one of those anti-slavery proponents who went beyond the words to take up arms to fight slavery, and yet he is very little mentioned both in black literature and black history. "Sometimes he is portrayed as a heroic martyr, but most of the time he is vilified as a fanatic and even a terrorist, an insane zealot and madman who went to extremes for what he believed," we read in Wikipedia—a free, open content, community-built encyclopedia. Nevertheless, he was a sincere man, devoted to fight slavery, who even gave his life for the anti-slavery movement.

*   *   *

The history of the atrocities committed against blacks and Indians is not only systematically falsified by the white man, but also accepted without much criticism by the descendants of those who were brutally victimized by the avarice of the white capitalist. This degenerate conjunction, association, and complicity of the oppressed with the oppressor—by no means a symbiotic relationship that brings benefits to both partners—is one of the most bizarre classical examples of the cooperative work of the dog's gene and the master's gene—there are numerous cases of dark-skinned people (some of them not even American citizens) who hate Latino immigrants, support the Republican party, and do other things that are even more debased, such that it is shameful to even put it in writing. To give just one example, Lou Dobbs' wife is Hispanic, and she agrees with and supports his anti-immigrant, ultra-nationalist, doctrinaire, and ultra-conservative ideology. Why is this behavior of almost total complicity with the former slave master so prevalent among the dark-skinned races? The answer is given above, as we talked about the "dog's gene."

Refusing to give in to the dog's gene is not the same as refusing to cooperate with the white man, as long as the relationship is maintained on a basis of equality, which means that the white man also has to refuse to give in to the master's gene. We can all interact harmoniously within an environment of equality and respect.

The dark-skinned man has to respect himself by rejecting the pressure of the dog's gene to make him behave slavishly, like a domestic dog, so that the white man doesn't get the idea that he can take advantage of dark-skinned people. The white man, on his part, has to respect the dark-skinned people by rejecting the pressure of the master's gene to treat them like inferior beings. Once white and dark-skinned people level themselves to the same stature of mutual respect, the conditions will be given for the advancement of *Homo sapiens* towards *Homo spiritualis* within an atmosphere of friendly interaction.

But it is so difficult to get rid of the pressure of the "master's gene," and the citations given above represent a full, unconditional acceptance of its nefarious influence. For the white man of those days, a slave was either an animal or a sub-human—and even nowadays, for some contemporary white people, the dark-skinned man is an inferior human being. The next stage towards the humanization of the white man is when he accepts all peoples of all races as human beings, with equal rights as those of white people. But this is all external posturing; deep inside, without ever mentioning or letting others know—except perhaps when having a chat among peers—the white man still feels superior to the dark-skinned man, and will express it in attitudes like paternalism and some forms of protectionism and condescendence towards dark-skinned people (they use expressions like "affirmative action," the equivalent of giving back a meager penny of what the white man owes the black man). Even more, under certain circumstances of heated interaction with dark-skinned people, the white man will sometimes blow up and break down his moral barriers and will shout the *n-word* to blacks—remember Kramer? This is the equivalent of the black man fighting an internal battle between his suppressed feeling of inferiority and the realization that he is also a human being, except that here the white man thinks of himself as somewhat better than the dark-skinned person, while agreeing to accept him/her as a human being, with equal rights to his own. This is a stage of internal conflict and denial. The great majority of white America is still at this stage of humanization. They are still hooked up to the master's gene. And yet, it is undeniable that there has been progress, and that the white man is making a conscious effort to overcome, first his open racism, and lately his repressed racism, though there is also no doubt that there are still residues of bigotry, especially among conservatives that identify themselves as Republicans, but also among liberal Democrats. Still, the latter sometimes seem to be "More papists than the Pope himself"—"Más papistas que el Papa," very often exhibiting extreme paternalistic attitudes that hide their repressed feelings of guilt and superiority.

Getting rid of either the dog's gene, or the master's gene, begins by accepting the reality that we have it, and consciously realizing that it cannot continue to be within us. It's something similar to shock therapy that produces catharsis. Liberation from the master's gene is making sure that whenever you deal with a dark-skinned person, you have to consciously harbor the belief that this other individual, of different color, is not inferior or superior to yourself. He or she is just a different human being. Once the white man gets used to think this way, he is in his way of becoming a full-fledged *Homo spititualis*. Except that he is not there yet. Nor is the dark-skinned person who needs to get rid of the dog's gene. If, and whenever not under the influence of the dog's gene, the dark-skinned man must forgive and forget, and the white man must procure his redemption through some kind of penance. But this is easier said than done. Neither the white people feel that they need to apologize for what their ancestors did to the dark-skinned people, nor some dark-skinned people are exactly eager to forgive and forget for what happened to their ancestors. Therefore, the process of humanization of man is at a standstill.

Now, people who display uncontrolled hatred for persons of other races—which is an especially serious problem among whites: the "rednecks," the skinheads, the white supremacists, the anti-Semites, the anti-immigrant champions (the Minutemen Project), the KKK, and others, instead of going through a process of humanization, are going through the reverse process of de-humanization. These racist people are fighting within themselves the crude realization that they are indeed "white trash," an expression used by the rest of their white peers who are going up in the process of humanization, and encounter these freaks going downhill, in a reverse process that we can only characterize as "animalization." These ignorant, racist individuals are so deeply infested with a master's gene that does not fit their self-assessed inferiority that they will try to deal with this condition through violent bouts against the dark-skinned people that they resent for no other reason than not being inferior to them. And still we must love them, we must make an effort to help them restore their humanity. As a driver instructor at the company I work for, I had the experience of dealing with individuals—some of them came from Vidor, Texas—who would rather quit their newly-found job than be in a class conducted by an inferior Hispanic "wetback." If truth must be said, I would not visit Vidor even at daytime, because those people (no matter if it's only a minority of them) are perfectly capable of tying one end of a rope to my neck and the other end to a pickup truck, and drag me down a road, like they did to an "old black boy" they murdered some years ago. But, again, as I said before, love must prevail, and we must make a conscious effort to understand these people, because they also are our fellow human beings.

Now, coming back to the white people's redemption, this is usually preceded by penance, and unlike forgiveness, redemption is not free. Fortunately there is love, and if we love our fellow human beings, redemption is cheap to the point that it becomes a gift—such is the wonderful miracle of love. Therefore, white people must pay for what they did to the dark-skinned people of the world—and I am not talking here about the application of the *lex talionis*, because it's too late for that. Those people from Asia, Africa, and South America that suffered the crushing burden of empowering the white man with abundant free labor and wealth, must be paid back, and paid back they will be.

The argument that the deeds of the white man belong to the past and that we bear no guilt for the acts of our ancestors does not hold water, because just as people inherit wealth and properties, they also inherit poverty and misery. If my father made it possible that I be rich today, because his father made it possible for him, and my great-grandfather for my grandfather, in this chain of inheritance of good things and good memories, somebody must have been oppressed and exploited, and this someone inherited his misery to his children and his children's children. And just like we glorify the deeds of our ancestors and feel proud about them, we must also condemn their evil actions and feel ashamed of what they did, because if today I eat my bread with great satisfaction, it may have been because somebody else in the distant past must have eaten dirt, so that I can enjoy today's wonderful fruits of life. And the victims have every right to claim for justice, and time is not a good redeemer, time has never been a good redeemer; it cannot erase the agony and misery of the slave thrown overboard in the middle of an ocean storm in the middle of a never ending vastness of water. Time is not going to pay for the scalps of the Yaqui Indians, probably removed while they were still alive—for that's what the troops of the Mexican dictator Porfirio Díaz, at the turn of the 20th century, used to do to the Yaqui rebels. And yet, the white man may refuse to pay back out of sheer arrogance, or lack of a sense of responsibility, and there is nothing we can do about that, because we cannot force him to pay, but pay he will eventually do if he is going to be redeemed, and even if he doesn't seek redemption, the *continuum* can never be cheated, and will make him pay. The Templars have no authority to use violence, except in self-defense, which means that we cannot obligate the white man to change his ways. All we can do is protect ourselves doing what will keep us away from exploitation, and work for our own well-being.

When we affirm that the Templars are monk-warriors, it is because we follow the lead of Jesus Christ, who was, and still is, a monk-warrior. He first came as a monk to fulfill His promise of love. His second coming is going to be as a warrior, to fulfill His promise of justice. This is because love is ever an ongoing solution to the problems of the material world and to the problems of the spirit, while justice is a one-time swift blow of the sword to cut off evil from its roots. For the time must come when all avenues of love are depleted to the point that the monk-warrior will have to get rid of his robe and pick up the sword to combat evil. But this fight must never be premature, and we, the Templars, learned this ever since the time of the Crusades—which explains why the Templars, the ultimate warriors, did not respond to the vicious attack upon them ordered by Philip IV, the king of France. Jesus Christ was the first Templar that realized that the use of the sword was premature when Peter cut off a soldier's ear. The Crusades taught the Templars that the use of the sword was far too untimely in the fight against evil, and the Holy Inquisition learned that the fight against spiritual evil cannot be done by punishing the physical body. Saint John's apocalypse shows what's going to happen to those that cannot be conquered with love, and it is then that the monk will become the most terrible of the warriors. In the meantime, we must give love a chance, and only when love loses all hope, will the blow of justice strike mercilessly, for where there is no love there can only be evil, and evil must forever be eradicated.

We understand the position of the Arab jihadists in their fight against what they perceive as evil. But they have two fundamental problems that the Templars try to avoid at all costs. First, the jihadists lack a good understanding of what is good and what is evil. Second, they never try all avenues of love before they resort to violence, since love is patient, love is indulgent, love is pampering to peace, and love is a silent dialog between spiritual beings. In short, their fight against evil can be too premature, and this is something that the Arabs didn't learn from the Crusades: That the fight of the warrior must always be swift and timely, but never premature—this misconception is due perhaps to the fact that the Arabs didn't start the Crusades, but rather became the target of what the Crusaders interpreted as a menace to Christendom.

Nowadays, things have changed drastically for how the Templars prepare themselves for the fight against evil. First of all, a would-be Templar has to learn to practice doing what is good constantly and relentlessly. Second, and without ever yielding as to the practice of good deeds, the Templar must have a perfect understanding of what is good and what is evil, and this is not easy at all—being able to differentiate good from evil is the most important step for becoming a Knight Templar, since evil can always intentionally disguise itself as good (while good can sometimes be perceived as evil, but only accidentally). Third, the Templar must ruthlessly fight evil, but only when he is absolutely certain that he is fighting evil, while always being prepared for the great final battle against evil, if and whenever he follows the lead of the Christ, utterly rejecting the lead of the flesh.

Ego-intelligence vs. Spirituality

But let's now continue with our task of dispelling the notion that dark-skinned people are less intelligent than whites.

The famous (or should I say infamous?) Bell Curve is "crushing evidence" that dark-skinned people are less intelligent than white people. If you look at this curve for whites and for "darkies," and compare them, you should be able to notice that the curve is much steeper for whites than it is for "darkies"—or conversely, the curve is flatter for dark-skinned people than it is for white people. This is the strongest statistical evidence yet that proves that white people are more intelligent than dark-skinned people. Except that these Bell Curves only show correlation among race, social and economic condition, and intelligence, as measured by the notorious

IQ measure of intelligence, and they don't explain cause and effect relationships among the variables. Now, we know why white people are richer than dark-skinned people, since it is no secret to anyone that we have had a history of white domination throughout past centuries. Besides, there is the dog's gene and the master's gene, which would add to the confusion of who is more intelligent than whom. Wouldn't it be logical to assume that because the white man dominated the dark-skinned folks, the white man is more intelligent than them all? As for the correlation between social and economic status versus intelligence, of course, white people are more intelligent than dark-skinned people, because the IQ measures, not intelligence per se (which needs to be defined anyway) but the size of the individual's ego—and a rich and ambitious person has a monumental ego (even a desperate and ambitious individual that happens to be poor is going to have a monumental ego) as measured by the IQ, because these IQ measures rely on "science" and logic, both of which are tools of the ego. I bet that gamblers, entrepreneurs, chess players, politicians, drug dealers, mafia godfathers, military generals, evangelist preachers, etc. have a big ego, and also a big IQ. As for the big IQ of scientists and engineers, their knowledge is also subservient to their ego, and it doesn't take a genius to know that education increases your IQ. I myself practiced quite a bit taking these intelligence tests until I achieved an IQ score superior to 120 points.

A brief digression is in place here. The dichotomy of the self dictates that 'intelligence' be measured with respect to the ego, which I will denominate ego-intelligence, and with respect to the anima, which I will call spirituality. Most measures of intelligence are really measures of ego-intelligence (IQ's), while there is no known measure of the level of spirituality of any given individual, though we have known great masters of spirituality, like Jesus Christ, Buddha, Zoroaster, Confucius, St. Augustine, St. Thomas Aquinas, and many others, too numerous to mention. Ego-intelligence is imposed on man by the necessity to survive, and depending on the race of the individual, and his/her level of greed and avarice, it may rank very high, or very low, the correlation being (in most cases, but not all): The higher the IQ, the lower the level of spirituality, and conversely, the more stable the IQ, the higher the level of spirituality (we use IQ stability here to weed out possible individuals with mental impediments who may score low IQ's). Spirituality is manifested in society's ethical principles, moral and religious values, culture, tradition, myth, art, and the capacity to care for others, and—although it is not necessarily nurtured by a given social milieu—it is mostly a product of social upbringing and education. In the final analysis, spirituality is a characteristic of individuals that may be reflected as a characteristic of societies. Our human evolution is, thus, to follow the path from *Homo sapiens* (*sapiens*, meaning knowledge, as an intelligent manifestation of the ego) to *Homo spiritualis*, or man imbued with a high level of 'spiritual intelligence' that is not based on science, reason, and logic, but on intuition, introspection, and meditation, and yet this 'spiritual intelligence' is deeply rational in its external verbiage as a vehicle of communication, so that we can share, in the communion with others, the bliss of the spirit world. Finally, ego-intelligence and spirituality are not exclusive of each other, and a person may be highly ego-intelligent and highly spiritual at the same time.

Another observation is in place here. People whose egos have been crushed continually for several consecutive generations are going to show a higher sensitivity to spirituality than those who dominate and extort them, on the condition that the victims of such oppression and exploitation rid themselves of the negative baggage that results from a relation of oppressed to oppressor—if catharsis never happens, the results are all too visible in our world populated by dark-skinned people who can only envision a future without hope and without faith. The victimizer, on the other hand, as he/she grows ruthless, vain and avaricious, gets more and more insensitive to the things of the spirit, and his relationship to God, even when manifesting a profound 'spirit' of (false) religiousness, is all but lost.

Since the IQ is a measure designed for the ego, if we want to compare the ego-intelligence of two individuals, we should at least bring them down to the same start level. Thus IQ should measure the capacity of the individual to survive, given certain initial conditions, and not the capacity of the individual to solve problems, given certain final conditions (like social status, education and wealth). Under this criterion, Ann Coulter, Pat Buchanan, and other ultra-conservatives would not do very well. Strip Pat Buchanan of his identity, paint him in darker colors, rid him of all his relations, in other words, level him with Juan Charrasqueado (the Mexican stereotype) or Juan Valdes (the Colombian stereotype), and ask them both to go across the border, on the Arizona side of the US, to see who makes it. As for Ann Coulter, I don't see how she is going to make it without suffering multiple gang-rapes before she even gets close to the Mexican-American border.

This discussion is different from the discussion we had before about race and intelligence, where we determined that science is a cultural manifestation of a particular race, mainly the white man—not that other people of other races cannot do science, but that the white man is specially suited by nature to discover science—which makes scientific development a poor measure of intelligence to be applied to peoples of different races. Here we say that social and economic status determines intelligence, and not the other way around. The fact is that individually speaking, there are plenty of smart "darkies" who will succeed, and who have succeeded in the white man's environment, and once they make it, they will be able to inherit (pass on to their children) their newly acquired "intelligence," much in the same way they will inherit or pass on to their children their newly acquired riches. And this happens simply because intelligence, as defined by the white man, is intrinsically tied to the size of the ego. So much for the argument that intelligence is passed on through the genes . . . but, of course, intelligence and social status have always been together!

The fact that dark-skinned people seem to be less intelligent than white people is an accident of opportunity. Since the white man happens to be the dominant individual through the history of humanity, the white man had the upper hand, the opportunity for education, progress, and achievement, giving the impression that the white man is mentally superior to dark-skinned individuals—and some white men, especially the most ignorant ones, neo-Nazis and white supremacists, believe this to be the case. But white and dark-skinned people are all members of the *Homo sapiens* family of men, and intelligence is evenly distributed within the same species of animals—in other words, intelligence is evenly distributed within the species of men, irrespectively of their race, which is to say that intelligence is internally discerned among individuals of the same species (intra-species discerned), and externally (collectively) differentiated between individuals of one intelligent species and individuals of a different species, e.g. *Homo sapiens* is definitely more intelligent than *Canis lupus*, by the standard of intelligence of *Homo sapiens*. This means that an individual *Homo sapiens* who live in a tribe of savages in the Amazon basin, or the islands of Borneo, if taken from childhood to live in our Western Civilization have the same chance as any other child born in the western world to become a renowned scientist, because the ego-intelligence naturally wired in the species of *Homo sapiens* may be found in the jungles of Borneo, as well as in New York (USA), or the University of Oxford (England)—the ego, in other words, is in its origin the same "size" for all peoples of all races.

Again, we are talking here about individuals, science as a collective endeavor of white people are culturally imprinted in them, and hence, the white man is more inclined to make scientific discoveries than other people of other races—which has nothing to do with the fact that one non-white individual can learn science. We must never forget that the white man's science is a strict by-product of the avarice of the ego—both to grow fame and riches, and also to conquer through the application of scientific knowledge to the development of weapons—a fact that let the white man be dominant among other races of people. For a man, or group of men, to be superior to another group of men, their historical genetic development would have to have encompassed far more varied inter-relationships with their environment than it would be the case with the "inferior" humans, which would make them members of a different species of "men"—and this contradicts the fact that all men have a common origin.

Using modern tests of IQ measurement, as designed for individuals that grew up in the western world, would be useless to measure the IQ of a person that belongs to an Amazon tribe. If not, let's compare the man from the Amazon and the man from a suburb of London by placing both in the same natural environment—say the Amazon jungle, with the same clothing (virtually naked), the same weapons, and the same circumstances—and let's find out who is going to survive longer. The amount of knowledge of the physical world, and the technological achievement of a civilized society, do not reflect the level of intelligence of an individual member of this society, just the same as the accumulation of knowledge of the members of a stone-age tribe in Borneo does not reflect the individual level of intelligence of a particular member of the tribe. Communication is at the core of ego-intelligence—if they can learn our language, and we can learn theirs, we can communicate, and as we make our communication more and more complex and sophisticated, we express higher levels of ego-intelligence that must be reciprocal, if communication is ever going to be possible. Once we get to the point that we cannot communicate with each other, the impasse reflects a lower ego-intelligence on the part of the individual who stopped comprehending—who could possibly be a so-called civilized man. This of course, doesn't preclude that some individuals within the same species have a specific ability that other individuals don't have—among men, this means that some individuals can be great mathematicians, while others can only be great carpenters or craftsmen that work with iron or clay, just like some dogs are great shepherds, while others are great hunters. Intelligence, defined as the ability to survive a certain environment is evenly distributed among individuals of the same species, and the Darwinian survival of the fittest will take care of those who fail to tackle their environment, which is something that applies only to animals—we humans are endowed with something superior to the animal ego and to the human ego that I call the anima (the soul or spirit), which is what makes possible the practice of the Principle of Love with our fellow human beings. The degree that the anima exerts control over the ego (the degree of an individual's spirituality) is what makes a man more or less intelligent.

The Fixation of the Dog's Gene

In nature, we observe the behavior of animals when confronted with danger, and it invariably turns out to be the flight or fight reflex or reaction. When animals feel threatened they either run away from whatever is threatening them, or they turn around and fight. Next, when forced to give up the fight, they either take a posture of submission (surrender) or continue to fight to death. Similarly, if they are cornered, they will submit or fight. I don't know of cases in nature when animals will surrender without fleeing or fighting first. This behavior of gutless cowardice, by the way, I have noticed only in human beings and in some domesticated animals, especially dogs.

It is said that about 10,000 to 15,000 years ago, man domesticated the dog. In other words, an animal species very similar to the wolf, or the coyote, became the domesticated animal we now know as the dog. Man also domesticated other animals, including the cat, the horse, the sheep, etc. but it was only the dog that developed this extreme behavior of total submission to its master. Total surrender, even to the point that the master can mistreat the animal and kill its offspring, is a unique characteristic of the dog, and the dog will display an attitude of total obedience to its master, under any and all circumstances. The problem is that this process of domestication was not only applied to animals. Some men managed to "domesticate" other men.

As man moved from one part of the world to another, he encountered other people who, at first, would offer resistance to the invasion of the newcomers. At the end, one group of men would prevail over others, conquering them. Now, since with human beings this process of continuous domination took more than 15,000 years, and it is still going on in some regions of the world as we speak, it is small wonder that some men would probably developed the "dog's gene." Conversely, the dominant group of individuals, through thousands of years of domination over other peoples and tribes, would eventually develop "the master's gene"—the gene of domination. The slave and the master would accept their condition naturally, once the adaptation became biologically entrenched—that is, if it ever became biologically assimilated, and the evidence seems to suggest that it did. Could this ever have happened? Let's take a quick glance at the history of humanity to see if we can explain the behavior of some social groups confronted with domination by other social groups. It all seems to indicate that the white man is poisoned with the master's gene—there is little doubt about this, since it has been mainly the white man the all-domineering force throughout the history of mankind, subjugating and controlling other people from other races. Of course, this is by no means something unique of the white man. The Mongols, Chinese, Japanese, and some of the Arabs, at one time or another, developed this eagerness to dominate and control other people of other races, but it has been more prevalent and more psychologically conditioned on the white man. The black people of Africa, the American Indians, and some other tribes from the Eurasian continent have also developed some sort of a master's gene within their own family of races, which is to say that these dark-skinned people dominated, at one time or another, and with some degree of continuity, other groups of people of their own ethnos.

It may be argued that all peoples and tribes in the world naturally have this gene of domination. But, through history, some people have been always stronger than others, and still, some people have known nothing but oppression and domination— the African people and the Indian people of the Americas have lived traditionally under subjugation for centuries. This is an undeniable historical fact.

The problem with "the master's gene" and the "dog's gene" is that their influence, in some cases, seems to be biologically imprinted in such a way that they make people react instinctively to the condition of master or slave, respectively, without those people under the influence of the said genes being able to control the urge to dominate or be dominated. Now, as far as humanity as a whole is concerned, both genes are nefarious, and the only way to combat the inclination to surrender the spirit to their influence is by consciously recognizing that we have one gene or the other, and then work hard to eliminate it from our system, and if it is imprinted in our human biology, work down through successive generations, until being able to suppress it altogether—this would be something like an uphill battle (against an instinct) that eventually will be won through generation after generation of constantly making a conscious effort to suppress the urge—to be a master or to be a slave—dictated by the said instincts.

The dog's gene seems to be extremely prevalent among the Latin American Indians. The Chronicles of the Conquest of Mexico by Bernal Díaz del Castillo relate multiple examples of native Mexican Indians displaying the dog's gene behavior. The classical example was the Indian woman Malinche, later named Marina, who was given to Costés as a slave-mistress, and who seems to have been instrumental in Cortés' success in the conquest of the Aztec Empire. Also, anybody who has read some other Spanish Chroniclers would have noticed that in Guatemala and Mexico, for example, the descendants of the Mayas and the Tlaxcaltecan Indians would come running to greet the Spanish invaders and shower them with gifts, even as the Spanish objective was to conquer them. One chieftain named Nicarao, who possibly gave his name to Nicaragua, didn't even wait to be catechized before converting to Christianity and pledging allegiance to the King of Spain. The Tlaxcaltecans felt that they had to choose between two masters, either the Aztec rulers or the Spanish Conquistadors, and they preferred the latter. The Tlaxcaltecan Indians didn't even dream that the Spanish conquerors were far worse than their Aztec masters-to-be—they had been fighting the Aztecs for more than 100 years. All throughout the conquest of the continent we see this indigenous servile attitude towards the Conquistadors, Spanish or otherwise, as long as they were white. Acts of betrayal were abundant in the conquest of Mexico, as well as in the conquest of Central and South America. And even long after the conquest, fighters like Zapata, Villa, Sandino, Ché Guevara, and many others fell victims of treason triggered by the dog's gene. Montezuma could never bring himself to annihilate less than 400 Spanish soldiers trapped in the city of Tenochtitlan, even if 1200 more, under Pánfilo Narvaez, were on their way to take Cortés prisoner, making of them all an insignificant force of 1600, compared with the military might, at least in the number of warriors, of the Aztec Empire. This blunder cost Montezuma his life, and almost 500 years of unspeakable suffering for the American Indians.

Atahualpa, in Perú, didn't fare any better with Pizarro, when he practically placed himself in Pizarro's hands to be taken prisoner, and later executed. The North American Indians saved the Pilgrims from starvation, an event that gave origin to Thanksgiving Day in the USA. If only the Indians of the American continent had had the wisdom of the Inuit, who avoided any contact with the Viking invaders, letting them perish of hunger and disease, we would still probably have a homeland that we could call ours. Nevertheless, the conquest of the Aztecs, the Mayas, and the Incas may be partially justified as a way of ridding the native American cultures of their repugnant practice of human sacrifices—even if anthropologists try to excuse these practices as something that sometimes came as an honor to the victims. It was only recently that evidence was found that corroborated the account of Spanish chroniclers and priests that the Aztec and Inca cultures even sacrificed children to their repulsive gods, like Tlaloc, the god of rain, and Huitzilopochtli the god of war of the Aztecs. Who knows? . . . Maybe the American Indian cultures were long overdue for an apocalypse that came right on time with the European invasion of America. We must not forget that the *continuum* is unforgiving when society oversteps the limits of corruption that triggers their own demise—it is not God who punishes the evil acts of men, it is those very same acts that in the milieu of the *continuum* hit them right back, like a cosmic boomerang.

But not everything was submission on the part of the indigenous people. There were brave Indians, like most of the Indians in North America, notably the Apache, Comanche and Cherokee Indians that could never be conquered—they had to be driven almost to a total extinction. In South America the Araucans and Mapuche Indians were also impossible to subdue, and up to the present time, they remain autonomous and indomitable, just like the Yaqui Indians of northern Mexico. And how could we forget Cuauhtémoc in Mexico, Lempira in Honduras, and Tecún Umán in Guatemala? Unfortunately, by then, the main Indian strongholds had fallen into the hands of the Conquistadors, and the heroism of these natives was nothing more than a symbolic gesture that marked the beginning of the American Indian unbearable holocaust at the hands of the Europeans.

Another attitude taken by some Indian tribes was to get as far away as possible from the Conquistadors. In Nicaragua, the Miskito Indians fled deep into the jungles and wetlands of the Atlantic coast, infested, then and now, with all kinds of mosquitoes and disease, and yet they managed to survive up to our present time. The Miskito Indians, even today, are ever so mistrustful and suspicious of the white man. The Subtiava Indians in León, Nicaragua, were "dominated" by the Spanish—in other words, accepted the Spanish conquest, but remained fiercely independent. The same thing is true of the Monimbó Indians of Masaya, who tolerated the presence of the Spanish, and worked with them, without totally submitting to them. The Chontales Indians, on the other hand, submitted to the Spanish, but turned out to be treacherous, and every time they had a chance, they would attack their masters. Even in our present time, the descendants of the Chontales Indians are willing to work with the white man, but deep down in their guts they hate the white domination, and would take vengeance whenever possible, if and always they could get away with it.

There is a whole gamut of attitudes on the part of the dominated race of Indians of the American continent that runs from unconditional and unsolicited collaboration with their white masters to complete and total insurrection, as we saw only recently in Nicaragua and El Salvador. The armies of the Salvadoran oligarchy of whites and *mestizos* and of the Somoza family in Nicaragua were composed mainly of Indians that were more than willing to brutalize their own people, as long as ordered by those they perceived as their white masters—not knowing that their masters were sort of willing slaves of the Grand White Master of the North, the USA. As for the black people, both of Africa and the Americas, the story is always the same. Some of the black slave-spirited people would give their lives for their white masters, and a very few (the Black Panthers, the followers of Malcolm X, among others) would fight fiercely for their autonomy and for the dignity of their people. But most of the blacks, the ones who go to fight the white man's wars, the ones who participate in the white man's government, and the ones who "represent" their people in Congress (they really and truly represent their white master), they need to be awakened to the fact that they probably have the dog's gene. Furthermore, all the *mestizos*—and I include myself in this category—should be aware that we must examine our conscience to determine whether or not we have the dog's gene, and those who are white, bossy and always looking down on the dark-skinned people should examine their conscience to determine if they have the master's gene—which is as pernicious as the dog's gene. Our humanity dictates that we must all be treated and treat others as what we are, human beings. We cannot be either masters or slaves, because either condition lessens our condition of human beings. Finally, I know that there is going to be a lot of slave-spirited people that are going to raise their voice in protest for what I am saying here, and their master-spirited counterparts will support them in their protest because it is convenient to their ego. They will say that I am a racist, but I am not, because somebody who is Indian-white-black-Arab-Jew-Spanish-German is in a much better position to say "I most definitely am not a racist, because I represent several races of *Homo sapiens*." No one who is the result of a wide combination of races is in a better position to say that he/she is not racist.

In order to establish my own identity, and in order to determine whether or not I had the dog's gene, I had to do a lot of self-examination. First, on my mother's side I come from a combination of Indians and Jews. My mother's last name on her father's side is Mena, of Spanish Sephardic origin. Her mother's last name Escobar also came from Spanish Jews. But in our family we had also Indians, and even blacks and Germans, so I come from a whole gamut of races and combination of races, and thus, cannot be a racist or anti-Semite. As a person with traces of white origin, I have to look at the Indians in the eye and ask them to forgive my white ancestors for enslaving them, and as an Indian and black, I have to look at the white man in the eye and tell him that I forgive him for what he did to my ancestors. If the Indians don't want to forgive my white ancestors, they are the only ones who have to deal with their conscience and with their problem. If the whites reject my forgiveness, because they feel they have nothing to be forgiven for, that's their problem. I was on the path to find my humanity, and to find it I have to both, on the one hand, forgive and forget, and, on the other hand, repent and do penance. This is the only way I can get rid of the dog's gene, and if I ever had the master's gene (which I doubt) I would also get rid of it the same way, by self-examination.

Something about the dark-skinned people that must be said at the outset is that we could very well classify them in three categories. Similar and more specific classifications could be made for Blacks, Indians and *mestizos* of Central and South America. Hispanic Americans could be grouped as *Hispanics proper, H. Lackeys, and H. Vassals*. I, on my part, developed from H. Vassal to H. Lackey to Hispanic proper. We must look onto ourselves and determine what we are. When I was a boy, I found out that my ancestors were Indians and blacks, and I felt deeply ashamed for that circumstance, while at the same time feeling that I was white—and I do look very much like a white man—which made me feel very proud of this accidental fact of life. Being proud to be white and ashamed to be Indian and black made me an H. VASSAL, because I was deeply infested with the dog's gene. So, *Vassals* are those who are infested with the dog's gene and don't even know about it, and certainly don't care, as long as they can be in good terms with their white masters. *Lackeys* are those who play the white man's social and political game, are very much infested with the dog's gene, while at the same time giving the appearance that they care about their people. *Blacks or Hispanics or Indians* are those in the process of ridding themselves of the dog's gene, but who still need to overcome the hurdle of their own feelings of inferiority masqueraded with forceful opposition to the white man's rule and a strong sense of independence. The white man has also his own classification. *Whites proper* are those white people still infested with the master's gene, who deny that they are racist, and appear even friendly and condescending to dark-skinned people, though they act paternalistically towards them; a good majority of white Americans belong to this classification. *W. Lackeys* are those who set themselves apart of the so-called liberals, hate illegal immigrants (who most of the time happen to be non-white)—which is a way of masquerading their racism with a strong sense of nationalism and deep, almost reverent, respect for the law—and in general may be characterized as conservatives; while strongly denying being racists, more so than Whites proper, they are not paternalistic or condescending towards the dark-skinned people. *W. Vassals* are those white people who are hopelessly enslaved by the master's gene, and comprise people like the KKK, the rednecks, skinheads, and other groups who are openly and unabashedly racist.

The classifications given above are meant to be a guide to an introspective examination of ourselves, in order to know what we are at a certain stage of life, so that we can make the necessary conscious changes to go up in the classification scale. It's not meant to be a label, and it should not be used as a label, for it is certainly insulting to call somebody a lackey or a vassal. My intention is not and should not be construed as pretending to insult the whole world with negative labels. Not included in that classification, because barely anybody has reached that state of consciousness is being an *Homo spiritualis*. I myself don't feel that I have reached the level of spiritual trans-achievement to call myself *Homo spiritualis*.

Again, racial slurs have nothing to do with the classifications given above. Whenever somebody insults people of a particular race, we should make an effort not to get unduly upset about it. In fact, it usually happens that those who use racially loaded words or expressions are willing to apologize, and we should accept their apologies. You have to remember that white men have been mercilessly submitted to the dogmatic belief in white superiority, generation after generation, and it is not going to be easy to get rid of this doctrinaire racism that is already ingrained in their psychology—maybe even in their biology—which is why we have to give them time to correct their ways, and be willing to help, if and always they are willing to be helped. White men have been intimidated to such a degree by the sensitivity of dark-skinned people about racial slurs—most white people are literally held hostage to this acute racial sensitivity to the point that they are scared to death to be labeled racists whenever they talk about dark-skinned people—that they very often opt to hide their racism, when it is better to bring it out into the open—not that we are encouraging white folks to popularize racial or ethnic slurs, but sometimes it is good to know who we are dealing with: If they are willing to apologize, we should help them deal with their problem; if they are reluctant to recognize that they have a problem, and are unwilling to mend their ways, then we should stay as far away from them as possible.

Racially loaded words and expressions are just words, and although they are ugly and hurtful, it is not a good line of defense to ban them words like the *n-word* (as a matter of fact, it doesn't help much to use the substitute *"n-word,"* because it brings to mind the original word, anyway) to hide the fact that we are black, dark, or Hispanic. If you have any doubts about what you are, just look at yourself at a mirror. Black and Hispanic leaders who are constantly working to disinfect the English language from offensive words and expressions are living in a dream-world, if they think that that's going to ameliorate discrimination. Racial discrimination is not words, but specific actions that affect minorities. Thus, as a Hispanic, I challenge the white men to call me *wetback, speck, greaser, bean*, or whatever other epithet they may think of. Even more, I will give them some ideas. What about *mojado*, which translates into wetback, or a similar-sounding Spanish word like *mojarra* (a fish, which also happens to be wet), or better still *mojón* (translated into dumdum or idiot; mojón being the Spanish word for sign-post). Are the use of those words going to make me worse or better? Not one or the other, although it will give me a good and healthy reminder that I must stay away from people who use them.

Those Reverends (and I don't know what they should be revered about, since they are a classical expression of mixing church and state in politics, which shouldn't be bad if it weren't for them race mongers) who claim to represent the black people, and are always appearing on TV to demand the resignation of somebody whose racism slips through the cracks of a poorly designed psychological defense against anti-racial intimidation, are nothing more than modern Pharisees, "white-washed tombs" like Jesus used to call them, because they are so ready to blame of racism anyone who, by whatever psychological sublimation slashes out (more than anything, innocent or poorly framed) racial slurs, while giving out the impression that they are the highest moral authorities on the subject of racism—remember Kramer, Imus, and others who seemed to be sincere about their apologies for what they said, and yet their inquisitors wanted more? They use the shield of their race and their religious titles (like Reverend) to assign to themselves the task of being the defenders of the black or Hispanic peoples, when they should be working hard within their own communities to free their people from the infestation of the dog's gene—which is like *"pedirle peras al olmo,"* anyway—since they themselves are infested with the dog's gene, and worse, are unwilling to recognize their problem, which makes them play into the white man's game of dishonest politics and social hypocrisy. [What's unbelievable is that Imus got criticized for saying "nappy-headed hos" in reference to the Rutgers female basketball team. Didn't anybody realize that "nappy-headed" is a description that fits black people, just like "pale-faced" is a fair description of white people? What everybody failed to mention is that Imus should be censured for calling those women "hos"—a popular slang for *whores*, especially among black people—which in the final analysis has nothing to do with racial discrimination or racism.]

I grew up with my grandmother, and I loved her dearly, but she transmitted to her children and grandchildren the dog's gene. She could not help it, it was a social malady that ran through many generations, and made of my grandmother a vassal, by the definitions given above. Thus, according with the definitions given, what can we say about Dr. Martin Luther King? He was not, for sure, a vassal or a lackey, but sometimes he gave the impression that he relied too much on the goodwill of the white people, which raises the suspicion of the dog's gene presence. The truth is that Dr. King could not help but be soft on whites, since white people had the repressive machine and the repressive will to suppress any would-be forceful actions led by him. There is absolutely no doubt that Dr. King was a champion leader of the peaceful fight for justice, and that's more important than what he was, or was made to be. He was, most assuredly, a pious and a great persona, and perhaps a greater preacher and father, but many a times he might have given the impression that he thought like an individual still in bondage. At the end, Dr. Martin Luther King was made an instrument of the white man's domination. The white man transformed him into both the white man's and the black man's martyr, because Dr. King's legacy is a good shield of protection for the white man against the ever increasing demands of the black people, especially in reference to monetary restitution to the heirs of the former slaves—and since it is only fair that inheritance rights be applied to both actual assets to be inherited, as well as payable pending debts to be accrued, the black people are plainly justified in claiming restitution. How could the black people not see that the white man even tells them what model to follow to claim their God-given, sacrosanct, inalienable, inviolable, natural and sovereign human rights, giving his seal of approval to the Martin Luther King model, consisting of mainly *begging* for those rights, until he decides to grant them? Other models, like the Farrakhan model, the Malcolm X model, and even the Nelson Mandela model, consisting of *demanding* those rights (sometimes even forcefully), are out of the question, because the white man is not willing to give in to demands from minorities. On the other hand, if those US minorities not only had equality under the law, but also social, political, and especially economic equality, there would be no need of any of the models previously mentioned.

Now the question arises: Can we forcefully (violently), claim restitution, both for the black people and for the American Indians? The answer is absolutely no, because we would be violating the spiritual dogma that *might never establishes right*, which morally disqualifies any violence to restore our historical rights—this, of course, doesn't disqualify self-defense, if ever dark-skinned people have to resort to self-defense. Nevertheless, from the said dogma it follows that **the white man occupation of the American continent will forever remain illegal**, and it is not those people crossing the border between Mexico and the USA who are illegal, but the white illegal occupier of our ancestral land. Would we be morally justified in asking the white Europeans to return to Europe, and take the black people they brought from Africa with them? Would we be justified in asking African-Americans to go back to Africa, when they came to America in bondage? A rhetorical answer to the first rhetorical question would be a resounding yes, and a rhetorical answer to the second rhetorical question would be totally and absolutely no. Why, then, after less than 500 years of domination of the American continent, white Europeans claim it as theirs? Don't they know that the Arabs dominated the Iberian Peninsula for more than 700 years, and still were expelled and pushed back to where they came from?

Again, I am not trying to offend anyone; I am just trying to point to the fact that we must reexamine what we are. I am not trying to assert that the Indian, black or other races should take an arrogant posture against the white man; they couldn't, even if they tried, because some blacks, and probably most Indians, have grown up for so long believing that they are inferior, that awakening to the fact that they are just like any other human being, would paralyze them, if and when leaning towards arrogance. In fact, I think the white man should take a good look at himself and determine whether or not he has the master's gene. We all have something within ourselves that makes us dominant or dominated, and this is a product of human evolution and the historical development of humanity. But we must strive to be simply *Homo sapiens*, simply men, members of the family of men, while fighting to become what I call *Homo spiritualis*, or spiritual members of the human race. The fact is, if we don't respect ourselves, we will not only be hurting us, but hurting the white man, by giving him the reasons to think that we are indeed inferior human beings, which would make him take the wrong turn in his self-assessment.

The key to the freedom of the dark-skinned races from psychological slavery is not in shouting slogans and hurling threats to the white man, and least of all resorting to violence—again, self-defense is a different story, remember? Self-segregation will not work either, because the white man is in control of most of the means of production, and he is also in control of the main institutions that make up the capitalist society. The dark-skinned man has to lift himself up from his bootstraps, stop whining and begging the white man to treat him as equal, and to the contrary, demonstrate (not to the white man, but to himself) that he is as good as anyone else of any other race at doing a good work, both mental and physical. Yes, we must fight racism and discrimination wherever we encounter them, but we must fight it with dignity, proud of being what we are, without turning into intolerant arrogant bullies. In other words, we must demand, not beg, for our basic human rights, and for our basic rights as Americans. If the white man doesn't want to work with us, too bad for the white man (and the dark-skinned man too, but mainly to the white man), because with the newly-found strength of believing what we really are—not what historically the white man made us believe that we were—we can do a lot, and participate extensively in the economic growth and social advancement of the country.

The dark-skinned people must stop participating in those racially charged debates in right-wing TV channels, like Fox, where Sean Hannity is always reposting that we are racists, when he clearly understands—if he doesn't, I will be shaken in my "belief" that he is a superior white man—that dark-skinned people cannot be racists, because historically we have been hammered down in our psyche that we are inferior, until we got to believe it. The dark-skinned people, through hundreds of years of domination by the white people, have been emasculated of any "sense of racial superiority." This is tough; some white people are going to say that what I sustain here is racism, and some dark-skinned people are going to follow suit with their masters, but racism can never—not ever, I emphasize—come from the so-called "inferior races" to the "superior races" (and I belong to most of the "inferior races") because dark-skinned people learned to assimilate the belief that we are indeed inferior. Racism is a one-directional parameter, from the white people to the dark-skinned people, and not the other way around. Something that seems to have been hard-wired in the brain of people through hundreds of generations is not going to dissipate overnight: Just as the white man will never feel inferior to the dark-skinned man, the dark-skinned man will never feel superior to the white man, irrespectively of whether or not the feeling of superiority/inferiority is real or imagined. An individual who believes, consciously or subconsciously, that he/she is inferior, is hardly ever going to discriminate against anyone, especially against the "superior" white man. What the Black Panthers and all those radical organizations bark in desperation and frustration is their profound psychological insecurity of being inferior, disguised in reactive violent talk and behavior. Don't they know that the white man is teasing and taunting them into becoming what right-wing supremacists are, although preceded by a minus sign, as absurd as this may be? The solution, then, to the problem of racism must be that the white man steps down from his sense of superiority, and the dark-skinned man steps up from his sense of inferiority, so that hopefully, both groups meet in the middle, reaching a sense of equality.

When I was a boy, my grandmother and other members of my family gave me a special treatment because I was light-skinned. My grandmother made sure that I, and everyone else, understood that I was better because I was "white," and she used to tell me, and my brother Francisco—who, by the way, was very dark (she used to call him "el negro," the black one)—that we had to improve the race, meaning that we had to look for a fair-skinned partner for marriage. And my grandmother, in addition to being an Indian, was very dark—she was so saturated with the dog's gene, the poor soul of my grandmother. In contrast with this, talking to Robert Jones, he once told me that he was part Indian and part white, and that in one occasion his mother took them children to see grandpa, a Blackfoot Indian, and that he overheard his grandpa tell his mother to get her "half-breed children" out of his house. As cruel as it sounds, this underlies the fact that Bob's grandpa may not have had the dog's gene in his psyche, like my grandma did. North American Indians faced almost total annihilation for their lack of the dog's gene, which may or may not have been an advantage, depending on how you look at it. It breaks my heart to see how the North American Indian is so distrustful of the white man, trying, as much as possible, to keep his distance from whites. The Native American's pride and dignity, as noble and beautiful as they are, nevertheless are just symbolic expressions of their hurt, and calls on our humanity the need to bring them back to the family of men.

But this phenomenon of wishing to be white was not restricted to my family. It was very much generalized. The Indian, and most of the Nicaraguan population were either Indians or *mestizos*, were profoundly despised. All the negative epithets that you could find were attributed to the Indians: "Indio haragán," "Indio bruto," "Indio igualado," "Indio feo," "Indio chirizo," "Indio ignorante," and hundreds of others—the blacks were practically unknown, but there existed very negative myths about black people, that they stunk badly, that they were ugly, that blacks were stupid, that black people were more akin to monkeys than to humans, etc. The Indian was considered to be lazy and the white people were revered. And light-skinned people reciprocated to this negative concept we had of ourselves, and even reinforced it by looking down upon us. Since light-skinned people also happened to be rich, we were always begging to get the attention of those people and were always ready to comply with their desires. The dog's gene was even more prevalent and more rooted down in the countryside, especially in the *haciendas*, where the *patrón* could do anything he wanted with the Indians—for the Indians it was something of a great honor to have a daughter that would become the *patrón's* mistress, and the fruit of these relationships, the illegitimate children of the *patrón*, would become a higher intermediate layer of the social order, always under the white man's layer of the Latin social organization. In essence, we were like dogs, submissive, loyal and obedient to the white man. I have met Mexicans nowadays that deeply despise the Mexican Indians, just like the Nicaraguan oligarchy used to do, and still does it today.

As for the white man, we must be aware that very rarely we see white people disagreeing among themselves about substantive issues. This is one of the reasons why they are Republicans or Democrats in the USA, and liberals and conservatives in most of the other countries of the world. These political tendencies have very little differences as far as the white man is concerned, but offer nothing to the slave-spirited people, or the dark-skinned people of both the USA and the rest of the countries of the world. The truth is that if you are dark, you have to have the dog's gene to be liberal or conservative, Republican or Democrat. Those ideologies are not for the people who are still bonded with their psyche or their biology and need to free themselves from modern psychological slavery.

The Africans, on the other hand, had a tradition of selling their own people as slaves to Arab traders and to the European slave traders. These African chieftains would be too willing to make war on other African tribes as long as these raids provided "meat" for the European slave traders that they could exchange for money or other goods. The same behavior could be observed in the Americas—abundant examples of treason among the Indian tribes could be found in Mexico, Central, and South America. In North America it was common for some Indian tribes to ally themselves with the white European against other tribes of Indians. This all attests to the fact that the dog's gene is more prevalent among dark-skinned people than among the "white devils" of Mr. Elijah Muhammad.

Elijah Muhammad described the white man as a "white devil," and I believe this description corresponded very much to the fact that the white man was infested with the master's gene, except that Mr. Muhammad gave it a religious and mythical twist. This description, though biased and inaccurate—there are definitely a substantive number of white people who are against modern slavery, and who don't seem to possess the master's gene—reflects somewhat the condition of today's world, since a great number of white people are contaminated with the master's gene that turns them into manipulators, dominators, and even dictators. Also, except perhaps for the Irish, who have suffered the domination of the English, there has been very little domination of one sub-group within the white people by another sub-group—there may be other white sub-groups in central Europe that have suffered the domination of other whites, but this domination has not lasted long enough to turn these people into slave-spirited individuals. And all this is one more reason why the white people will give support to each other more than we see dark-skinned people giving support to their own. With the dark-skinned people we find that there are groups subservient to the white power, always ready to butcher the people of their own race to satisfy their master. This behavior is seldom seen among whites. Even Hitler preferred to attack the Russians, whom he didn't consider whites, rather than attack the British or the Americans.

Mr. Muhammad could only see Mr. Hyde in the white man—I am making reference here to the famous story *The Strange Case of Dr. Jekyll and Mr. Hyde*—and we have to make sure we don't make the same mistake. People like Bill O'Reilly, Sean Hannity, Pat Buchanann, Ann Coulter, Rush Limbaugh, Glenn Beck, Lou Dobbs, and others, are possessed by their powerful, horrible, and overwhelming ego, but deep inside them, hidden to the eye, there may be a pristine, transparent, clean, and beautiful anima. [So many Irish names . . . Thank God that I've known plenty of beautiful Irish people!] We never truly understood Jesus when he said that we must love our enemies. He meant that we must love the Dr. Jekyll that dwells in every one of us—even as we hate Mr. Hyde. The people mentioned above bring to the surface the ugly face of their monstrous ego, and sure, we must be careful with them, because they may bite us, or do a lot of harm to us—they are truly dangerous people, make no mistake about that, even if from the pulpit of the national media. But we must help them, we must love them with spiritual, Christian love, even if we can't love them with human, mundane love of the flesh; even more, we must patronize them in a very real sense of the word, help them to step and stump over their ego, and push it to the gutter, so that they can bring their anima to the surface of their being. We must do this because conversion sometimes happens, and out of the rough, ugly shell, we may witness the miracle of the pupa becoming a beautiful butterfly. And if conversion never happens, it is advisable to stay away from them, always ready to exercise our right to self-defense—which would be an unfortunate option of last resort. As far as the other white people, the ones that patronize on us, the ones conservatives love to call "lefties" or liberals, we must also try to understand them. They have to deal with an occult sense of guilt that sometimes overwhelms their feelings of superiority, which is why they suffocate us with their excessive attention. We must ask these people to stop it, and easy up on their help. We can do this, because once we've got rid of the veil of the dog's gene that covered our eyes, we can see clearly the veil of the master's gene that covers the eyes of some white people.

The White Man's Democracy

Democracy is not necessarily the best system—the collective wisdom of the masses may not be better than the individual wisdom of one person, or the collective wisdom of the few, though most of the time the will of the majority goes hand in hand with democracy. We don't want the dictatorship of the majority, and we certainly don't want the dictatorship of a minority or of one single individual. But what we take for democracy is a gross misrepresentation of what is considered to be the will of the people, especially when the will of the people is manipulated by the media to such a degree that it becomes the will of the manipulators—a system made out of the media and the establishment, which only changes hands and faces every four years or so.

If we define democracy as the *will of the people*, the will of the people is made up of the will of the individuals that make up the people. Thus, the will of the individual to be right must be a) rational, which is to say based on sound judgment; b) free of external interferences, like culture, tradition, and indoctrination; and c) based on accurate, unbiased, neutral information. The will of mentally deranged people doesn't qualify as democracy, nor the will of people fed biased information or brainwashed by the media, nor the will of people unduly influenced by culture, tradition and/or misdirected education, much less the will of the people unduly influenced by the specter of fear. But this is only half of what democracy is—it is so good and sound to say that democracy is the will of the people, when we don't specify what we mean by that. We seem to easily forget—or rather the "managers" of democracy make sure that you fail to notice—that the will of the people has an object or objects, and this object or objects have to be freely and equally accessible to their subject, mainly the people, who shall *will* on them. This means that every valid issue, every viable candidate, and every sound political position must be freely and equally accessible to all the people, so that the people can judge on them. The criteria above immediately disqualifies the USA as a model of democracy for many reasons, the most important one being that you have to have money to have access to mass communication that would freely and equally let your political views available to the people, so that the people can make a judgment about them. Funny thing about capitalism, pretending to follow democratic principles when the capitalists control even the most basic avenue for democracy, mass communication. There can never be freedom of the press when the press is in the hands of people like Rupert Murdoch, a capitalist of the right-wing media, while the rest of the "free press" is in the hands of left-wing media capitalists—yes, the media, like education, health, and everything else is in the hands of capitalists who promote capitalism, and whose ultimate goal is reaping profits. And that's without even considering the powerful lobbying of special interests, whose muscle comes from nothing less than money, and money directly or indirectly exerts an unduly excessive external influence—which is an external interference—in the main source of democracy, the free will of the people. In addition to the USA, there are a lot of other countries in the world where democracy is really the will of those who can exert and buy influence through the mass media.

Whenever you participate in the democratic game, you are legitimizing what the winning candidate is willing to do. Those who voted against Bush, cannot say that they don't support the Iraq war, because once you cast your vote for or against a given candidate, you are approving of whatever the elected candidate does as a president. Those who didn't participate in the game of democracy can rightfully claim that the elected president is not their president—why, we are talking about democracy, are we not? In the United States alone, it is not unusual to have 50 percent or more of people eligible to vote not participate in elections. And this means, that the will of the majority is not respected. Those people who refuse to vote, because of apathy, disinterest, or whatever you want to call it, in the global game of democracy are casting their vote against anyone who gets elected by those who do participate in the actual electoral process. Therefore, many times, the elected president of the United States is not the president of the majority of citizens of the country. And that's without taking into account that in the USA choosing a president is not made by direct popular vote.

One more thing. It is extremely dangerous to have a person in positions of high authority, yielding a lot of power, like the presidency of a country, who will be virtually irremovable from office for four, five, or six years, whatever the number of years the elected candidate is going to be an important public official. And the same argument could be made of those chosen to be members of congress, or of any critical institution of the Republic. Human beings are intrinsically unreliable, especially when they reach positions of power, and they should be removable any time they give signs of being dangerous, pedantic, intransigent, stubborn, fanatics, or just plain out of contact with reality, to say the least of those showing signs of morphing into tyrants, or being insane, by rejecting all criticism, by doing things without consulting other branches of government, by doing away with the law and the constitution, by just plain overriding national and international law and institutions, and dismissing other people as traitors, anti-patriotic, anti-God, or whatever epithet they use to denigrate others. If democracy is ever going to have any meaning, the tool of *public referendums* should be available to the people, for anything from the removal of a would-be presidential tyrant, or inept and inefficient congressman, to the approval of law or public policy. No argument of expediency, practicality, or desirability about referendums is justifiable in today's world of computers and the Internet. Other countries (like Venezuela and Nicaragua) even hold public meetings where people may express their desires about one public policy or government project, as against another. Of course this *permanent democracy*, or *democracy on the works* would lose its meaning if people are not firmly convinced of their position with respect to a given national issue, without external interference, threat, or undue fear, instilled by either yellow journalism or other repressive institutions of the state.

The white man—first the Greeks, then the Romans, and finally the leaders of the French Revolution, until it was transplanted to America, both North and South—invented the concept we commonly call democracy, which in its crudest form (the dictatorship of the majority), and in the absence of anything else, was the best political system ever known to humankind. But democracy implies freedom, absolute freedom of choice, and slave-spirited people don't have absolute freedom of choice. Hence, democracy is a hollow word for the dominated dark-skinned people of the world. This clearly explains why millions of Indians in Mexico, Central and South America will participate in the elections organized by their white masters, and they will even vote for the lighter-colored demagogue of their choice—this one normally responds positively to the whites that in turn dominate the entire world, the USA—who will promise everything and will deliver nothing. The elections in Bolivia, Ecuador, and Venezuela, as of late, seem to be the exceptions to this rule. As we said before, more than five hundred years of uninterrupted white domination is possibly deeply rooted already in the biology of the American Indian in the form of what we called the dog's gene.

And we must be careful in the task of bringing these people back to consciousness, out of this brainwashing handiwork that has lasted for so long, and still is being exercised. These people are so screwed up mentally that they would be willing to kill in defense of their masters. And just to give an illustration of what I mean by this, check the following: On May 1, 2007, in Los Angeles, some Hispanic organizations, made up mostly of Mexicans, decided to take the streets in peaceful support of the migrants—mainly in favor of legalizing the 12 million illegal migrants living in the USA—but were dispersed by the use of force by the L.A. police, notoriously well-known for its brutality. The footage shown on the news was clear as to how the police behaved. Nevertheless, the next day, "Radio La Norteña" was justifying the police action on the grounds that there were a few provocateurs that provoked the police, making them fear for their physical integrity, which prompted the indiscriminate attack on the crowd of protesters. Talk about the dog's gene. Like I said before, these people are like the domestic dogs that may bite you in defense of their master, even if you are in their favor. I am sure the estimated 30,000 to 40,000 people who participated in this demonstration in Los Angeles went back home dreaming the "American Dream." Even that *H. lackey* (see my definition of *H. Lackey* on page 187) of Pedro Sevsec from Telemundo was abused by the police, and yet, within a few days, you can bet your life he will be back praising democracy and the "American Dream" of the "greatest nation of the world," the USA. And this "American Dream" cliché is another peace of marketing propaganda used to stuff the immigrants' heads with bull. Why is it that Telemundo and Univision don't speak the truth clearly? People come to the USA because this is the only country in the Americas where they can work to feed their family, and for no other reason whatsoever. They would gladly go back to their country if they had the economic means to do it. The "American Dream" is another invention of capitalism to sell their over-priced, neat, compact, and pretty-looking "wood and plaster" houses that, by the time you finish paying for them, the capitalist investor would have pocketed more than twice (maybe even thrice) its original cash value—which already includes an outrageous margin of profits.

The same thing is true of the black and the rest of the Hispanic population of the USA who vote Republican or Democrat (but mostly Democrat). The majority of the black people of the United States of America are so blinded by the dog's gene that even when they are being openly discriminated, they will inevitably follow the lead of the white man with respect to war, domestic and foreign policy, and with respect to immigration policy. It is a fact that, very often, even black people abuse Latinos as an act reflex of the discrimination they themselves are victims of. Ethnic discrimination on the part of both white and black people against Latinos in the USA comes to the surface when dealing with immigration. It is said that more than 70% of the US population oppose illegal immigration (and these stats include black people)—in actual fact, they oppose both legal and illegal immigration, because immigrants are usually Mexicans and Latinos—giving US lawmakers a real problem, since they have to balance the labor needs of capitalism, versus the majority of their constituents' opposition to Hispanic immigration. But we will expand on immigration in the next section.

The white man may not have invented the concept of nationalism and national pride—given that this sense of nationalism is prevalent in all countries of the world, with their different racial and cultural components—but he sure gave it a tremendous boost by revering their heroes of past wars of aggression, and by brainwashing their children at home and school, so that they learn to die for their country, not for humanity. And as we speak, there is no country in the world where children are not taught the concept of nationalism, and the concept of the national hero and national pride. A morbid sense of national vainglory is of paramount importance for the imperial domination of one country over another, and especially for the domination over the dark-skinned people of the world—but even some dark-skinned nations raise their pitch of nationalism to such extremes, that very often it amounts to sheer bigotry, especially if nationalism is also mixed with religious fanaticism. Nationalism transfigured into patriotism is taken with religious fervor: the flag is sacred, and the national anthem has to be sung in the native language only, which often times is the official language of the country in question. We have to be constantly reminded that there are people willing to destroy and trample, for some, their Muslim religion and culture, and for others, their Western Civilization and values, and to take away our freedom. Fighters are raised to the category of martyrs and heroes, because they are the protectors of either Islam, or democracy and freedom, even though those soldiers were transformed into killing machines that must swear absolute obedience to their commanders for the cause of their religious beliefs, for the cause of their nation, for the cause of their people. Soldiers must rid themselves of their absolute freedom of choice, so that their killing instincts remain sharp, so that they can kill and destroy without mercy for a misperceived concept of strict religious orthodoxy, freedom and democracy, and ultimately, for the sake of the country where they were born. There is barely anyone in the whole world willing to die and make sacrifices for humanity.

On Illegal Immigration

It is undeniable that the United States of America is probably the only country in the world where immigrants are sincerely welcome. This may not be a result of the sympathy that the general population of the USA feel for people from other parts of the world, but rather a product of the scarcity of cheap labor that some businesses constantly require to operate. Just to mention one sector of the US economy, farmers would not be able to deal with their farming activities without immigrant labor, which means that we need foreign workers for the harvesting of grains and staples, picking fruits and vegetables, raising chickens, collecting, sorting and distributing eggs and other dairy products, as well as processing and packaging meat. Similarly, the construction industry, including home, highway and bridge building would run into a deep crisis if it were not for the Mexican laborers that do the back-breaking work. And so would the hotel and restaurant services.

In essence, we can say that the United States of America is one of two places in the Americas, and one of the few places in the world, where there is a scarcity of common unskilled labor workers. Coupled with the comparatively high pay-rate for unskilled and semi-skilled labor, the USA constitutes a magnet for cheap Latin American labor, and as long as the American economy grows, there is always going to be a strong need for immigrants. The common American citizen and the Minutemen activists have to get used to this fact of life. Besides, labor migration Northwards is a consequence of the consumption culture that capitalism has created. Many would-be migrants would probably manage to subsist in their country of origin, but the lure of consumerism is too great for them to ignore. They crave for themselves and their families the modern conveniences of the capitalist world that only the dollar can buy. It is frequently the case that a good number of migrants don't leave their country of origin because of financial pressures, but because they want to move up in the social scale. The absolutely penniless peasants of El Salvador and Guatemala would think it twice before they move to the big cities of those countries, let alone to the USA. To be able to ride the dreadful adventure of coming to the USA illegally you must be absolutely courageous, irresponsible in extreme, hopelessly desperate, or else have the money to pay the "coyote" that will bring you here. Furthermore, the drama of going across all those borders (especially the Mexico-Guatemala border and the Mexico-USA border) is so traumatic that only those ignorant of the savagery of the Maras (in the Guatemala-Mexico border) or the "polleros" (in the Mexican-USA border)—added to the rampant corruption of the authorities of all those countries—could possibly risk their lives to launch themselves to such a dangerous adventure.

Migration is such a delicate theme that it should be treated with care. Nowadays, when we talk about migration, we think of Latinos coming to the USA. But there is also another kind of reverse migration that, although legal and still in its embryonic phase, has to do with humanity, or rather with the inhumanity of the capitalist system of production. It is a known fact that old people in the USA represent the human scraps or leftovers of capitalism. It is close to a tragedy to grow old in the United States of America, because those who do are bound to end up in nursing homes, which are almost no different from modern "penitentiaries" (for the old)—and old people, or their relatives, have to pay for the "service" they get at these places. The universal excuse is that old people need special attention that their children cannot provide, because they have to work. So, the only options left to the elderly are either to pay expensive nurses to care for them (and you have to have plenty of money to do that), or else to be sent to nursing homes (and you also have to have money to pay for it). For those with no money, or little money, there are only two ways out: impending abandonment and eventual death, or migration to a third-world country. There are places in Mexico, Nicaragua, Costa Rica and other countries where these old people can live, and believe me, they are welcome with open arms by the people of those countries. Yes, the fact that they bring money has something to do with it, but it is also a question of humanity and the willingness to serve. As soon as Social Security in the USA enters a period of crisis, predicted for the years 2030 / 2040, these human leftovers of capitalism (the aging, the disabled and the sick) are going to have to migrate more and more to Latin America. The question is: What's the difference between old people willing to live in Mexico because they can't afford to live in the States, and the labor workers who wish to live in the United States, even if doing the hard work Americans don't want to do? In terms of humanity, there is no difference whatsoever. Thus, my advise to those Minutemen activists who inevitably are going to grow old is that they better have money to serve their sentence in a nursing home, or else migrate to the country of those people they mistreat and despise so much, because I can assure them that we will treat them with dignity, even if money helps to grant such dignified treatment.

Another common misconception about illegal immigrants is that they don't pay taxes. Nothing could be further from the truth. Illegal immigrants willing to work are forced to use somebody else's social security number, or invent one, and in neither case will they be able to get a tax reimbursement—as for the invented social security numbers, illegal immigrants actually give away money contributions to the Social Security fund. Those illegal workers who get paid in cash cannot be responsible for the delinquency of those who pay them without making the appropriate tax deductions—which they virtually make, anyway, since they are "stealing" those taxes from the government by not paying fair wages to their contract workers. Illegal immigrants are the source of immoral, and sometimes even criminal businesses of those who exploit them, from the recruiter and the "coyote" in their country of origin, to the "lawyer," slumlord, and employer in the USA who skim their earnings with the promise (or the excuse) of legality. The number of people who make a living of the plight and blood of these immigrants go from common peddlers to sellers of the "American Dream," which means that their contribution to the legal and quasi-legal (and unfortunately also the illegal) business activities of this country is much more important than it is usually recognized. An illegal immigrant gets extorted from the moment he decides to come to the USA, up to the very moment they incinerate him, once he dies—no funeral home will take less than cash from the illegal immigrants' surviving relatives.

Now, one of the reasons Anglos and Caucasians resent newcomers, especially Latinos, is that these newcomers fail to integrate (at least in the first generation) to the mainstream 'American culture' and American values. As far as the 'American culture' is concerned, it is not clear what the 'American culture' is. In our Latino culture we do most everything Americans do, except speak English, because the Latin American culture and the US culture are both products of Western civilization and Western lifestyles. Besides, it is always better to be a multi-cultural society, with an underlying background culture, or mother culture, that could be called the 'American culture,' and the English language would be one common language to speak, though not exclusively, for all the other members of this conglomerate of cultures. As for the American values, it is difficult to distinguish those values from the cultural, moral or religious values of people from so dissimilar countries like Argentina, Haiti, Nicaragua, and Mexico, and yet they all share a common set of moral values that is no different from the American moral values. Which means that the preoccupation of the Anglos and Caucasians to keep the 'American way' intact is unwarranted, and they have nothing to fear from immigrants. Latin Americans also have nothing to fear, and we really don't fear, the Anglo-Saxon cultural environment. Furthermore, we really appreciate some aspects of the Anglo culture, like punctuality, seriousness, hard-working habits, sobriety in dress and manners, and liberalism in thought and speech, and the Anglos should appreciate some of the positive aspects of the Latino culture.

Maybe Anglos like Lou Dobbs, Glenn Beck and others—I am not going to include Rush Limbaugh here—should enjoy salsa and merengue, have a piñata for their grand-children, learn to eat burritos and tamales, and if they don't like them, no problem, they can go back to their hotdogs and hamburgers. As for myself, yes, I can have a hamburger and a hotdog from time to time, but if you ask me, I prefer beans, tortillas, burritos and tamales. Never mind about Shakespeare and some of those cultivated English writers, because to tell you the truth, even Cervantes, the greatest Spanish novelist, is too sophisticated for me. I prefer Gabriel Garcia Marques and his nemesis Mario Vargas Llosa. But Hemingway, that's a different story, Hemingway was an Anglo with a Latin spirit, and so was Mark Twain (even if he never knew it), and Elvis Presley, and the Beatles. I love them all.

Do I love my adopted country, the USA? Yes, and I would even be willing to learn the National Anthem in English (believe me Anglos, the American national anthem is not easy to memorize, not for a Latino, anyway). But to tell you the truth, I am not very much inclined to invade other countries and provoke wars for the sake of democracy. I rather be friends with those other people of Asia and the Middle East, even if they don't enjoy the fruits of democracy. They do have strange customs, but this is a big world, and we should have a bigger mind to try to understand them. Let them be Chinese, Russian, Syrian, Iranian and Hindus, and if they eventually see the virtues of democracy, let them adopt it themselves. Why should I be preaching democracy, when I was born a Catholic, an easy-going religion that is always willing to forgive for whatever wrongs you do, as long as you ask for forgiveness before you die—at the expense of being criticized as cynical, Catholicism gives you a sense of sin-laxness. You see, Catholicism is not a very democratic religion, nor is our Catholic God. Protestantism? Nah, as much as I respect all religious beliefs, I think Protestantism is too dry, strict and stern for my upbringing. I like to participate in public processions, singing and carrying the image of Christ or the Virgin Mary, even if I sometimes dislike them images—the image of the Catholic Christ dying on the cross used to scare the wits out of me when I was a child, and once, when I was a young boy, I lifted the robe of a plaster doll-Christ figure, and to my astonishment found a frame of wood and nails that didn't hold good to my religious beliefs. Not that I am an unfaithful and loose Catholic, but the Catholic God seems to be less severe and more lenient than other gods from other religions. Whenever I am doing something mischievous—never anything criminal—I am wary about Him, because He's always watching me . . . Good thing that he also gave me a guardian angel. So Anglos, let me come into your country (our country now), but let me be different. You may very much appreciate England, Canada, and the queen and princes and princesses of England, and the sober and somber Anglo culture, but I am keen to enjoy my life one day at a time, and I love to talk about anything under the sun. I like to sit outside, at the porch of my house, and see my neighbors go by, and who knows, I may even talk a bit about them, but not because I want to invade their privacy or be mean-spirited, but because they are human beings, and human beings always have something interesting (or bad) with them that we like to know and talk about.

I know what you are going to say. Yes, we Latinos are a bit trashy (maybe more than a bit). If we are eating tamales, we throw the wrappings to the gutter; we also may sometimes spit on the floor, and pick our noses and scratch our asses, but these are bad habits that can be overcome. We may sometimes eat without washing our hands, but we don't need, and we certainly don't want, to disinfect the world, which is why we get sick and grow worms (parasites) in our guts, but if we don't die young, we get to enjoy a long and not very "gringo-sanitized" life, which is not so bad. Should you, then, be afraid of immigrants? Nah, they are not going to take over your world . . . Not by force, anyway.

The Herd Instinct

Ever since man gathered together to hunt and look after each other they had to develop what I call the "herd instinct," which is the tendency for groups of individuals to stick close to each other due to a sense of solidarity or for their defense against a perceived danger. So the herd instinct presents two facets: one is just the sense that members of the same species should stay close to each other; the other is the tendency to increase the capacity of defense in numbers—the higher the number of individuals, the stronger they will be to face dangerous situations, enemies or animals. Again, as with the dog's gene and the master's gene, I am not saying here that the herd instinct is a biological reality—it's more than anything a behavioral characteristic of certain groups of animals, men among others. All species of the genus Homo, including *Homo sapiens*, had to develop this instinct if they were to survive in a world filled with dangerous animals and dangerous situations. The problem with these biological defenses is that once they get rooted, they don't disappear promptly after the circumstances that caused them also disappear. And this is why we still carry within us the tendency to group together, even though there may not be a direct threat to our security—we carry with us the historical hurdle of the first cavemen hording together to hunt or fight against their enemies.

The herd instinct would not be so bad if we had inherited just the tender facet of it that makes humans find comfort with each other. Notice how in a natural setting some animal species fight danger in numbers, without developing the aggressive weapons to fight predators, and we see this behavior in schools of fish, herds of sheep, etc. where these animals have completely suppressed the instinct of territoriality—all cows and horses graze together in the same pasture, because being together is more important than preserving food for the future. A different story is found in animals like the wolf that get together for more than just solidarity of the species—they join with each other to defend their territory, and kill in the hunt for food. The herd instinct in man presents both facets described above: for solidarity and for defense. Whenever there is a natural disaster, people get together to help those hurt, but whenever there is the need to be aggressive against the presence of enemies, or the perceived threat from other nations, people with a common heritage or origin get together to fight other nations for dominance, or to protect their territory. Nationalism and all manifestations and representations of nationalism are a consequence of the workings of the herd instinct. But there are other ways as well that people show their infestation with the herd instinct.

The herd instinct has varied and subtle ways of manifesting in human attitudes. Behind the lead of a politician there is always the herd instinct. A rock star or singer would not be as famous if we didn't have the herd instinct. Sports facilities and stadiums filled with people exist thanks to the herd instinct. Churches, preachers, and even the gang leader on the streets owe their presence to the herd instinct.

203

Have you ever seen in the news how in certain countries like Guatemala and Perú mobs lynch petty criminals, guilty or not? Have you ever seen in the news how fanatics of soccer go against each other fired up by the herd instinct? The herd instinct is such a powerful force that it completely shuts off the capacity of man to act rationally. Whenever you have a crowd of people, all it takes is the appropriate trigger or detonator to convert a peaceful group of rational human beings into a crazed mob ready to destroy everything and anybody it encounters in its path. The herd instinct is dormant in every crowd of people, and all it takes is certain cue—a scream, a speech or harangue, a sound, a shot, a target of destruction—to convert them into a source of tremendous devastation. The important thing to notice about this behavior is the incapacity of the mob to act rationally—all the rational controls of the human being get shut off once the herd instinct gets fired up within a mass of people. The herd instinct is the way nature prepared certain species of animals to fend for themselves.

I remember (when I was young and restless) casually witnessing a brawl in the street among two groups of people I didn't know. As I approached the place where they were fighting, four or five individuals broke off from the mob and got inside a house to get machetes. When they came out, everyone started to run, except me. "Why should I run?" I asked myself, I am not part of this fight. But my rational thinking only lasted a couple of seconds, for I soon realized that the mob was coming towards me brandishing the machetes. I ran like hell, like I had never run before. And yes, the mob was chasing me, they sure as hell were after me, and if for any reason I had fallen, or stopped running to explain that I was just a passer by, they would have hurt me or killed me. This is the herd instinct in action—every individual, part of a furious mob, loses all contact with their rational inner being, and they follow the instinct to kill, or to run away from danger, whatever the situation may be. But this kind of mob behavior has more or less been suppressed in "civilized nations" like the USA, which is not to say that it has not taken other more subtle forms of mob behavior; it has metamorphosed into something called nationalism, and into something even more subtle called democracy.

The media has known for a long time how to take advantage of this very human tendency to display the herd instinct, and so have the politicians and other public figures that rely on wide dissemination of information through the media outlets, like newspapers, the radio and television, and most recently, the Internet. There is no single artist, singer, well-known writer or politician who is not to be known through the media. And this means that the media holds a powerful control over the masses—and this is one of the reasons why the old school of communism tried to control, and even suppress, freedom of the press and freedom of speech—not because they wanted to keep people ignorant of what was going on in the rest of the world. For our modern democratic system, freedom of the press is of the utmost importance, especially since the press is part of the capitalist system of production, and the press is the ideal weapon to control the masses. The press holds the drum-beat to move the masses in a certain direction, to slow them down, or to speed them up. No wonder it was the American media that gave the signal for most Americans to go along with president Bush's war in Iraq. It was the media that made almost everybody in this country, Democrats, Republicans, or independents support something as immoral as a war of aggression, giving it the slant of a war of self-defense. Another strategy used by the politicians who hold certain control over the media is to outright lie about something. This was learned from Goebbels' Nazi propaganda: repeating a lie more than one time eventually settles in the people's mind and becomes a "truth." American politicians, and politicians from all over the world, including communists, applied extensively this strategy in a very successful way. This is nothing less than mind control—and don't you ever think for one minute that the Western press doesn't do it, except that sometimes they try to correct the information when it is too late, and some people already believe it in spite of the "effort" the press made to correct it—CNN did it to president Hugo Chavez, linking him "erroneously" with Al Qaeda. Like I said before, and this is far from being a triviality, the press holds a powerful grip on the people by not telling the truth (lying), by withholding the truth, by giving the information with a twist of their own, by self-censure, by just plain not giving the information, by keeping certain people without a media outlet to air their grievances, by taking out of the airwaves something that reflects negatively on the government, etc. This means that you have to exert your own judgment and skepticism when being fed information by the media.

In a capitalist society, governments don't need to control the media, because the media controls itself to preserve the very capitalist system of which they are an integral part, which is why there is no need of censorship. Communists, on the other hand, didn't have the luxury of letting the media control itself, which it wouldn't do anyway, since, as we said before, they are an integral part of the capitalist system of production, and they are going to fight for capitalism, and against communism. Never mind what the general population thinks or believes; the media that has always served the interests of the capital is going to feed what's convenient to the capital. The reason we don't see this maneuvering is because we can only contrast the crude, open and visible communist censorship of the media, against the subtle, and often invisible, self-controlled, self-censorship of the capitalist media. In essence, we can say that the media is an instrument of the capital—how do you think media companies would subsist without ads and commercials? And it can never be transformed into an instrument of a communist system, because, in principle, a communist system doesn't need of an independent media—which is why the communists would establish state controlled media outlets that would inevitably respond to the needs of the communist government. But recently, with the advent of computers, things are bound to change, even within a capitalist system of production—the capital will no longer control the media, and this is going to bring the wonderful end of classical capitalism as we know it. We will explain how and why.

Here is the how. Politicians will no longer be able to present their case through the filter of the standard, regular media outlets (radio, TV, movies, newspapers and magazines, books, pamphlets and flyers). Whatever a politician says or offers will be validated in the Internet by a jury of universal Internet users—just like in a regular court jury. The different blogs of the Internet will act as the politician's defense (if for the politician) or the politician's rebuttal (if against the politician), and it's going to be the general population, the Internet jury, who will decide who presented the best case. Even more, the time will come when candidates will be elected by voting through the Internet. The technology exists; if we can very well buy things online, I don't see why we won't be able to choose our public servants online. The "why?" is very much a consequence of the "how?" And this all means that democracy, the old democracy based on the herd instinct, will be forever dead, and the new democracy will let people get well-informed before making their choices, without the nefarious interference (through the filter of the standard media) that will let a well-informed citizenry vote for or against their choice of politics and politicians. Therefore, democracy of the sort generated by the herd instinct will forever be *requiescat in pace*. YouTube, and similar Internet sites, are going to bury the democracy of CBS, CNN, ABC, FOX, and other TV networks that for so many years monopolized and controlled the flux of information to the general public.

Since democracy as we know it is a consequence of our human herd instinct reaction to demagoguery of our politicians, it doesn't really represent the will of the people—although people will argue that they are indeed making their own decisions when choosing a public official—because the will of the people under the herd instinct influence is like the will of the mob when participating in the lynching of a person. Have you ever notice how some politicians win elections by so-called "landslides"? It's the herd instinct at work. This kind of democracy produced the government of Nazi Germany and other "democratic" governments around the world. Furthermore, the lethal combination of the dog's gene and the herd instinct produce the kind of anti-indigenous governments in countries like Mexico, Perú, Bolivia, Guatemala, and other Latin American nations, where the majority of the Indian population are controlled by a minority of white capitalists with the "democratic consent" of the Indians themselves, who are truly the people. If not, why a ragged illiterate Indian of the northern states of Mexico would vote for Vicente Fox, who represents everything Indians should hate the most? Why a Peruvian descendant of the Incas would vote for a thief like Fugimori or Alan García?—Imagine, Fugimori, who, as we speak, is running for congress in Japan, the only country he really cherishes and recognizes, which makes of Perú a good candidate for the Guinness Book of Records: The only country outside Japan who ever had a Japanese president. Why indeed a former shoeshine boy like Toledo, grown into a man who became president of Perú, would turn his back on his own people, mainly the poor, hungry and exploited Peruvian Indians? Why indeed, if not because of the dog's gene accompanied by the herd instinct, both of which make such a lethal combination? But that's what we call democracy today.

11

THE CITY OF GOD IN THE CITY OF MAN

The contrast between St. Augustine's city of God and the city of man is the contrast between the spiritual world of God's heavenly order and the terrestrial world of greed, crime, sin and disorder. Augustine wants to make a clear separation between the state and the church, and the secular control of the administration of the state can only be made easier with the help of the church that controls and regulates the moral aspects of the social order. It is not the business of the church to participate in the affairs of the state, which in a sense makes the church subservient to the state, without the contrary reciprocity. This insistence on the separation of state and church was a lethal blow to humanity as a project of spiritual development, and facilitated the growth and almost unlimited strengthening of the brutal capitalist system we are now living. The synthesis of the conflicting roles of the church and the state, to the detriment of the church, must be placed then in its rightful position, with a new re-synthesis of church and state, in which the balance of the material and the spiritual move to a superior level of syncretism, giving birth to *Homo spiritualis* as a better, more advanced offshoot of *Homo sapiens*. It is only in this way that future generations will look at *Homo sapiens* in the same manner we now look at *Homo Neanderthalis*.

Although Augustine's view is valid, and the difference between the spiritual and the material is still maintained, when we look at the life of man as a harmonious interplay of the body and the spirit, there is no separation of body and spirit for those individuals in the path to salvation. Man reaches to God through other men and through the actions they do for other men, and given that everyone that follows the same moral principles is guided by the same objectives of humanity, there should be no contradiction between what one man does as a physical entity, to a certain extent influenced by the ego, and what other men do in the same guise, if and always the anima leads their actions towards the common spiritual goal embedded in their physical world. Church and state are no longer in contradiction, and need not be separated. And the same is true for the individual man: the conflict between the ego and the anima can be resolved in a higher synthesis transcending both the realm of the physical needs of man's ego and the realities of the spiritual needs of man's anima in a self that may need to climb to a higher level of being. Thus, the city of man can reach to the City of God if and always the City of God extends its reach to the city of man, always within the realm of the physical world, and the journey towards the heavenly kingdom becomes an integral process of body and spirit that happens in and on the *continuum* that runs parallel to the visible world of matter.

This *continuum* is not God, but the activity of God, God's Work, which in Latin is *Opus Dei*, and everything in the Universe vibrates and moves to the tune of the *continuum*, which inexorably leads to the spiritual City of God. Should man, influenced by the evil one, turn out to be an obstacle to this spiritual ascension of humanity, the Apocalypse would result—which is going to be the inevitable outcome, in any case, and after *Homo sapiens*, *Homo spiritualis* would have to move to a higher rank of spiritual hierarchical classification, maybe even becoming par with angels. Therefore, humanity, as of today, is at a crossroads where a decision has to be made: If we choose the path of righteousness towards the City of God in the city of man, Apocalypse will ensue in a gentle transition from *Homo sapiens* to *Homo spiritualis* and anything that follows; but if we choose the path of greed and avarice towards more and more radical capitalism and individualism, Apocalypse will also ensue, but no longer as a gentle transition, but as a violent and catastrophic confrontation of the forces of good against the forces of evil, and whatever remains of humanity afterwards, will still move towards *Homo spiritualis* and the City of God.

The End of Pax Americana

Robert J. Samuelson of Newsweek asks the following rhetorical question:

> *The United States has unmatched military and economic strength, but is it losing its role as a force for global stability?*

Then, he starts his article as follows:

"By objective measures, Pax Americana's legacy is enormous. Since Hiroshima and Nagasaki, no nuclear device has been used in anger. In World War II, an estimated 60 million people died. Only four subsequent conflicts have had more than a million deaths (the Congo civil war, 3 million; Vietnam, 1.9 million; Korea, 1.3 million; China's civil war, 1.2

million), reports the Center for International Development and Conflict Management at the University of Maryland. Under the U.S. military umbrella, democracy flourished in Western Europe and Japan. It later spread to South Korea, Eastern Europe and elsewhere. In 1977, there were 89 autocratic regimes in the world and only 35 democracies, the center estimates. In 2005, there were 88 democracies and 29 autocracies."

And this is all thanks to PAX AMERICANA, it is claimed, without taking into account that perhaps the world was going to go the way it went without the intervention of the United States of America. Furthermore, nothing is said about the source of the authority that the US took for itself. Winning a World War is not a ticket for world domination, because might does not make right. Who assigned the United States the task of patrolling and policing the world? Hiroshima and Nagasaki were indeed the result of Pax Americana, although the nascent imperial Japan started the conflict with the USA. The Pacific War was the result of the imperialistic ambitions of the two countries involved, and Pax Americana, together with the two atomic bombs, decided which imperial power was going to be the sole imperial power of the Pacific Rim, and Japan lost.

Nothing is said about the fact that the Congo Civil War was sparked by the European colonial powers, especially the Belgians, so the Europeans and the white man can be credited for the 3 million people killed in Congo. With respect to the Vietnam War—where the USA lost nearly 58,000 troops, a puny number compared with the Vietnamese loses—Mr. Samuelson does not give credit to Pax Americana for the death of the 1.9 million Vietnamese killed in the conflict. Even more, the Korean War may be rightfully attributed to Pax Americana, with another 1.3 million deaths more to its credit. Only the Chinese civil war can be attributed to a strictly internal Chinese settlement of scores. As for the 89 autocratic regimes mentioned above, nothing is said about the fact that Pax Americana was responsible for a good number of dictatorships in Africa, Asia and Latin America. The author of that passage conveniently forgets that Pinochet, Somoza, Papa Doc, Batista, the Argentine Junta, Stroessner, Ferdinand Marcos, and other gorillas of Africa, Asia and Latin America were allies of the USA, encouraged and protected by the USA to maintain a stranglehold of domination on their people.

"Prosperity has been unprecedented. Historian Angus Maddison tells us that from 1950 to 1998 the world economy expanded by a factor of six. Global trade increased 20 times. These growth rates were well beyond historic experience. Living standards exploded. Since 1950, average incomes have multiplied about 16 times in South Korea, 11 times in Japan and six times in Spain, reports Maddison. From higher bases, the increases were nearly five times in Germany, four in France and three in the United States."

"It is fatuous to think all this would have occurred spontaneously. Since the Marshall Plan, the United States has been a stabilizing influence— albeit with lapses (the Vietnam War, the 1970s inflation, now Iraq). Aside from security, it provided a global currency, the dollar. It championed lower tariffs and global investment, which transferred technology and management skills around the world. It kept its markets open. It's doubtful that any other major country would have tolerated present U.S. trade deficits (now approaching $800 billion) without imposing pervasive import restrictions."

Again, the author of the above passage wants us to believe that the prosperity he describes may be all thanks to the United States of America and Pax Americana. Whenever these fools—on the payroll of capitalism—handle macro-economic figures that reflect the benefits obtained by the huge capitalist corporations— which right after World War II became transnational companies, with their main headquarters in the European capitals and the USA—they never give figures about how impoverished a good portion of the world population has grown (inflation means nothing to them), thanks to the huge prosperity of the good corporations that pay their salaries.

Pax Americana has always meant the USA keeping the world order, a world order dictated by the needs of Pax Americana and the imperialist ambitions of the USA.

One wonders why the Russians don't have to worry that much about whether or not the Iranians and Koreans acquire the bomb. Brazilians, Argentineans, Chileans, and Venezuelans can sleep with tranquility because they don't have any enemies. Mexico is busy exploiting its own Indian population—while the "coyotes" and drug lords are busy in the business of exporting Mexico's population surplus and the Colombian drugs to the United States, respectively—and has nothing to fear from its powerful and rich Northern neighbors. Pakistan had to develop the atomic bomb because India had it, not because Nicaragua was a threat to its national security. Israel may rightfully worry that Iran develops a nuclear weapon, but there is no reason to think that because Israel has gone nuclear, Iran should be thrilled about the peace and tranquility that a nuclear Israel may bring to the region. North Korea would probably assign its resources to something other than building weapons, if it didn't have to fear the United States. Japan would have no reason to fear North Korea, if it wasn't an unconditional allied of the United States (remember the dog's gene we talked about above?) The South Koreans don't show any signs of uncontrolled paranoia because the North is going nuclear—in fact, it is the United States of America that shows signs of extreme concern about what the North Koreans do, more than the South Koreans that share a border with the North. The British have every right to be fearful of Al Qaeda, because they decided to remain non-neutral to a conflict that only concerns the United States. France and Canada don't seem to be that freaked out because Iran is trying to go nuclear. Norway, Finland, Holland, Spain, Belgium, and other European countries that barely ever get involved in international problems with other countries, can dedicate their efforts to growth and development, as long as they don't get involved with the Arab conflicts. The United Nations doesn't resolve anything, except cultural and economic pseudo-problems, organizing meetings that lead nowhere, and from time to time participating in whatever the US wants it to participate. It is mainly the United States that is in trouble, especially with the Arabs, because the United States is either siding almost openly with Israel—whose creation was a problem generated by the British and the League of Nations to begin with—or is worried about the oil that the Arabs would not know what to do with, if they didn't have buyers that burn it. In essence, if every nation minds its own business, helping whenever prompted to help, the world would not be such a difficult place to live in, and we, in the United States, would not be so fearful of terrorists who are nothing more than common criminals taking their frustrations on the United States, because the United States controls their country by proxy or by force.

Pax Americana, which in reality has always been Bellum Americanum—in which case it is good news that it seems to be getting to an end—would not be getting to an end, if the US and its Asian and European proxies, instead of interfering in the internal affairs of other countries, had implemented a system of international relations based on mutual respect among nations—and this would be the true Pax Americana—a more appropriate substitute for the all-too-easy decision to go to war in order to resolve human conflicts. We should make it a habit of working for the building of the City of God in the city of man, doing God's Work, and treating everyone with the due respect that *Homo spiritualis* deserve.

The End of Humanity's Dark Ages

We read in Kiwipedia, the Internet Encyclopedia that:

> "In historiography, the term Dark Ages or Dark Age most commonly refers to the European Early Middle Ages, the period encompassing (roughly) 476 to 1000."

> "This concept of a dark age was created by the Italian scholar Francesco Petrarca (Petrarch) and was originally intended as a sweeping criticism of the character of Late Latin literature. Later historians expanded

the term to include not only the lack of Latin literature, but also a lack of contemporary written history and material cultural achievements in general. Popular culture has further expanded on the term as a vehicle to depict the Middle Ages as a time of backwardness, extending its pejorative use and expanding its scope . . ."

With the timid, late flourishing of the sciences, and with the meager geographical discoveries of the early second millennium, the dark ages can be extended well past the 15th Century to encompass a historical period of humanity when religion was more powerful than science. Things began to change at the end of the 15th Century, and by the 16th and 17th Centuries humanity had left behind the period of obscurantism. This was a historical period in Europe called the Enlightenment, preceded by the Age of Reason, with a rapid development of philosophy, mathematics and the physical sciences, times that saw Voltaire, Rousseau, Hume, Galileo, Newton, Leibniz, Lavoisier, Pascal, Descartes, and others. At the same time, and as a spiritual reaction to the Age of Reason and the Enlightenment, art and literature also flourished, and the period that followed the dark ages is also called the Renaissance, dominated by people of the caliber of Dante, Boccaccio, Petrarca, Raphael, Donatello, Giotto, Michelangelo, Leonardo, etc. The Renaissance was in reality a spiritual protest manifested in the arts and literature against the development of science, although the actors of this movement profoundly despised the clerical establishment. It is right after the Renaissance that science turns from being a meek interpreter and accommodator of religious writings, to become more and more emboldened with the new discoveries in Biology, Physiology, and Medicine. The 19th Century opens up the door to scientists like Charles Darwin and his theory of evolution. Science takes the lead, and religion and spirituality become synonymous with ignorance and backwardness.

The bullying of religion and spirituality by science was a response to the bullying of physical knowledge and learning by religion. The misunderstanding of the function and methods of both science and religion led to a conflict for the primacy of human knowledge, where there shouldn't have been any conflicts. The dark ages was a period where both material and spiritual learning were almost completely lacking, the present dark ages is a period where there is abundance of material learning, but almost a total lack of spiritual knowledge. So, we can rightly say that the dark ages of humanity really began in the 5th Century, continued through the Age of Reason and Enlightenment, past the Renaissance, and it is still with us in the 21st Century, because if there is lack of spiritual knowledge, there will also be intellectual darkness in spite of the plentitude of material (scientific) knowledge. To pass and leave behind the period of the dark ages of humanity, we must become illuminated by the spirit; we must metamorphose into *Homo spiritualis*.

This extended Dark Ages of humanity will come to an end with the advent of the City of God in the city of man. As we said before, the dark ages are not only the medieval times of human history, but practically the whole of human history. The wars, the crimes, the genocide will eventually come to an end, and this will not happen thanks to "democracy" and to the modern political systems that preach the equality of all men—but at the same time fight with tooth and nails to protect the sacrosanct capitalist system of production—but thanks to the advent of the City of God in the city of man, impelled by the Fraternity of the Templars. The idea that we will eventually end poverty in the world by raising the standard of living of the lowest people in the lowest social stratus will not hold fast, because poverty is not measured at the bottom of the human condition, but at the top of the human glamour. A man is not poor because he can hardly provide bread to eat to his family, but because the multi-millionaire can throw to waste the abundance of the things that could satiate the needs of those at the bottom of the social scale. It is the waste of the human effort in the form of accumulated riches that makes a man poor, and not the failure to satisfy the bare necessities of life. I may be making enough money to buy all the food my family needs, but I will still be poor because the multi-billionaires can save their money in the banks to remain idle, money that will do nothing for me and for the rest of the people of the world.

The end of humanity's dark ages will also be marked by a stop of domination of one country over others and/or by the erasure of all borders among nations. We are now witnessing the first part of the disjunction. The American Imperialist era is coming to an end. This end was started with the Korean War, continued with the Viet Nam War, and it made the empire collapse with the Iraq and Afghanistan wars, both of which will be lost—even if eventually a (Pyrrhic) victory is claimed—because there is no way to fight a war of aggression with all the modern weaponry that the United States has, if at the end we have to place soldiers on the ground who will be forced to fight guerrilla insurrections indefinitely. The argument that we are fighting terrorism doesn't hold, because terror is a police enforcement problem, not a problem to be solved by invading those countries that allegedly give cover to terrorists. In the case of Afghanistan, all we had to do was to force the government of the mullahs to get rid of Osama Bin Laden, or allow us to do the work, not replace a government that only the Afghan people know how to replace. It just doesn't make sense that people who defeated the Russian Army would not be able to get rid of a government they didn't want. Now that we invaded their turf, the same thugs we got out of power have plenty of justification to "liberate" their nation and clean their country of foreign invaders. Afghanistan will never be pacified if the Western armies don't get out of the country and let the nationals settle their own scores the way they have done it through past centuries.

In order to preempt attacks from those who will say that I am not a patriot, I am going to reiterate here that, as far as my ego is concerned: a) I hold principles of moderate patriotism, and love and pledge loyalty to the United States of America, my adopted country; b) I also love my country of birth, Nicaragua, and my Latin culture; and, as far as my anima is concerned: c) I believe in humanity, I love humanity, and I am a spiritual citizen of the world, which is the cradle of my soul. Having clarified my position with respect to my ego and anima loyalties, I also would like to add that I oppose all wars without exception, yet I recognize that sometimes there may be no alternative but to fight the only wars that I would ever reluctantly fight, and those are wars of self-defense. I also recognize that at certain times, and under certain circumstances, nations may be forced to fight wars for the defense and protection of their people, though these wars may not always be justifiable on moral grounds. Having said this, I will continue with the present chapter.

Never has the United States of America—a country that I love dearly, to reiterate what I said before—acted in self-defense throughout its history, except when it was attacked by Japan at Pearl Harbor, which gave origin to the Pacific War, fought mainly by two imperialistic powers, the USA and Japan, both bound to collide in their expansionist march across the Pacific rim. All other wars in which the USA has been involved have been either preemptive (and thus aggressive) of the expansion of other imperialistic powers, like Germany during World War I and World War II, and the Soviet Union during the Cold War (with the Korean and Viet Nam wars), or wars of aggression, like the Mexican-American War and the Spanish-American War, plus all the multiple interventions in the Caribbean, Central and South America that also qualify as aggressive interventionism. The reason why the USA has very rarely had to fight wars of self-defense has been because of its mighty military and economic power. And this reason holds true today, as it has held true in the past. The United States of America has no reason to fear any other country in the world, which means that all the modern wars of 'self-defense,' or wars for the protection of our national interests and national security, are really wars of imperialistic expansion. But fortunately, thanks to the modern trend of the world towards globalization, there is no longer any need for the USA to pursue further military expansionist ventures, opening the door to restricting itself to engage in peaceful economic, political and cultural cooperation with other countries. The era of colonialism and imperialism is practically dead, and former imperialist powers like the UK, Russia, France, and Japan now have to adapt to a world where the distribution of power is more or less balanced by nuclear deterrents, rather than by conventional armies—not that going nuclear is any good for humanity, but it gives some countries a false sense of security, but a sense of security nonetheless, at the expense of the world's safety and security. Thus, if nothing catastrophic happens before we reach total world economic, political, and social globalization, there will be no further need of nuclear deterrents.

The weaknesses of the American imperial thrust are now visible for the entire world to see. The United States of America just doesn't have enough men to invade a medium-size country like Iraq, and I don't think it can gather enough soldiers to invade a country like Iran, especially since Iran has already organized its own guerrilla forces, the Hezbollah fighters, invisible and diffused in several countries, including Lebanon, Syria, Iran itself and Iraq, with the potential of transforming its national army (the Iranian army) into a broader and more deadly guerrilla force. The Iraq war and the Israeli invasion of Lebanon widely exposed the flaws of the Western machinery of war. The fact of the matter is that people learn and adapt themselves to changing scenarios. For Iran and Al Qaeda, the continuation of the Iraq war is of the utmost importance, because it serves a triple purpose: First, it keeps the empire bleeding; second, it serves as a convenient training ground for their forces; third, it discredits the western world, especially the USA, favoring the recruitment of their own combatants. Under these circumstances the Iraq war has no end in sight, especially since it serves the purpose of the insurgents to keep it alive for as long as they want and need to.

Another sign that signals the end of the American imperial venture is the increased capacity of other countries' armies to fight standard classical wars. The dream and delusion of the American nationals that we are the only super-power left at the end of the Cold War era, is nothing but dreams and delusions, and falls by its own weight. How can the United States of America be a super-power, militarily speaking, when we can't even win a war against a third-world country like Iraq? Besides, there are countries like China and Russia—not really the best of our allies—which we can't wipe out of the face of the earth without running the risk of being wiped out ourselves. There are other smaller countries, like Pakistan and India that, although not really our enemies, can do lots of harm, if we were to get into a conflict against them. In fact, not even North Korea would be a country easy to get rid of in a classical confrontation, without running the risk of a serious defeat. Therefore, the notion that the United States is a super-power cannot be disputed, if super-powers can also be blown into oblivion, or kept busy fighting puny, never-ending guerrilla wars.

What good is all the sophisticated weaponry of the United States of America, if China can blow our satellites to pieces, rendering the GPS computers in our modern submarines and bombers inoperable? What good are our modern, sophisticated, expensive weapons, if we can't use them in a classical, everyday war, against a bunch of ragged terrorists, guerrilla fighters, insurgents, or whatever you want to call them? The fastest of the fastest F-16's or F-17's cannot do absolutely anything against a subversive hiding in a house of a poor neighborhood in the city of Bagdad, because if we care about collateral damages, we have to send somebody on foot to get him out of there. And just try to run one of those modern super-tanks, or armored vehicles, on the streets of an Anbar province town in Iraq without being hit by the infamous IED's—which, by the way, are no longer either infamous or improvised. So, let's get up and take a cold shower, so that we can face up reality wide awake.

The days of the super-power imperial master of the world are over. Finished. Kaput. The Imperial America is going down in history as one of the shortest-lived empires that the world has ever seen, with barely 150 years of existence (the Roman Empire lasted for more than 500 years, according to some authors, and for more than 1000 years, according to others), and we could discover this thanks to president George W. Bush.

And if the observations above are not enough, just think about what follows. What makes the USA powerful is its capacity to ship troops to other countries, and America is flanked by two vast oceans. How do you think we are going to transport massive amounts of troops and airplanes, if not in aircraft-carriers, which are floating fortresses crying out to be hit by one of those Russian-made "Sizzler" missiles? Furthermore, those huge floating fortresses eventually have to get to shore, or very close to shore, where they are going to be extremely vulnerable. Sure, an imbecility-dunked idiot like Sadam Hussein never thought that the way to neutralize the USA was with modern anti-aircraft weapons and missiles that can hit and sink aircraft-carriers. By now the Iranians, the Pakistanis, the Indians, the North Koreans, and any country that cares about its own defense know what to do with our super floating fortresses, and probably are working very hard to develop the firecrackers that can take care of them—so as not to depend so much on the Russians. And to exclaim "Nuke them!" is to no avail, because some of those countries may nuke us as well.

Yet, if the truth be said, we are still an economic hyper-power, and this is much more important than all the sophistication of our modern army. We are the most technologically advanced country of the world, with the most productive economy the world has ever seen. With our solid economic strength we can feed ourselves and feed the world several times over. We are, in other words, the only economic super-power of the world, and if we hold imperialistic ambitions, we can conquer the world with the dollar, and effectively shelf the gun. With all the money we have wasted in Iraq, we could have built a buffer zone several miles wide on the Mexican side of our border that would effectively have stopped illegal immigration. We can show Chavez, Fidel Castro and all the socialists of South America how to raise the purchasing power of the Latin American people, and how to set up businesses that would keep the labor force of those countries in their own countries, and still make money, lots of money. Such is the magnificent uniqueness of the capitalist economic system the United States of America polished, if not invented. But we lack the will to do it, because we still hold deep down within our beings the nefarious master's gene that pushes us to conquer the world by force, rather than by the use of green persuasion—and as much I sympathize with environmental conservation, I am talking here about money, and money is a powerful persuasive force.

Imagine, we could make the immigration buffer zone produce articles to be consumed in Mexico and the United States, and if making money is not that important, we could do lots of charity work in Africa and the rest of Latin America, sending them what we want potential illegal immigrants to produce. This immigration buffer zone, paired with a restructured subsidy to American agriculture, would be cheaper than building a wall that will slow down the invasion of this country, but will not stop it. Instead of giving away money to farmers for nothing in return, we could pay them for hiring American legal workers, breaking the incentive of American businesses to hire illegal immigrants.

I am sure that if we had placed all our efforts in devising a way to destroy a country at the expense of almost half a trillion dollars to good use, we could have certainly found an effective way to spend all that money in something twice as constructive as the invasion of Iraq was destructive, and perhaps with even an added bonus, like stopping the flow of illegal drugs, and making people love us in the process—and I mean literally drive them crazy with love for the "compassionate conservative gringo." But we chose the way of hatred and destruction. Why would you think anybody would like to destroy a country that would generously give for the betterment of humanity? And I am not talking here about charity. The United States of America can give and receive at the same time, if we only use our ingenuity to find ways of investing in poor countries.

The Real New Age of Mankind

The real new age of mankind will become a reality when we turn the city of man into the City of God, or when the City of God reaches down to the city of man. The first part of the disjunction is possible, but the second part is not. Good cannot reach towards evil, but evil can be purified, cleaned up, and reach towards that which is good. In simple terms, good can get corrupted into letting evil be manifested—not originated or created, because good cannot be the cause of evil—and this is precisely what happened with both the turpitude of Lucifer and the fall of man in Paradise. Similarly, evil cannot be the cause or origin of that which is good.

Nature is controlled by the law of entropy, which means that the sub-systems of the physical world move towards chaos in a single direction. Matter and flesh tend to corruption, which is one reason why time is irreversible. Why chaos? Because all processes in nature depend on heat transfer in order to originate work, change, transformation, movement, assimilation, adjustment, as well as other physical, chemical and biological processes, and a system that is under the influence of a flow towards equal heat distribution (heat equilibrium), generates no work once it reaches equilibrium; this in turn will cause the assimilation of the said system into a more inclusive system that will also tend to heat equilibrium, but not before increasing the overall entropy of the more inclusive system—take for instance life, which depends on heat flow in the form of caloric energy that comes from food and produces work; after we die, we reach heat equilibrium, and there is no production of work (no life), but the body enters another process that involves heat transfer, mainly organic decomposition; so, in the flow of time we are continuously stepping down the ladder of orderly phenomena from more orderly processes to less orderly interactions, i.e. we continually descend into greater and greater chaos.

Simply stated, heat energy tends towards equilibrium (equalization of temperature) from hot objects to cooler objects, which amounts to a transfer of heat capable of producing work; this instability of systems trying to reach a point of equilibrium, translates into an increase of the (more inclusive) system's entropy, sometimes interpreted as an increase of chaos within the system, if only because its similitude with things getting older and decaying. This is the reason why we are born, grow, and eventually perish in old age, if there isn't a drastic impediment to this process. Fruits ripen and eventually rot; the same thing happens to living organisms that die. Human inventions, like motors and engines, are more notoriously subject to the law of entropy than other natural processes. A good running engine eventually stops working—and it never happens that something that is not working will fix itself. Things can fix themselves in nature, but only as slow responses to systemic changes in the external and internal environment of such said things (like overcoming a disease) but we must eventually age and die. We can say, thus, that good is the catalyst of that which is bad—not as an organic transformation of good into evil, but as a process of letting evil *be* in order to enhance and appreciate the presence of that which is good—and not the other way around, because from order we descend into disorder. I am not talking here about what humans can do as a matter of practical everyday life: if we find a situation of disorder, we can go ahead and move things from one place to another and generate order from disorder; but in a much wider context, we would have in fact sunk things into a greater disorder.

Just as it happens in nature, spiritual good is the pretext for spiritual evil to be, but only through the exercise of the free will. Free will in this context is the spiritual equivalent of entropy. God created Lucifer a good angel, but Lucifer's free will gave origin to his desire to be par with God; his newly acquired spiritual energy, free will, generated or gave origin to the desire to be not just like God, but God—according to the Bible one-third of the heavenly angels followed suit and sided with Lucifer, and this is the equivalent of increasing entropy and transfer of heat in the physical world. In a similar fashion, God created man, innocent and probably with no willingness to exercise his free will to do what is wrong, and it was the serpent that lied and tempted man, so that he would disobey God through the exercise of Eve's free will—can you see the fine thread of entropy here? We would not be able to appreciate goodness if not in the background of that which is bad, and this doesn't carry the implication that good gives origin, or is the cause of evil—in other words, whenever and wherever there is goodness, there is the potential for evil to sprout, which is to say that evil is opportunistic, and comes into being upon the presence of that which is good. In all cases, then, good is the opportunity of evil to be as a result of a misstep of the free will, but it never happens that evil originates good, meaning that from what is evil nothing good can be derived—just as it is inconceivable that a rotten fruit can ripen again and become good to eat, or an old person can stop the process of physical aging and grow to be young again. But how then, is sin cleansed, and thus forgiven? Through the intervention of goodness: what's good can only give origin to what's good, and when dealing with sin, only good can erase what's evil, bringing the maculated entity to its original pristine purity.

To summarize, we can say, then, that God created good spiritual beings and gave them freedom of the will, so that these beings could be like God, but some of the spiritual beings that God created exercised their free will to do what is wrong, and this was precisely the genesis of evil, which in turn is necessary to appreciate the good things that God made. In other words, we (first Lucifer and then us) did and created bad things that could only enhance the appreciation of the good things that God gave us.

According to what we said above, it was historically necessary that men would create a social order and a powerful production tool (inherently good), the capitalist system of production, and the presence of this powerful production tool gave the opportunity for evil to be, and eventually prevail, throughout the history of mankind. This social order, integrated within the capitalist system of production, became a tool to extort other human beings of their property, represented by the things in which they invested their labor. This system of things was seen to be good in the eyes of the ego, though the ego is not morally qualified to judge what is good. At the same time that the ego was devising more and more ways of accumulating property, the anima came to work against the ego. The anima created a moral order that would restrain the ego from going to excesses, and as this moral order becomes more and more strong, it will eventually turn things around towards a more egalitarian society, towards the City of God from the city of man. But make no mistake, the physical world will still be submitted to the law of entropy and will inevitably march towards greater chaos, while the spiritual world will follow the contrary path towards a heavenly order. We cannot make of this world the permanent residence of the spirit. Eventually the anima moves towards a purely spiritual heavenly order. The city of man, even if in the City of God, still belongs to the ambit of "the things of this world."

Now, as for the necessity of evil, that's a different story. We could never appreciate what's good if we didn't have a sense of what's bad or evil, which points to the necessity of that which is good, evil being just an incidental (not necessary) attribute, for evil is only a parasitic entity that attaches itself to goodness and can only *be* if good *is*—and by this argument, and the argument above, what is good may get corrupted and turned into that which is bad or evil (again, making of evil something that accidentally accompanies or attaches to what is good). It is evil, through the perceptions of the physical world, what gives form, shape and substance to spiritual good, but only as a way of contrasting one with the other. Spiritual good, on the other hand, is not and cannot originate spiritual evil.

Therefore, evil can only exist in the material world and through the material world. If Satan had never had the intention to outmaneuver God, he would never have been sent to the abyss of the material world, and humanity would never have erred against God. But once humans fell victims of evil, never again would evil go back to wreak havoc in heaven; thus, spiritual evil is here to stay in this, the world of material things. It will remain forever in the realm of the physical world, until we are cleared of all sin and go back to where we belong, the City of God. Then, and only then, will we leave spiritual evil behind. Now, since the processes in nature run sort of parallel and out of view to the processes of the spirit, the latter moved by the *continuum*, whatever we manage to distort and deviate of its natural path, will eventually be brought under control with an air of inevitability by the ultimate Work of God, the Opus Dei, which is the *continuum*. Even apocalypses are the work of the *continuum*, and we have witnessed several of them: the discovery and conquest of America was an apocalypse; the enslaving of the black African man was another apocalypse; World War II, and the near annihilation of the Jews, was a major apocalypse. Thus, humanity runs the risk of a total apocalypse that may affect the whole world, and one of the objectives of the Fraternity of the Templars is averting this global (and perhaps final) apocalypse. It should be clearly understood that St. John's Apocalypse is a spiritual event, and thus a timeless event, that whenever it materializes, it does it anywhere in the world, and in any period of human history.

Thus, the real new age of mankind seems to be taking shape in the American continent with the United States of America as its main actor. And it is in relation to the modern developments of the USA that the *continuum* takes an enormous relevance. It all started with the British model of colonization, whose predecessor goes back to the Pilgrims and the *Mayflower* in the New World. The British (and to a minor extent the French) had two ways of colonizing the newly discovered lands: one may be characterized as genocidal racial sanitation (to distinguish it from modern ethnic cleansing), and the conquest of the United States and Canada are classical examples of this model. This method consists mainly of clearing the land of any native peoples, just leaving some remnants of the original inhabitants, too small to constitute a threat to the new rulers of the conquered lands. New Zealand and Australia are two other classical examples of the British genocidal racial sanitation model of nation building—to be fair, this genocidal racial sanitation method of colonization used by the British may have never been completely planned and premeditated by cool-headed British genocidal planners, it was just a *de facto* way the British Empire executed its imperial ambitions. Another model used by the British may be called the segregation and bondage model of colonization. This method was applied in those places where genocide was impractical, due to the monumental task of getting rid of populations too numerous to be annihilated by a far smaller repressive force, opting for the strategy of ruling and keeping the natives in bondage, while holding them at bay by sheer military power, all this without absolutely no racial integration. This last method was used in India and Pakistan, South Africa, East and West Africa, and other places in the Middle East.

The problem with these British methods of colonization, especially in the American continent, came with the Spanish and Portuguese alternative methods of conquest and colonization that drastically botched the British experiment of genocidal racial sanitation of the Americas—again, I would like to reiterate here that this may have been a *de facto* genocide, not a premeditated one. In other words, the Spanish and Portuguese blew it big by giving origin to a mixed race of people who call themselves *mestizos*, and who are neither white nor Indians, but both, and in some other instances adding black to this color cocktail of races. Black Africans constituted another important element that helped thwart the British genocidal experiment in America (forgive me, Britons, this is just a way of stating the truth) since the institution of slavery needed a vast source of free labor that had to be brought from Africa.

Consequently, the American continent never became completely white, as it happened in Australia and New Zealand, except for the Northern part of the continent that makes up the USA—with small black patches all over the place—and Canada, which remained pristine white. Thus, most of the American continent is bronze-like in color, and due to Darwin's natural selection—it is a law of evolution that a successful species will reproduce quickly, and will develop internal genetic mechanisms for better adaptation to environmental changes—is becoming more and more bronze-like, and even darker than bronze in color, manifested as a demographic tidal wave pushing northwards, and whose boundaries are far beyond the Mexico-USA southern border, reducing, little by little, the area occupied by whites. And this is all happening without premeditation, because nobody has planned it. We could say that it is the *continuum* at work. This bronze-like tidal wave is inevitable, because the typical races of humanity reached an evolutionary dead-end: white people are not going to get whiter, and blacks are not going to get blacker. The typical human races can only overcome this evolutionary dead-end by varied, though gentle, interaction with their environment, which could happen over hundreds of thousands of years, or by evolutionary stagnation of the species (like in the case of the coelacanth fish), which is basically an evolutionary dead-end. It is easier to produce rapid biological changes, and thus an increased variation in the gene pool, with the intermixing of races, and this is what's going to happen eventually, and in the shorter term, meaning within the next hundreds, or thousands (not hundreds of thousands) of years.

[Had the Nazis been successful in wiping out the "inferior races," and left only the "superior" Aryan race, and perhaps other white races, they would probably have effectively succeeded in exterminating *Homo sapiens*, because racial purification reduces more and more the total variation of the "pure race" gene pool, making it less and less adaptable to sudden environmental changes. A table of genetic differences for 26 groups of races prepared in a study by Masatoshi Nei and Arun K. Roychoudhury from *Evolutionary Relationships of Human Populations on a Global Scale* (1993) shows that average heterozygotic differences among those 26 groups of races go from a low 21% for Australian aborigines to a high of 36.1% for Iranians. Racist theories of human differences imply that these genetic variations among the different peoples of the world are nothing but an idle capriciousness of nature.]

Of course, white people can put a stop to this demographic tidal wave that is moving North by using methods that may go from building (from coast to coast) a wall across the Mexico-USA border, to militarization of the USA southern border, to genocidal racial sanitation. But it may already be too late for that. Besides, as we said at the introduction to this book, we can never outwit the *continuum*, because sooner or later, it will adjust itself in such a way that it will do what it has to do (and often times we don't know what it "wants" to do), and the most we can effect is to ride with the flow of the *continuum*.

Therefore, at the end, neither the Indian, black or white peoples will inherit the American continent, but the new race of humans that we may appropriately say will be superior than its constituent races, not in terms of ego-intelligence—we already said that ego-intelligence is a characteristic of all human races—but in terms of spirituality, and perhaps even in terms of biology, since it is entirely possible that the genetic composition of the new race of *mestizos* would better withstand environmental changes than any of its component races—again, this is on the assumption that we may one day rid ourselves of our old demons, including the dog's gene. Which comes to show that, in the final analysis, the "wisdom of the ages" may be more judicious than the "impetus of new knowledge," and perhaps my grandmother was right (even if under the duress and influence of the dog's gene) when she advised us to "improve" our race by marrying lighter-skinned partners—not precisely because light skin is better, but because the mixture is better—instead of inter-marrying among people of our own race. The *continuum* indeed works in strange and mysterious ways.

To end this book, I will finally say that we have to learn to ride with the *continuum*, because it seems to be taking us to a brave new world where the City of God will be in the city of man, and where all races will be either integrated into the *mestizo* race, or integrated within the new social organization led by Orbis Unum, God Enterprises, and the Fraternity of the Templars.